American Folklore and the Mass Media

FOLKLORE TODAY

Linda Dégh, *General Editor*

AMERICAN FOLKLORE
AND THE MASS MEDIA

Linda Dégh

Indiana University Press

Bloomington and Indianapolis

Library of Congress Cataloging-in-Publication Data

Dégh, Linda.
American folklore and the mass media / Linda Dégh.
p. cm.—(Folklore today)
Includes bibliographical references (p.   ) and index.
ISBN 0-253-31677-4 (cloth : alk. paper). — ISBN 0-253-20844-0
(pbk. : alk. paper)
1. Folklore—United States. 2. Mass media—United States.
3. United States—Popular culture. I. Title. II. Series.
GR105.D44 1994
398'.0973—dc20
93-7543

1 2 3 4 5 98 97 96 95 94

Contents

Introduction

FEW FOLKLORISTS OF our time have impressed me more than Rudolf Schenda. His profound knowledge of the cultural history of western civilization and his sober, no-nonsense evaluation of the social processes of folklore through the ages lack the euphoric enthusiasm and worshipful compassion for the folk that is so common in the works of professional folklorists. His pioneering approach to narratives and narration in the frames of the social communication of culture is far from romantic; it is a model for studying folklore in society. His approach is particularly attractive to students of folklore in the industrial age. Schenda never separated lore from the folk, nor did he speak of an independent and superior oral tradition. For him, the folk was never an idealized rural isolate unwittingly preserving national values but rather a collaborative product of negotiations between social classes. Implicitly, for Schenda, the folk are the common people constituting social, economic, occupational, and age subcategories that share a cultural tradition but at the same time are influenced by the consumer-oriented culture industry (Horkheimer and Adorno 1947). Folklore thus is the product of an ongoing historical process that consolidates the interaction of literary and oral, professional and nonprofessional, formal and informal, constructed and improvised creativity. With the advent of mass production—book printing and audiovisual reproduction—the earlier harmonious give and take between oral and nonoral folklore ceased to exist, and technical reproductivity (Benjamin 1963) dictated a different pace for folklore communication through new media.

Can we say that printed or electronically reproduced folklore, out of the normal context of traditional spinning rooms, firesides, and wayside inns, is not folklore? It retains all the criteria by which we judge what is folklore and what is not: it is socially relevant, based on tradition, and applied to current needs. As old wine in a new bottle, it appeals to a much larger population group than ever before, in fact, to a much broader array of diverse social groups than ever before. As we will demonstrate in this discussion, the phenomenon we identify as folklore permeates all society assisted by mass media; it is not ruled out as folklore simply because its bearers manipulate new instruments to fit the needs of modern consumers. Folklore blossoms and proliferates before our eyes as it emerges from new conditions more vigorously and forcefully, empowered with more authority and prestige, than ever before. Can we afford to retreat to the horse-and-buggy days, instead of wading into the slippery marshland of the new, mass-mediated cultural universe, and as orderly *bricoleurs*, collecting and classifying the emergent data?

The mass media liberate folklore from its earlier confinement to the so-called lower layers of society and from the prejudice—both pro and con—that stigmatized it. Folklore belongs to everyone, not only to the underprivileged, uneducated masses. It is a common cultural property characterizing our ways of thinking, believing, and dreaming, and our modes of defining our identity. The observer of emergent folklore may be able to decipher the meaning of basic human ideas that continue to recur in myriads of new interpretations through the accessibility of modern media. We are eyewitnesses to a new era in which folklore gains power and prestige as an authoritative voice: the voice of the urban-industrial folk; the voice of concern, fear, daydream, and hope; the voice of all humanity alienated and fractured by electronic efficiency. The task of folklorists is to read these meanings of folklore, and this task makes folkloristics an important interdisciplinary science, now more than ever before.

In a 1990 address, Schenda asserted that "Never did folklore fare better than under the flag of mass culture" (1992:30). In fact, "folklore reproduced and placed in new contexts produces new folklore genres, . . . it became evident that the mass media contributes to the maintenance and the creation of folklore" (1992:29). Even more thought-provoking is Schenda's observation that folklore has become more prolific than previously:

> For a long time, not only has folklore been adopted from *parole* into the *langue*, but it also has entered a realm of which Bogatyrev and Jakobson (1929: 900–13) could not have had comprehension. Namely, in a discourse, featuring a 'communicative package,' various coexistent actions and intentions may be considered. For example, sales strategies of the capitalist-inclined market; psychohygienic allusions to comfort people concerned with the destruction of the environment; allusion to the 'good old days' to enhance a political campaign. . . . The attraction of folklore so appealing to the general nostalgia trend should not mislead us because the mask of innocence can conceal a string of not-so-innocent ideologies. To trace the roots of mask-parades seems a pressing task for contemporary folklore study. . . . *Folklore—a peculiar form of creation?* The old question still has its justification. But sixty years later in a radically changed world it needs a whole set of new answers. The folklore debate has not yet been settled. In fact, it will become truly actual in the totally electrified year two thousand (Schenda 1992:30).

This book is an attempt to probe into Schenda's observations concerning the role of the mass media in the maintenance of old and the creation of new folklore genres. In essence, it takes its departure from a view of folklore as a process in time and space, in constant motion and change under the influence of an epochal transformation of western civilization. The three questions that lie behind the chapters are the following: (1) What are the constants and what are the variables in content and style, what kind of dressing is needed to make old ideas work for modern practical and utilitarian purposes? (2) How are text variables created, or how is fixity achieved by writing, printing, photocopying, tape-recording, or photography? (3) How are the media used to promote consumption and how do individuals take media instruments into their own hands to maintain, reconstruct, create, and transform traditional practices? In the following chapters I hope to illustrate the routines that produce folklore by way of collaboration between professional and non-professional arbitrators—that is, between professional media communicators and the folk in given social contexts utilizing the mass media.

These broad and perhaps vague questions do not allow a strict developmental continuity between the chapters but rather open a larger spectrum in which the complexity of retroactions between folklore and mass media can be documented and characterized through a handful of arbitrarily chosen, conspicuous examples that I have encountered and that I was able to explore. The themes discussed in each chapter reflect my personal interests in folklore in the industrial world—folk religion, worldview, tale, and legend—and exhibit my way of thinking, the learning process I underwent during years of research and writing. Mass communication, mass society, and the related concept of popular culture have been studied in the social sciences and the humanities for decades, but folklorists have been shy about participating in the numerous collaborative efforts undertaken. The most that folklorists have done is to adopt certain terms or pay lip service to ideas gleaned from the works of philosophers, literary theorists, social historians, sociologists, and anthropologists, without contributing to the interdisciplinary dialogue from their own disciplinary vantage point. This makes my venture a lonely (or shall I say deviant) attempt.

The first chapter, in which I discuss variability as a pivotal trait of folklore in the making between oral, literary, and mass mediators, presents a theoretical frame for the following chapters, which are case studies of diverse phenomena related to mass media in diverse ways. Both chapters 2 and 3 deal with sales strategies: how merchandise is advertised by the exploitation of the general audience's belief in supernatural agencies and magic solutions, and how promoters utilize and reformulate traditional legends and magic tales for sales purposes. Chapter 2 deals with television commercials inserted into general programs, while chapter 3 describes printed newspaper ads promoting products for mail or telephone order. Chapter 4 examines illustrated magazines designed for modern women. By publishing short stories, interviews with popular public figures, and advertisements promoting fashion, beauty, health aids, and kitchen accessories, magazines follow and confirm a 'happy housewife heroine' career script fashioned after the guidelines of traditional folktales and literary fairy tales that have been used in the education of young girls for centuries.

Both chapters 5 and 6 explore the use of popular media to communicate folklore; each chapter describes a subcultural phenomenon ethnographically, presenting mass-mediated texts in situational contexts. In chapter 5 the practice of multiple telling, recording, and replaying of miracle legends in a Pentecostal congregation demonstrates personal creativity in performance, transmission, and variation through the use of cassette tape recorders. In chapter 6 the custom of placing memorial poems in the classified ads section of a local newspaper is explained by tracing its roots to traditional beliefs, practices, and rituals surrounding death in the family, and by field inquiry into poetry composition technique and the meaning and function of memorializing the dead and maintaining family cohesion in the community.

This book is based on data I have obtained through ethnographic fieldwork, which included collection of printed and handwritten materials, notetaking, tape-recording of both spontaneous and audience-oriented formal performances, informal conversations, and photography, as well as observations and impressions scribbled on notepads or memorized. This ethnography, unusual as it would seem to some, included collection from both professionals and nonprofessionals: from the creators and disseminators of media folklore and from the creators and consumers of traditional folklore. As a folklore fieldworker, I positioned myself in a place where I could observe both in relation to each other. I read the popular press—magazines, tabloids, local newspapers, and other print materials at the disposal of customers in doctors' waiting rooms, beauty shops, and law offices; and I listened to the radio and watched TV in order to discover folklore messages and get a basic impression of how the popular media intrudes into the privacy of people, and how it influences existing folklore expressions. My divided interest between folklore in the media and mass-treated folklore among people is reflected in the way this book is structured. Chapters 2, 3, and 4 focus on media presentations of folklore, relying on only occasional and nonspecific informant commentary, whereas chapters 5 and 6 probe into community interplay with media-manipulated materials. These two final chapters are *lege artis* community studies prepared by reliance on both media and folk information.

My informants were consumers of mass media folklore gleaned from everyday exposure; they were repeaters, revisers, or creators of new folklore and applicators of media to create new folklore. Actually, I relied on two kinds of sources: folklore disseminators whom I met personally, and unmet media folklore consumers and performers whom I could observe on TV and radio or in print. The two groups were not kept separate from each other; it was through my local informants that I understood the relevance of the media to living folklore. Their contribution to my work was crucial because they were interested in my project and they helped me in collecting. I was able to discuss my ideas with them and they corrected me if they thought I was wrong.

These people were members of the same community to which I belong; their daily lives do not differ significantly from mine. We hear the same news and share a similar set of values, symbols, and behavioral conventions, so communication among ourselves is not difficult. We can rely on a common vocabulary of everyday living, a common referential framework. I am talking here about people who could be my next-door neighbors, my equals, handling similar daily routines. They shop in supermarkets, watch TV, borrow video movies, drive cars, and bowl. My relationship with my informants was based on mutual trust and respect, without being subordinated or obligated to each other. I was the curious one who listened to things I wanted to learn about; they were the respondents who because of my interest were forced to construct an image of themselves that they considered presentable to an outsider like me. This kind of relationship between researcher and informants is basic in creating a suitable ethnographic database enabling one to produce problem-oriented scholarly works in modern folkloristics.

The time is ripe for folklorists to think about a new type of fieldwork for a more systematic, scientific study of folklore transmission in the age of the electronic explosion. We are slow in theorizing and keep hopelessly far behind inventors who keep changing the world at breathtaking speed with technological magic and clairvoyance. I feel that during its long history, the discipline of folklore has developed some useful ideas concerning transmission and variation that can be reviewed and developed further for future research.

Fieldwork as the method of data gathering for folkloristic study was first considered when the discipline had graduated from its basically nationalistic-political orientation. In the nineteenth century, this orientation was concealed behind the propagation of primitive (peasant) poetry. Collectors of "wild roses" felt obliged to "restore" the perfect "beauty" of an oral literature that had eroded in the oral wear and tear of the uneducated folk. Later on, ethnography targeted the "lower layers" (*Unterschicht*) of society, for both ethnographic museum displays and comparative text studies, with emphasis on the communal nature of folklore. This approach effectively prevented researchers from paying attention to the real people behind the texts or their immediate social conditions.

For a long time, field study was a rescue operation, a reconstruction of the past from relics in the memory of old people. Interest in the ethnographic present, in the individual creativity of tradition bearers within cultural entities, first emerged during the interwar years, in the paths of Emile Durkheim, Max Weber, Bronislaw Malinowski, and Richard Thurnwald. The question of genuineness and authenticity arose then, and not only as a technical problem of recording accuracy. Holistic approaches required the unselective collection of everything functional in a culture, at a time when folklorists were still busy separating things "sanctioned by tradition" from the "corrupted" (*zersungen*), the "alien," and the "fake." By this time, shortly before World War II, the subjects, goals, and approaches of folkloristics began to show their limitations. Soon a critical review of the discipline and plans for a complete overhaul on the basis of ethnographic observation of the present were put on the agenda. The task was to create a new frame for the observation and description of the new style of mass society that was emerging, characterized by advanced industrialization, urbanization, commercialization, technological growth, political and economic population mobility, population explosion, alienation, ethnic, racial, and confessional strife, an upsurge of claims for ethnic identity recognition, and the restructuring of the layers of society.

Fieldwork-based, problem-oriented folkloristics began during the late sixties in Germany. It was a watershed, in the spirit of regeneration, regaining dignity devastated by Nazism. A group of young members of the Gesellschaft für deutsche Volkskunde and students of Hermann Bausinger's seminar in Tübingen took issue with the ruling nationalist ideology of folklore, which in its extreme form had supported Hitler's Third Reich. Bidding farewell to the old canon and the old concepts and methods of inquiry, the group proposed a new folkloristics, one that would be "a critical social science" based on empirical reseach and problem-oriented culture analysis (Geiger, Jeggle, and Korff 1970; Schenda 1970b; Jeggle 1984; Dow and Lixfeld 1986). The ideas initiated by this group were inspired by the philosophers and social critics Adorno, Marcuse, Benjamin, Habermas, and others of the Frankfurt School. Adaptation of a critical, analytical approach to field observation was further developed by Ina-Maria Greverus (1990) and others. The dominant role of the fieldworker was also convincingly argued by Bente Alver (1990). Her "personal narrative" about her qualitative method "creating the source" for scientific study reveals the importance of deep personal involvement with the objects and the subjects of observation.

A great number of other folklorists in Europe and in America have tried in different ways to modernize their approach to the field. They know the difficulty of bridging the gap between two cultures, that of the fieldworker and that of the host culture, and of creating a platform of mutual understanding for collectors and informants. As an ethnographer of mass media-ridden society, I have had to come to terms with my own researcher persona in my presentation of folklore in the American mass media. Folklorists deal with intentional information, subjective expressions in created situational contexts that cannot be neutral or objective. We cannot know if the information is true or false, or if the informant is deliberately misleading us. For the folklorist it really does not matter—we are not expecting our informant to tell us the truth. We want the spontaneous reaction to the situation, deliberate or unintended truth or falsity, not the objective (or subjective) fact. The folklorist wants to observe the informant's creative ways of thinking, expressive behavior, and artistry. However, the fieldworker's behavior, personality, and reaction to informant's gestures precipitate the informant's performance of folklore, commentaries, and accompanying body signals. These variables make fieldwork an interactive product of fieldworker and informant.

The cultural distance between fieldworkers and informants is a factor that weakens the quality of the data between the two. The fieldworkers are initially biased by their culture, and their inquiries are guided by the conviction that their view of the world is the authentic one and that the other's, of which they know little, is an anomaly. The same is true of the informants with the difference that they are forced into the situation without being prepared. As Wagner explains, the fieldworker invents the field and all we can hope for is a relative objectivity (1981). How can we avoid distortions? We are aware of the fact that the researchers can open only a window to inspect the segment as far as their vision reaches into an unknown universe. Anthropologists working with preindustrial tribal groups realize that data gathering and the writing of an interpretive study are largely determined by the ethnographer's personality (Marcus and Fischer 1986; Clifford and Marcus 1986). It is actually two cultures that collaborate and conflict in this relationship so that the addition of the author's self-portrait, as truthful as it can be, would make a more complete analytical ethnography. It would seem, in this relationship, that the researcher has multiple identities as visitor, investigator, apprentice, tourist, guest, intruder, and voyeur, and is an active, aggressive initiator of a contact, whereas the native (or natives—actually the single personality of a community) has the identities of the source of knowledge, the expert, and the host and is the passive, involuntary recipient of contact. Together they conduct a dialogue to negotiate their identities, playing roles they assume for each other. Anthropologists suggest in-depth analytical and self-critical descriptions of this encounter from the participant researcher's viewpoint, to make the "impossible attempt to fuse objective and subjective practices" in ethnographic writing (Pratt 1986:49), and perform anthropology as cultural criticism.

Should folklorists engaged in fieldwork in complex modern western population groups closer to their own groups follow this suggestion? They certainly need to deal with their personality biases as much as it is possible, but their handicap in achieving ethnographic accuracy differs from those of field anthropologists dealing with tribal, preindustrial cultures. The native ethnographers share only general cultural traits with the targeted subcultural group in their own country, but otherwise they are aliens. What they are searching for in fieldwork is the local variable of the prototype, the specific of the general. This search can be attempted only if one can minimize one's intrusion into the normal conditions which the fieldworker must observe. Furthermore, the ethnography that folklorists perform is quite demanding. Studying folklore in the making by individuals in conventional social settings requires a readiness to record spontaneous events and performances, avoiding direct questioning and manipulation of subjects. It is the collecting of folklore and subjecting the data to analysis in the context of performers and performance with the purpose of understanding the processes of human creativity that demand refinement. I mean here the recording of not only live but also media folklore performances and their variations. Being there and talking to people make one capable of exploring the ethnography of media-influenced folklore.

Be that as it may, I do not want to delay any longer the declaration of my own position as fieldworker gathering data for this book and my motivations in writing it up. It will not be a penetrating self-criticism, nor a confessional, just a statement of facts. I do not like to talk about myself, but I believe that my background has something to do with the way I gather, organize, analyze, and interpret my data.

When I was appointed to the Folklore Institute of Indiana University in 1964, my special commission was to teach European ethnology and folklore in the newly formed graduate folklore curriculum. Richard Dorson, the founder and director of the Institute, met me at the First Congress of the International Society for Folk Narrative Research in Kiel (Germany), which was my first trip to the West from my native Hungary. At that time, I taught folklore at the Eötvös Loránd University, Budapest, and my fieldwork-based research included storytelling, ritual life, folk religion, and ideology in archaic peasant villages, as well as historical and revolutionary songs, ethnic and interethnic folklore contacts, industrialization and village transformation, and urban and working class folklore. In Indiana I began to teach East and West European folklore, fieldwork, folk narrative, and ethnic folklore. Curiosity about the culture of Hungarian-Americans, triggered by my previous encounters with resettlers in Hungarian villages, took me to northwest Indiana's Calumet Region.

As I continued study of Hungarian-Americans over the years, my own acculturation—as a European folklorist becoming a midwestern small-town resident and an academic employee, torn between town and gown—led me in a new direction. I was not totally unprepared for the urban-industrial scene; I had done some fieldwork in the working-class districts of Budapest and studied the life of migrant construction workers. Going to the Calumet Region in northwest Indiana was motivated by the same impulse that dominated my interest in folklore from the outset: namely the processes of transmission, variation, and social change. Since natural processes cannot be followed through in one's own lifetime, I looked for extraordinary situations that speeded up the normal pace. The situations in which I observed the uses and modifications of folklore were crisis situations: the resettlement of ethnic cultures, labor migration, urbanization, industrialization, and interethnic integration and the disintegration of communities.

Settling in Bloomington meant discovering an unknown but familiar world in which village neighborliness and industrial paranoia coexist and accommodate two extremes: an archaic, indeed anachronistically traditional and yet hypermodern view of the world expressed in terms of folklore. As a professional, I went through developmental stages from visiting anthropologist to native ethnographer. How did I become a native folklorist? By being there, living there, listening to people and participating in community affairs, I became one. My earliest informants, my tutors and advisors who gave me the key to the understanding of American culture, were students in my introductory folklore classes: they were the "natives" whom I coerced to collect folklore from their peers or from themselves. They gave me a lesson in American lifestyle and ways of thinking through their peculiar ways of collecting folklore. They offered me a cross-section of the folklore of three generations: their own and that of their parents and grandparents. A representative sample of this folklore gave me an idea of proportions and dimensions: what was commonly known and what was unusual and exceptional; what was artistic and what was vulgar; all the rest, revising first impressions and correcting misconceptions, came informally through everyday living. I did not have to collect—I learned by instinct, noticing things, then checking them out through informal chats, casual questions at the farmer's market, bake sales, ice cream socials, the beauty salon, the gas station, the dentist's waiting room, standing in line at the Halloween Haunted House, reading local news, hearing local radio announcements. I discovered things that were sensational for me only; all the natives thought I was being ridiculous.

I had to decide on my own what was and what was not folklore in this context because I have found things European folklorists would have thought do not exist anymore and certainly not in the world's leading technological country. I did not expect to discover that in a world of mass-mediated print culture, archaisms persist in viable, meaningful reformulations, and that calendar and life-cycle rituals, cults, magic practices, and belief narratives are alive and well. My preoccupation with ghost stories, haunted houses, horror legends, witches, and psychics was not celebrated by my colleagues. Like everybody else, they had grown up with these notions; the supernatural world was part of everybody's adolescent education. So was Halloween, the grandiose feast of the dead, the most complex, revealing, elaborate, and widespread folk drama in the western world. I felt left alone when I stubbornly continued research in legend and in Halloween. It took some time until others also realized the worth of these topics for folklorists. No one thought much of mass-mediated folklore either. In fact, many colleagues told me that folklore was contaminated and destroyed by the mass media, that Halloween paraphernalia were prefabricated and sold in drugstores, and that the ghost stories I collected were not coming from oral tradition but from books. . . .

While doing my fieldwork—collecting by listening to people, and gleaning from media sources—I learned much about American folklore, its creators, communicators, and audiences, and its social contexts. My curiosity drove me further, away from the "purely oral" and deep into the folklore of the day irrespective of its source: oral, print, or audiovisual. While I was diligently clipping folklore from printed sources, recording folklore from the audiovisual media, and attending the meetings of UFOlogists, spiritualists, occultists, and fundamental sectarians, I became enculturated into the American folk culture. As an alien with a European prejudice, I had the advantage of discovering culture-specific forms of symbolic behavior that for the natives were harder to identify. If this book is a report of my present state of acculturation, my ability to integrate my cultural past and present, it is also a probe into the value of the study of American folklore by a Europe-based resident participant observer.

I owe thanks to many people who helped me in the writing of this book. In the first place, I want to thank the people of Bloomington, Indiana, and adjacent settlements in Monroe County. I will never be able to express my heartfelt gratitude to them for reciting their folklore to me, and for introducing me to a universe I never knew before. It was their kindness, understanding, and patience that I particularly appreciate; answering my awkward questions, explaining views and philosophies obvious to them but odd to me. They have contributed to my knowledge of the norms and etiquette that set and regulate the smooth running of their social network, manifested in the practice of religious belief, patriotic pride, hard work, strong family ties, neighborliness, and general good will—things that helped me understand the uses of folklore in present-day rural Indiana. They are people, engaged in farming, the stone-cutting industry, factory work, and other occupations. Some are salespeople, others run small businesses or are skilled artisans, office, health, or clerical employees, old and young, men and women, married and widowed. They live in lovely, spotlessly clean houses with porches adorned with flowers and front yards decorated with animal lawn ornaments, symbolizing, perhaps, the harmony of the lost Garden of Eden or maybe the old-fashioned farmlife of the good old days. I learned to understand and appreciate folklore as the conscious aspiration of modest people to create art in domestic life, be it decoration of practical tools and objects, writing occasional ritual poetry, or telling legends. I admired my informants' openness, honesty, and wisdom, their eloquence in speaking any sound reasoning in interpretation; their education was tradition-based, learning through life's experiences. I dedicate this book to them.

My informants were very supportive of my work; they allowed me to interview them, and to transcribe and use recordings I made. Some have read parts of the manuscript that concerned them, corrected my errors, and made helpful comments. They authorized me to publish their photos and their oral and written folklore materials.

I would like to express my special thanks to the Rev. Lee Coffman, Leatha Smith, Leah Leahy, Sarah Bartlett, Thelma Crohn, Jack Hoard, Reba Harris, Kimberley Deckard, Susie Dick, Jackie Smith, Gregory Quillen, Donna Benham, Martha Frame, Sherry Lee Meadows, Lynne Bruner, Kay Smith, Thelma Hays Blackwell, Velma Skinner, and Ernest Detmer. I would also like to thank those whose names are too numerous to mention—their presence and participation assured me of their good will.

Last but not least, I would like to remember my professional friends and colleagues whose encouragement was crucial during the process of research and writing. Some inspired my thinking indirectly by their own writings, others more directly through informal discussions, or reading chapters in progress. As a team player, I do not like to be left alone with the field-acquired data when I am in the process of writing, unsure of where I am going. I like to think aloud and subject my ideas to the critical reading of others. I presented early drafts of the ideas in these chapters at professional meetings and published less crystallized versions in conference proceedings and journals. The first version of Chapter 2 I wrote in the company of my husband Andrew Vázsonyi, honoring Max Lüthi on his 70th birthday (Dégh and Vázsonyi 1979). Andrew's ideas were crucial in the development of my thinking about legends and magic tales; he guided me in the exploration of the marketing of occult subcultures. I am grateful to my commentators, critics, and advisors who helped me feel secure and polish the rough edges. Of course, the responsibility for any remaining weaknesses is mine. In alphabetical order, my warmest appreciation goes to: Linda Adams, Inta Carpenter, Alan Dundes, Henry Glassie, Roger Janelli, Bengt af Klintberg, Reimund and Karin Kvideland, Carl Lindahl, Max Lüthi, Beverly Stoeltje, Kay Stone, and Libuše Volbrachtová.

A good part of this book was written during my Fellowship at the National Humanities Center, Research Triangle Park, North Carolina, 1990–91.

1

The Variant and the Folklorization Process in the Basic Forms of Narration

Märchen and Legend

Variant and Type

> The large number of incidents making up the story or stories are like the pieces of glass in a kaleidoscope. You may shake them as much as you please, constantly producing fresh combinations, but the pieces making them up always remain the same. In a similar way the incidents in fairy tales were constantly shaken, producing almost any form.
>
> Andrew Lang, International Folklore Congress, 1891

"Variant" is a well-established term in the vocabulary of folklorists, particularly in relationship to the dynamics of repetition, transmission, and dissemination of oral or literary texts. "Every repetition . . . displays variation" (Thompson 1949:1155); "usually it constitutes, with other variants of the same tradition, a type" (Bødker 1965:310). The variant, thus, may be understood as a life sign of an existing species, a single utterance which reports its current status in the course of a folkloric process (Voigt 1972:180–210). Others view the variant as a defining feature: "Constant change, variation within a tradition, whether intentional or inadvertent, is . . . a central fact of life for folklore" (Toelken 1979:10). Unlike literature, which has independent existence, "folklore can persist *only* in its function, in its momentary topicality, as a part of tradition, . . . not the firm Gestalt but the *variability* is the essence of its existence" (Bausinger 1980:48).

Although the concepts type and variant were established by scholars who took it for granted that folklore was a self-contained, self-perpetuating art of an illiterate folk, free from literary influence, they remained central for the study of narrative folklore in the modern technological world. However, we need to reconsider the implications of knowledge gained from new field research methodologies that deal with existential problems of our field. We need to ask ourselves: are we able to deal with our data, which is proliferating unpredictably and out of proportion because of the multiplication of conduits (Dégh 1979b) in the eighties, on the basis of conclusions reached in an entirely different socioeconomic system almost a century ago? Are our measuring tools, constructed in a conceivable, familiar world, still useful for understanding a strange, new, boundless, mass-media dominated world? Are our definitions and delimitations still valid and dependable for helping to understand narrational units in the industrial world of many contradictory values and norms? Folklorists who feel it their duty to improve on the definition of folklore in order to make room for their new discoveries, cannot keep in step with the speedily changing social climate that brought these discoveries to life. It is the nature of definitions that they are biased by the personal interest of the definer; they are too narrow, simplistic, and enumerative; too broad and general; too abstract and philosophical. Yet all are useful building blocks that clarify ideas, that help in identification and rethinking of concepts that strengthen the lifeline of the discipline (Dégh 1983a). In discussing the concept of variant as a crucial ingredient in the definition of folklore, I do not propose to play the "definition game" (Ben-Amos 1971:15). My goal is to suggest that an orientation (Oring 1986) toward variability opens new perspectives in folkloristics, folk narrative study in particular.

Folklorists may differ in many ways, particularly because each has gained competence in only one, or some, but not all cultures. Some folklorists work with materials from Third World cultures (of which we still know very little), others with ancient civilizations (where classic literary tale collections abound but basic classificatory works are just emerging). Others are competent in Europe, where the tales upon which research methods and theories were founded are dwindling, or in the USA, where folk tradition mediated through print (Dorson 1945) gave rise to new narrative formulations by newly structured social groups. What we share, though, is our folkloristic education, the terminology and classificatory principles developed for the convenience of historic-comparative theories and methods of tale study. In recent publications and conference papers, I see a tacit revival of some routines of the discredited Historic-Geographic school by those who have graduated from more interpretational trends influenced by structuralism, behaviorism, sociolinguistics, semiotics, communication—or performance theory (Dundes 1986; Georges 1986; Goldberg 1986; Jones 1986). In a redressed form, interest is directed toward a cross-cultural search for narrative universals on the basis of text abstracts—episodic outlines, in critical opposition to the field-based repertoire analysis of individual narrators in regional, local, or ethnic groups (Dégh 1986).

The 'Variant' is one of our inherited terms. If we speak of it (and sometimes we call it 'version,' which is simply a synonym [Thompson 1949:1155]), we must have a referent in mind, the master-term, the *type*, whose variant we mean. "The type constitutes the ideal unit of the multitude of variants," wrote Honti (1975). But what is that "ideal" or "normative" unit? If the type is the summary result of variants, and there is one type and a limitless number of variants (since there are as many variants as there are utterances), who determines which is the type among the available texts and which are the variants? Evidently we folklorists do. We examine the narrative content of the texts and use our common sense (I could have said subjective judgment) to create our personal analytical construct (essentially a "literary" endeavor), which may be different from the type construct that others would make on the basis of their ethno-cultural experience. We take what we consider the most complete variant (the one that contains the greatest number of ingredients established by the *Motif Index* [Thompson 1955–58]) as the type, or the ideal type, including the deviations of all accessible variants of a modest and unrepresentative corpus (compared to the virtually limitless number existing in the world). It is also up to us to determine the boundaries of the type: to mark the point where variants depart so radically from the main story, with some regional consistency, that they have to be called a redaction, subtype, or oicotype, or have to be assigned to another type.

Type determination, however, is not so difficult if it concerns more or less stabilized and objectified complex (multiepisodic) narratives like the magic tale, or short narratives like the joke and anecdote that are set in the real world and characterize real people. The task is far more problematic if it concerns such short, unstructured, fragile, unstable, and subjective texts as, for example, legends or autobiographical experience stories, whose efficacy depends not on the art of telling a captivating fiction but on the importance of the message they contain and convey to recipients for variable personal interpretations. Unlike legends, tale variants are never fragmentary but are carefully structured, depersonalized, and balanced wholes, coherent and complete parallels of the type. They are symbiotic in nature (Sirovátka 1964) and must be told from beginning to end following a clearly outlined episodic sequence. In my own experience as a collector of tales, narrators who named their repertoire pieces by title, and often had these ready written out on a piece of paper, could never summarize contents. When I asked what the tale was about, they began to tell the whole, beginning with the due introduction: "Once upon a time . . . "

Legend variants, on the other hand, are not shaped by the same stylistic convention even in the case of a lengthy, elaborate text rich in motifs, produced by an inspired legend teller, or legends taken from a literary source by an avid reader or constructed by the analyst in order to derive a type. During the 1960s, when European and American members of the International Society for Folk Narrative Research were engaged in constructing an international legend index, they failed in their attempt to describe the legend as a classifiable entity because they could not accept the fact that not all texts accumulating around the same theme could be defined as oral narrative

(Tagung 1962; Tagung 1963; Hand 1965). They recognized that legends may appear as real or imaginary experience accounts, but they could not accept that reports on belief concepts (*Vorstellungsberichte*) without a story should be included in the type index (Harkort 1966:208–23). Even some of the more recent proponents of legend definition insist that the legend must be an oral narrative (Nicolaisen 1984a:113–17; 1984b:167–78; Brunvand 1986:47, 178). On the other hand, the kernel or core of the legend may be contained equally in textually elaborate or underdeveloped variants, or in a single episode or statement; with or without a narrative content, reference, or allusion; and a legend may be either orally told or signaled. Any related utterance conveying the same message is capable of independent life because legends rely on common knowledge, a common frame of reference, that exempts the legend proponent from telling them in detail with explanatory comments, as if an outsider (such as a folklore fieldworker) were present. For the folklorist, all elements or ingredients are important to register with the type, whose extent and function cannot otherwise be discerned. Some of those who realized this textual inconsistency of the legend suggested using the *Motif Index* for reference because it registers the smallest narrational units to be found in legends. Unfortunately, however, the *Motif Index* items are so unspecific that they cannot be used to describe legends: the same motif number may be assigned to quite diverse legendary accounts (Halpert 1971:50).

This difference in the determination of type and variant in tale and legend originates in the social history of these two basic and contrasting genres, or, as Lüthi saw them, "zwei Grundmöglichkeiten der Erzählung" (Lüthi 1966:6). The tale—generally understood as a multiepisodic, fantastic, biographical adventure story of a central hero—(which constitutes only a part of the tale categories listed in the Aarne-Thompson type index) has been recognized and appreciated by authors, scholars, and educators as a fantastic and dreamlike fiction, a naive, childlike, but exquisite literary art, as far back in history as written documents can show. The entertaining effect of tales made storytelling an important skill for all layers of society seeking amusement, relief from boredom, and escape from everyday drudgery into the world of illusion. In the mid-seventeenth century, Pascal called the tale a "superbe ennemie de la raison," and a hundred years later Wieland, "the German Voltaire," noted that tales may spread through oral tradition, "aber gedruckt müssen sie nicht werden" ("but they must not be printed"). The telling of tales became routine, and the texts were stabilized by printing and reprinting "für nacherzählen" ("for retelling"), as Achim von Arnim suggested to his friends the Grimm brothers when they prepared their collection for the use of women and children. This practice established a peculiar interdependency between oral and written forms, both having a share in the creation of the ideal types described in folklorists' classifications. In many cases, however, folklorists did not have to deduce the type from the accessible body of variants. Instead, they located their models in prestigious early recordings and assigned the names and outlines of classic literary stories to basic type models. No one noticed this inherent feature of the type index, contradicting claims for the oral (folk) origin of Märchen.

Just a glance at the Aarne-Thompson type index (Aarne and Thompson 1961) shows how many of the listed names refer to classic themes of world literature, many of which are problematic to accept as folktales. The maintenance of titles from early epic poetry, classical literature, court epic, romance, novellas, medieval exempla, chapbooks, and broadsides[1] from the sixteenth to the nineteenth century, and from tale collections from Basile to Grimm,[2] demonstrate that the models of early tale classifiers such as Georg Hahn, Reinhold Köhler, or Lajos Katona, who were limited to these sources in defining and tabulating type models, are still accepted. Since the bulk of the tale corpus upon which folk narrative scholarship has developed was collected and guided by quite different principles than ours, it is time to question the justification of using non-folktale models as ideal types and of determining the extent of variation by comparison to their standard.

Evidently, it is more comfortable to incorporate new materials into an existing system than to build a new one on the basis of new principles. This is particularly true in the case of the folktale corpus, which has a broader international distribution than any other folklore genre and therefore needs more international cooperation in research. More sophisticated classification attempts were doomed to fail because their cross-cultural applicability is limited. While the shortcomings of the *Type Index* are known and taken into consideration, their overall usefulness is proven by the fact that new national catalogs keep being projected and published. Among the latest are the Korean, the Persian, and the Malgasy (Choi 1979; Marzolph 1984; Haring 1983), and since humanities foundations judge such endeavors favorably, more indexes are in progress. One is tempted to raise the question: is it worthwhile to try to create another, maybe less practical and more imaginative interpretive system of classification for international use? Or is it any more reasonable to index only field-recorded folk items which have all the information necessary to answer more ambitious questions which our ancestors never raised? Would such a restricted body of materials be more helpful than the all-inclusive index of diverse dependability, which, like an old tree trunk, shows the layers of its history? It seems we cannot afford to omit the vast resources stored in archives by generations of folklorists as their most cherished contribution to scholarship, their legacy left to us. These archive materials have survived the barren years when folklorists felt it necessary to debunk archives in order to liberate themselves from traditional erudition and discover the living storytelling event (Georges 1969; Dundes 1966). It did not take two decades to show the validity and indispensability of the evidences of past storytelling hidden in scholarly archives (Apo 1986; Holbek 1987; Herranen 1987).

Oral and Literary

A reassessment of the history of the folk narrative from the perspectives of social meaning and function and also the scholarly motivations for its study would be useful and timely. It would not only help to get rid of numerous misconceptions concerning the goals of research, but also help in the reexamination of the social-political conditions in the background of subjective-nationalistic evaluations that have permeated folk narrative study for most of its history. Many attempts have been made to design a developmental scheme of narrative formation from simple to complex, from natural to artistic, from practical—magical, mythic, and genealogical (religious and historic)—to fictional, entertaining stories along the lines of both social evolution and recurrent universal needs (Jolles 1965; Wesselski 1931; Propp 1946; Meletinsky 1958). Prior to rare dependable oral recordings from the second decade of the twentieth century and the field materials collected by "Märchenbiologists" (Lüthi 1976:89–108) from the 1940s to the present, all source materials are literary. Nevertheless, scholars seem to minimize the part that literature—writing, printing, and reading—has played and continues to play in the shaping of folk narrative tradition. Throughout the history of research, naive nationalist-populist debates have been conducted to prove the primacy of oral (folk) tradition over the literary. *Kunstpoesie* was judged as constructed and artificial, unlike the natural *Naturpoesie*. I am referring here to the criticism of the heritage theory of the Grimms; the reception theory of Hoffman-Krayer (Bausinger 1980:19–55); and the attack of Soviet folklorists against the "aristocratic" theory, in which they claimed that epic songs did not originate among professional court singers but among the suppressed and exploited folk (Oinas 1973). After the much criticized Albert Wesselski, whose contributions to folk narrative study were considerable, fifty years passed before the source-critical research of Rudolf Schenda (1970a: 1976), Grimm philologist Heinz Rölleke (1975), and others could shed light on the relationship of oral and literary tradition in eighteenth- and nineteenth-century society without being suspect of hostility toward the folk.

Between Basile and Grimm, elite society developed an intellectual fascination with the complex tale. The landmark publication of *Le Cabinet des fées* (1785–86) in 41 volumes shows that "des contes des fées et autres contes merveilleux" had become fashionable. This first serial publication of tales included all that was then known as marvelous tale, *Wundermärchen*, or fairy tale: classic Arabic, Persian, Indic, Turkish, and Mongolian collections in translation, and the stories of Perrault, Countesses d'Aulnoy and Murat, and other aristocratic women of letters. No author claimed to represent the folk; style and tone were refined according to the contemporary literary taste of their audience: abstractedly naive and appealing to the tender-hearted.

The Grimm collection also depended heavily on literary texts, sometimes translated from non-German sources. Even if the source was secondhand, even if a reteller had read it from a book or heard it from another reader who read it from a book, the Grimms claimed folk (primitive, rustic, illiterate) origin. With the Grimms and their supporters, the Märchen—the same body of complex tales fashionable among the aristocracy—became celebrated as an ancestral German heritage preserved by the peasant folk and therefore nationally and politically important. The fashionable genre thus entered the household and the nursery of the urban bourgeoisie in nineteenth-century Germany through the book market, carrying the literary tradition undisturbed.

In the singular relationship of oral tradition and literary variants, who can tell them apart? Ironically, despite the efforts of folklorists to stay away from alien urban influences and record only the genuinely oral tradition, tales like Cinderella, Snow White, Beauty and the Beast, and The Kind and Unkind Girls reinforce their literary persona as shaped by the Italian, French, and German authors, only to be conveyed to further republishers and recasters, editors and translators, designers, composers, cartoonists, and filmmakers to influence the folk masses. Isn't it time we also include the study of the professional literary-artistic variants with those told by oral folk tellers? They tell more about the sociological causes of possible oral formulations— our traditional target—than if we have the consumers retell the stories to us.

The literary appeal of the *conte merveilleuse* (whatever it includes) led folklorists to false conclusions. They focused on the magic tale, and whatever they wrote about the nature of the folktale as a genre did not really include all tale categories registered in the tale type index but only the types numbered between 300 and 749, or between 300 and 1000 at best. We were also misled by noted storytellers who enjoyed recognition for their entertaining services among migrant laborers and gave preference to long-winded magic tales, making us forget to look for other kinds of stories in their repertoires that fill other needs and are structured differently. While the literary tale, commonly known by the readership as the fairy tale, and so much appreciated by elite circles, became popularized and in turn folklorized, then defined, scrutinized, and interpreted by scholars as oral folk (peasant) art, other narrative forms were largely neglected.

A cursory look at Johannes Bolte's listing in his *Zeugnisse zur Geschichte der Märchen* (1921) would have shown us that other kinds of narratives were no less popular than the Märchen. Bolte's list is a modest but realistic inventory of popular story themes, narrators, and occasions. The themes, however, are broad and representative of the miscellany of current narratives. Included with the tales are horror stories, ghost stories, mythic and demonologic legends, histories, romances, heroic chapbook novels, adventures, and anecdotes, as well as personal experience stories. The narrators (friends, neighbors, servants, nursemaids, other employees, family members, and guests) not only recounted their stories at the usual occasions (fireside talk, coffee hour, nursery entertainment of children, girl's spinnery diversion, occupational gatherings) but also often read stories to the listeners from popular books. Thanks to recent Grimm philology, particularly the studies of Heinz Rölleke, we now have an idea of the interaction of oral and literary narration and variation by the tradition bearers of the Grimm circle: teller-reader-rewriter-editor-reteller, from book to book. All this tells us something about the difficulty of isolating the folktale as oral art from its narrational context and its literary relationships.

Among the many genres in social use, the legend as we know it today remained for the most part unnoticed and unappreciated by scholars. When the Grimm brothers, the founders of our discipline, provided posterity with the first collection of tales and legends, they were well aware of the basic difference between these two genres, and this awareness is reflected in their treatment of the texts. They defined the Märchen as fictional, open to poetic fantasy. At first the brothers were hesitant to embellish the Märchen texts, which they regarded as the conveyor of a sacred ancestral heritage. But as soon as they found their responsive audience in urban middle-class women and their children, they freely used their artistic skill in transforming the raw materials they assembled to create new narratives fit for an "Erziehungsbuch" (book for child education). Consequently, the aptly transformed and revised *Kinder-und Hausmärchen* became an instant success in the marketplace. It remains today the world's prime best-seller for generations of the youthful, mainly feminine readership (Tatar 1987).

On the other hand, the Grimms knew that legends are nonfiction, have their place in the real world, and involve ordinary people as their principal actors. Their *Deutsche Sagen* never made it as a popular reader and remained on the bookshelves of scholars. No wonder: the stories are brief, dry, and factual, chronicle-like, unartistic, moralizing, dull reports. Although the Grimms did embellish the texts that they lifted from old historic sources (chronicles, chapbooks, local histories, travelogues, and other printed matter), they kept the semblance of historicity (Rosenfeld 1958:82–90). The most they did was to combine the factual accounts of several variants and make a better documented story. Although sometimes reference was made to a local oral variant (e.g., "from oral sources"), this was no more than an allusion, not a direct recording by the brothers. Like Grimm Märchen titles, *Sagen* titles (such as Kyffhäuser, Rübezahl, Die Kinder von Hameln, Tannhäuser, or Charlemagne) were taken from printed models by later German type indexers.

I hope I have adequately exposed the questions concerning the relationship between the oral and literary communication of tales and legends, in order to exorcise the revenant concept that keeps haunting our premises: namely, that folklore is a purely oral art which is in decline under the pressures of literary fixation. There can be no question that the folklore process, the creation and transmission of tale and legend types and variants, results from a constant interdependence between oral and written formulations. In a purely isolated oral community, no narrative tradition could evolve and persist: this is what the past has taught us. In our days, more than ever, no soundproof separation can keep professionally transmitted folklore from affecting the masses of the world. To modernize our discipline and cope with the problem of identifying currently evolving and varying folk narratives, we have to find new determinants and look at the forces that stimulate and accelerate variation.

It has been a legacy of the founders of folkloristics to view the peasant or the primitive as the folk, the unique custodian of national heritage. Patriotic zeal endowed the peasants (an abstract, collective entity) with superior qualities which were linked to their lack of education and lack of exposure to the intellectual world. The contrast between folk and nonfolk was also environmentally dramatized: idyllic countryside, simple agricultural and pastoral lifestyle, and closeness to nature were contrasted to life in the urban-industrial centers in which alienation from national values and loss of identity resulted from the infiltration of alien (urban and cosmopolitan) elements. Folklorists saw their task as to rescue and preserve the unconscious art of the folk for use in national education to restore identity based on tradition. These ideas, conceived in the nineteenth century, persisted with varying intensity and linger to the present day.

Among the ideas most consistent in the definitions of folklore is the emphasis on orality. Folklore is often regarded as synonymous with oral literature as contrasted to written literature. It is cited as "unwritten literature," "oral tradition," "oral literary tradition," "purely oral culture," "verbal art," or "spoken word." In one definition, "folklore . . . consists of oral tradition in variants" (Brunvand 1981:3), whereas in other definitions, orality—or more precisely, speaking—is emphasized as the technique of transmission: "The main forms of the communication within the domain of folklore are oral . . . " (Voigt 1980). Other definitions similarly emphasize orality in the transmission, not the overall attribute of folklore: "Verbal tradition orally transmitted," "oral communication," "literature transmitted orally," "orally transmitted popular literature," "unwritten literature" "handed down from one person to the other," and the "process by which tradition is communicated through speech from speaker to listener" (Hultkrantz 1960:192–93; Pentikäinen 1970:89–93; Ben-Amos 1971:13–14; Bauman 1977:4–5; Oring 1986:14). "Folklorists tend largely to draw the boundaries of the field to exclude forms that depend on the written word," writes Bauman (1989:180). An argument is also made to view oral literature and folklore not as identical but rather as reciprocal: oral in its manifestation but literary in its aesthetic quality (Lawless 1985). Alan Dundes and Carl Pagter appear to be the only challengers of this emphasis on orality (1975:xvii–xviii).

Regarding folk narrative research in particular, the illiteracy of raconteurs gained particular attention. From Radlov to Lord, Bowra, Finnegan, and others, students of epic poetry have been impressed by the remarkable memorizing and reproducing technique of illiterate epic singers (Finnegan 1977; Stolz and Shannon 1976). Similarly, the early discovery of storytellers with large repertoires, like the street sweeper Tobias Kern (Bünker 1906) and day laborer Mihály Borbély (Kálmány 1914–15), prompted folklorists to ascribe their art to the peculiarities of illiterate recall. Memory became a key clue for researchers, who ascribed individual creativity, communal variation, and generational transmission to the nature of remembering and forgetting by illiterates (for a detailed discussion of the issues raised by Bartlett, Anderson, and others, see Dégh and Vázsonyi 1975).

No one seemed to be bothered by the fact that the originals of the stories in one of the earliest folktale collections, George Gaal's *Märchen der Magyaren* (Vienna, 1822), had been written, not told, by the narrators. They were peasant youngsters from the Nagykunság, who had been drafted into the Austrian-Hungarian army; they obeyed a standing order from their commanding officer to write down a tale they could remember from their home village. Thus, this early Grimm-inspired book of tales represented not oral but written communication from folk to folklorist, without a trace of oral technique or style. In 1969 an international symposium in Budapest discussed the nature of oral transmission. Participants remarked on the timeliness of the topic because the majority of the world's population still lived in illiterate cultural conditions and produced folklore in its purest form. On the other hand, they also stated that evidence of erosion of the purely oral, the switch to literacy, and the impact of the electronic media could also be observed (Voigt 1974). The discussion of primary and secondary orality in relationship to literacy by Walter Ong directs us to a more realistic view of modern folk narration (Ong 1980).

Throughout my career as fieldworker in traditional villages I experienced the ubiquitous presence of literary tradition in the repertoires of illiterate and semiliterate as well as literate storytellers. There was no correlation between their creative act of recital and their degree of literacy. About sixty percent of the repertoire of illiterate Mrs. Palkó, for example, came from books which were either retold or re-read in her presence (Dégh 1989:146–163). During my several visits to this extremely tradition-minded community—Kakasd, in Hungary—I learned more of the standard community repertoire, which consisted of a balanced set of oral and literary traditions. Several of the story-tellers were keen readers, like the current star, 60-year-old Mrs. Maria Fábián, whose deceased father, storyteller Rudolf Györfi, had also been a reader (Sebestyén 1979:1:86). Moreover, on a recent return to Kakasd, Mrs. Palkó's cousin, illiterate Mrs. Jákob Erös, told me a well-embellished variant of the frame story of the chapbook *Historia Septem Sapientum.* Similarly, M. Kurcsi, J. Faragó's alpine storyteller, adapted his whole stock of Märchen from an abridged Grimm collection he owned (Faragó 1969).

András Albert, one of the most gifted storytellers I ever met, was an avid reader of chapbooks, adventure novels, romances, and storybooks. His creativity can be easily discerned by comparing his variant to the one he has read. I had the good fortune to find his chapbook source when I took inventory of reading matter in his village. In a text-analytical comparison, personal and regional stylistic features as well as features endemic to the genre could be identified (Dégh 1946–47). András, with whom I kept up correspondence, was also a writer of letters. Among other things, he sent me two of his tales by mail. I have published one in *Folktales of Hungary* (Dégh 1965a:28–45): a most original redaction of AaTh 400, displaying his adaptation of story structuring, style of description, and dialogue from literary sources.

From the viewpoint of the audience, it makes no difference whether the narrator learned his story in father-to-son transmission, made it up himself, memorized it from a book, or is reading it aloud in performance. It is the nature of the folktale that it has to be recited by sound to listeners (or read or played from a record or tape, and so on), just as a drama script has to be enacted (Dégh 1981). The provenance of the tale is irrelevant in this relationship. For the folklorist, it must be clear that behind the variant chosen for recital there is a long line of told, written, printed, illustrated, expanded, and reduced variants. Each of these, singly and collectively, contributes to the new variant's formulation, hand in hand with the situational context.

Under the influence of modern sociolinguistics, some folklorists have switched focus from folklore creation in the context of the interplay between storyteller, audience, and tradition to the technique and routine of verbal exchange in communicating narrative messages. For them, verbal art is performance, and the "way of speaking" is the target of observation at the moment of utterance (Bauman 1977), in the situated context, separated from the larger social, cultural, economic, and historical context. For the folk narrative specialist, the results of the microanalysis of conditions and mechanisms surrounding the emergent texts in verbal exchange may be useful but too limited to answer basic questions concerning cultural adaptation, persistence, and variation of story themes by narrators responding to changing social conditions. If the event and the text are taken as the data for scholarly interpretation in the framework of the act of communication (Bauman 1986), the personality and creativity of narrators fall to the wayside.

The Mass Media

The relation between oral and written, folk and the elite, the informal and the formal, the authorized and the unauthorized, the everyday and the ceremonial, the lay and the professional, developed hand in hand through the ages. The dynamic interdependence was regular, harmonious, and predictable. However, since about the end of World War II, there has been an upset in the equilibrium of the two. In the global village (to use the apt term of Marshall McLuhan) created by the media, a new communality has formed on the basis of the homogenizing effect of uniform information and the mass-marketing of stories to a mass society structured into occupational, ethnic, age, sex, religious, and other population groups, also identifiable as folk or folklore-transmitting communities. The even flow of identical information systematically enculturates the citizens of the world, turning them into the consumers of identical cultural goods by creating a symbolic egalitarian social order that supersedes segmentation by national boundaries. The choices in careers and lifestyles have become boundless, while the content of mass messages has remained as patterned as messages ever were, composed of traditional (conventional), reconstructed (revivalistic), and innovative elements.

The course of the folklore process that folklorists studied before occurred on a smaller and more or less observable scale and was understood as transmission and variation from one generation to the next, in historical depth. This worked well because normally no radical social change disrupted the system, in which generational conflict was reconciled by a rigid rule of generativity (Erikson 1964). Among the monograph studies of narrative repertoires, Kurt Ranke's collection of tales (1955–1962) is a good example of the process of tracing the flow of transmission by individual storytellers in regional, local, and family continuity.

Modern vehicles of communication technology have added to the slow-moving regularity of passing on tradition from "father to son" a new and more vigorous form of transmission: the passing on of tradition from peer group to peer group (Buchan 1981:2). Legend researchers in particular have noted that repertoires are shared by age groups; stories that circulate among teenagers are unknown to their parents. The media unites groups of common interest without physical proximity and supplies them with the proper information, the proper folklore, without hesitation, almost simultaneously with its actualization. This strengthening of synchronic over diachronic transmission, along with the simultaneity of repetitions within extremely short periods of time, inadvertently results in the multiplication of variants through diverse interconnected channels of communication. Thus, the "interference" of mass media vehicles not only accelerates the folklore process but also contributes to a numerical growth, indeed, a never-before-experienced inflation of folklore. If researchers at the turn of the century foretold the demise of folklore, seeking to salvage the last vestiges of the glorious past, our generation is witnessing the return of folklore on the wings of the media, with more vigorous circulation, gaining more significance than ever, emerging as a crucial response to the vicissitudes of life in the modern age.

Folklore forms—traditional, emergent, new, and reconstructed—appear in innumerable retellings, varied according to the need of the accommodating media that profoundly influences oral transmission. Appearances in the media outnumber oral variants, making it hopeless to determine the source or origin of field-collected texts. If under these circumstances folklorists still disqualify mass media-influenced variants, claiming that "they are not rooted in community life but commodified and imposed from without," "not participatory but are meant to be consumed by a mass audience" and "not variable but fixed" (Bauman 1989:180), they deny their discipline the right of existence. Folklorists in the modern world should keep pace with technological developments and not romantically idealize the preliterate folk. We have to recognize that we are a consumer-oriented society, that the market produces for us what we need to conform to tradition in our social interactions, to participate in ritual life and entertainment. Hallmark greeting cards prepare us for traditional occasions; we have no trouble finding Halloween paraphernalia on supermarket shelves, guidebooks on how to organize festivals, weddings, and burials, or occult books and botanicas to keep us feeling socially secure, faithful to heritage while creatively innovative.

The mass media has caused the dissemination of several pertinent didactic legends, whose Christian theology-based and folklore-stimulating thesis—"if we believe in God we must also believe in the Devil"—would otherwise have remained within the confines of fundamental Protestant congregations, implanting the fear of Evil into the hearts of the faithful. I do not think I have to go into detail describing the legends sharing this motif; thanks to modern journalism they have become familiar, appearing in headlines, front-page news, talk show discussions, docudramas, and movies. Just three examples in the abundant Devil legend cycle for reference:

(1) The Church of Satan is building its worldwide power through blood rituals involving children who are forced to participate in sex acts and the sacrifice of babies and animals.

(2) Supermarket bar codes contain 666, the Number of the Beast, in

order to seduce more souls before the Last Judgment, coming soon in the year 2000.

(3) The owner of Procter and Gamble made a pact with the Devil to give him his heart and soul when he dies in return for helping him prosper.

The choice of stories offered to the public is enormous, but not limitless. New stories ascend, others fade away, while old stories are brought back to life following the whims of public opinion. Favorites are reissued in books, magazines, and newspapers in more copies than ever before; they are narrated on the radio and dramatized in movie and television scripts. Depending on the nature of the medium—scholarly, popularizing publication by experts, journalistic elaboration, or literary or artistic recasting—the audience is exposed to professionally-shaped variants of tales and legends. The balanced give-and-take between folklore and the media has been upset by overwhelming media proliferation.

It is not enough to recognize that mass media play a role in folklore transmission. It is closer to the truth to admit that the media have become a part of folklore. Interacting with oral repetition, they may constitute the greater part of the folklore conduit. As the story travels and switches from conduit to conduit and spreads to parallel conduits (Dégh and Vázsonyi 1975), it also addresses through mass media devices a much larger audience, united by a common notion-inventory and earlier variants into which the just-received version is accommodated. In the midst of mass media storytellers, retellers, and variant-producers, the everyday oral transmitter is forced to take a back seat. The now-proliferating UFO abduction legends, for example, did not begin in Barney and Betty Hill's living room in 1961, when they told their memorate to their friends as is customary to do. The story was launched by the mass media with the participation of scientists and pseudo-scientists— experts in psychology, parapsychology, astrophysics, and religion—and presented to the global villagers. Twenty-seven years have elapsed since the incident, and the story keeps its attraction (Klass 1988). More and more people come forward to narrate their abduction stories publicly, relying on "abductee support groups," which have gained credibility in the public eye. Variants retold in books, movies, and tabloids, again and again, inspire new storytellers. Copycat cases emerge (Dégh and Vázsonyi 1983) and create new variants on the solid basis of previous media-supported knowledge and banalization. The influence of diverse occult establishments seems to be interacting in the production of more recent variables of UFO lore: e.g., fairies are walking on the streets of cities in broad daylight (Rojcewicz 1991:479–514).

The relationship between the Grimm brothers and the folk is very different from that between the mass media and the folk. While the creation of the Grimms can be distinguished from orally transmitted tale variants, the components of the relationship between mass media and the folk are practically inseparable; indeed, theoretically it is not even necessary to separate them. This is especially true of legends. In their fragile, diffuse, and often not fully developed forms, legends en vogue can hardly be followed through a labyrinth of diverse transmission media: immediate oral communication; letter writing; telephone messages; news reports in the daily papers and on radio and TV; more detailed accounts in popular magazines, weeklies, and scholarly publications, as well as in literary works, cartoons, and comics; converging, diverging and complementing the variants of the same story in the mind of potential retellers (Dégh and Vázsonyi 1976).

If we consult the current legend crops, passed on to us through tabloids, cartoons, and popular children's books, we learn that our beloved dead relatives have also found new electronic vehicles to communicate with us. In *Phone Call from a Ghost* by Daniel Cohen (1988), it is Grandma who calls from the grave. The following is a small assortment from May 1992 issues of *Weekly World News, Globe, Sun, Star, and National Examiner*: A man tells that his ex-wife has called him on their wedding anniversary every year for 22 years; A woman tells how her dead husband talks to her on the lower end of the TV dial; A widow is contacted by her spouse over the dial tone of her cordless telephone; Another widow finds the message 'I miss you' on the Xerox copy of her dead husband's will; A couple reports that their recently deceased son comforted them by telling them over the static between two AM stations that he is in a happy place; A concerned dead mother uses the toaster to burn the words "car port" on the bread when her son lost the key of the safe deposit box she willed to him.

Similarly, classic ghost stories have been rejuvenated by the application of the fax machine: Employees of one company report that the dead boss "still tries to run the company from beyond the grave!" His orders for shipping, invoices, and money decisions arrive at random intervals on the company fax. Another story tells of a fax received from London by a traveling salesman who was killed on the way to London a week earlier. We are far from the time when Bascom's statement that "all folklore is orally transmitted" was acceptable (1953). When so many agents contribute to the composition of folk narrative products, how can we identify variants as purely oral products?

Both folktales and legends continue to survive in industrial western society: pursuing their life history would be a worthwhile documentation of how basic human expressions—fears, hopes, and desires—continue to manifest in diverse symbolic forms in the process of social change. The scene changes, the social groups change and multiply, but what people tell about themselves in the frames of conveniently traditional narratives does not change or changes only in nuances.

In regard to folktales (magic tales), most folklorists express skepticism concerning their relevance today and speak of their demise, displacement, second-hand exploitation, and normalization. At the same time, it is almost incredible how much attention is given to this anachronistic fantasy genre, how much controversy it stirs up among child psychologists, educators, social workers, sociologists, and alarmed parents concerned with the mental health of society. With their fascination for the symbolic language of the world of enchantment, artists and literary authors exploit and propagate tale magic, while scholars in the humanities attempt to decode the hidden meanings of the tale. All these concerns—practical, artistic, and scientific—significantly contribute to the subsistence and further variation of the Märchen. The number of books written on the tale is breathtaking and approximates the number of storybooks published. Finding folktale structures, characters, and ideology in the burgeoning realm of science fiction movies, we may also speculate about the extent of variability and repeatability and the breaking point that the tale world cannot transgress.

That the magic tale is an important human expression was convincingly proven by the high regard accorded for centuries to the Grimms; why then this pessimism as to its survival? The answer is simple: most folklorists view the folktale as a product of preindustrial European peasant communities which were ethnographically experienced between the second half of the nineteenth and the first half of the twentieth century. The tale models (the types) were derived from texts collected from "illiterate" villagers, completely ignoring the fact that the wealth in tales was not independent from the Grimm collection. Even today, the Grimm variant is still regarded as the prototypical folktale, in the conceptualizations of both psychoanalysts (Bettelheim 1976) and literary folklorists (Lüthi 1966; Röhrich 1971). In fact, the Grimm-style story condensed and integrated elements of previous variants on the basis of nineteenth-century cultural norms that helped to homogenize, standardize, and disseminate tales, enabling them to be adapted to new needs and to survive (Dégh 1988).

The interaction between oral tale and book tale was evident to fieldworkers as much as to all those who cared to examine earlier sources. Fictive and real, professional and lay storytellers passed on the tradition in the past: Scheherazade, the Seven Sages of Rome, Lucius the Golden Ass, ma mère l'oye, Frau Viehmann, Agatuzza Messia, Natalja Vinokurowa, and Charlotte Rougemont. Today modern narrators do the same: the Americans, Brother Blue, Jackie Torrence, and Ray Hicks, the Germans Felicitas Betz, Carl-Heinz Mallet, and Janosch; the French Evelyne Cevin or Bernard Cheze, and countless others (Wehse 1983; Doderer 1983). What is the difference between Zsuzsanna Palkó of the village Kakasd (Dégh 1989) and my mother who told me a tale every afternoon while we walked to Grandmother's house? She told me Märchen she had heard from her mother or read from a beautifully illustrated book of European folktales we had at home, or she made them up herself.

In modern society, the home of the Märchen is more variegated and more institutionalized than ever. Storytelling guilds emerge as artificial subcultures, outside the mainstream of the modern cultural scene. Self-styled storytellers attempt to reimpose an anachronistic mode of behavior in an arbitrary, staged presentation. In the hope of capturing the attention of large audiences, they create storytelling festivals, weekends, and encounters, often also appearing on local and national radio and TV programs to perform staged, traditional, reconstructed, and invented narratives (Dégh 1985b:214–15). Like any literate storytellers, rural or urban, these men and women take their stories partly from books, partly from oral tradition, and also make them up. It is up to their listeners what will continue and what will not, how they will modify their stories and what they will drop, just as it was for illiterate narrators whose repertoire was a direct outgrowth of their society in the good old days. However, since the staged performance is uniformly patterned, involving the acts of heterogeneous performers and ad hoc audiences and lacking a homogeneous social base, its future is uncertain.

Nevertheless, like other cases of folklorism, storytelling revivals need to be studied.[3] The folk narrative scholar's task is not to stick to past standards and bemoan the loss of classic forms of storytelling, but to move on to the questions: What makes modern (urban, if you like) society maintain its interest in folktales? How does the folktale bear new variants to keep its audience spellbound? What are the successful media devices that carry the tales and adjust them to up-to-date needs?

Maybe it is needless to say that the legend has shown itself as the most viable among the narrative folklore genres. If tale variability is promoted indirectly, the legend benefits directly from the mass media and proliferates with increasing speed. The messages of the legend are universal; they are characteristic and even determinant of individual human thoughts, acts, and mass movements. The basic concern of legend is human life and its fragility, death and the mysteries of the spirit world—fearful secrets unresolvable by the human mind. It responds to current concerns and may appear in all walks of life, making its statement and commentary on critical events. This capability of the legend can be attributed to its compositional flexibility, its lack of the straightjacket of an artistic form and style. Legend tellers, as a rule, are considered as well-informed people insofar as they stress their experience and knowledge, as opposed to tale tellers, who emphasize their artistic inspiration and authorship. As I have said before, the legend can appear in any oral, literary, or media channel, presenting always a sensational, extraordinary, horrible, dreadful, ridiculous, baffling, or mysterious feat. It often assumes the style of experience story, autobiography, rumor, or anecdote, and stresses personal involvement. At the same time, the legend can easily be distinguished from other narratives because it is the only folklore genre that is dialectic and provokes controversy (Dégh and Vázsonyi 1976). When the tellers make their point, they argue against a contrary opinion held by the majority of society; and their assertion is followed by statements of belief and disbelief by the audience. Even if listeners occasionally happen to agree, the framework of opposing authoritative opinion remains the stimulant of legend performance.

Much has been said of the legend since the international experiment with classification mentioned earlier. After some resistance to leaving peasant villages, regarded as the hotbeds of legendry, researchers successfully explored the industrial society of which they and co-urbanite intellectuals were also part. It was not easy for them to see themselves as potential legend-bearers. This new treasure hunt indicates several things about the legend in the modern world.

First, legend types known before in preindustrial, feudal, and rural environments continue to live in current industrial contexts, and variants show great flexibility in adjusting to current needs. Yet legend transmitters are ignorant of previous variants, just as the tellers of local legends were ignorant of the legends that scholars knew as migratory (Dégh 1973, 1975).

Second, the recurrent stories may not be variants of a single *Urform* that can be traced step by step. Legends are too skimpy in narrative detail; and the factual core that carries them is both too unspecific and too banal to be unique. The legend as we all know it takes place in the real world, and the extraordinary event it relates is not impossible, not totally unimaginable, and can even sound plausible. It fits well into the everyday life of ordinary people and the contemporary value system that surrounds it. In fact, the event it relates might have happened not only once but many times on independent occasions at distant places. The ubiquitous *Mordeltern* story (Aath 939, Killing the Returned Soldier) is a good example of the many modern legends whose variants cannot be related in the spatial and temporal system of the deductive historic-geographic method (Kosko 1966). The technique of simple text comparison cannot establish the *Urform* or the generic relationship of single variants.

It is all the more amazing that scholars studying "urban legends" argue that a just-recorded story is "untrue" because it can be traced to a nineteenth-century predecessor on another continent. In this spirit, Sanderson (1981:10–11) criticizes my description of the legend of "The House of Blue Lights," whose life history and variation can be localized to the Indianapolis area by the great abundance of variants from the early 1940s fitting the worldview and lifestyle of adolescents. Yet Sanderson feels it unsatisfactory to call this a "dormitory story"—which I did simply because it was among the standard repertoire pieces of dormitory legend-telling sessions (Grider 1980), not because I intended to coin a scholarly term. Sanderson found an 1831 "variant" related to Queen Victoria's consort, and claimed this "earlier version" made it doubtful that "The House of Blue Lights" was an original Indiana legend with "truly historical facts" behind it.

What do we gain by looking for the earliest content analogy whose genetic connection to the legend in question cannot be established, instead of performing an analytical field-based study of the variation of a local story? Perhaps such a search is meant to reach the conclusion Brunvand reached, namely that the legend is a story told for true but is in fact untrue. By painstaking scrutiny of international and historic "variants," he argues that the just-spreading new legend or rumor cannot have happened because it has been heard elsewhere (Brunvand 1986). But is this all that defines the legend, and should this be all we need to know about it? The insistence by legend transmitters that their stories are true is not a necessary requirement for keeping the genre vibrantly alive. Conversely, for a researcher, a legend is not a legend because it is untrue. Actually, legends might be as much true as they are untrue, objectively or subjectively; it really does not make much difference. What matters is that the legend raises the question of plausibility and makes people reflect.

Third, because of the acceleration of communication, legendary information multiplies and produces many variants. The same core sent by newswire may produce many variants as different reporters write the story up for their respective papers. Responding to current rumors and events, syndicated columnists, opinion pages, and tabloids also make their more elaborate contributions to variation. A side ramification of the "razor blade in the apple" legend (Grider 1984), for example, erupted on the occasion of the Tylenol poisoning in Chicago in 1982. The fast-spreading legend cycle produced some sixty distinct stories, each proven to be an untrue variant of the true Tylenol case and reported during a period of three months by newsmen in local daily papers across America. Even as this book was in press, a new cycle of "hypodermic-needle-in-the-diet-drink-can" stories was blitzing the country. Legends, speeding on the expressway of the electronic media and news reports, are short-lived. They function until the related fact wears off, when they are replaced by another headline news item, to be later revitalized by the news media during dull seasons or on anniversaries or any other appropriate occasion reporters can find.

Fourth and finally, urban legend explorers emphasize the oral nature of the stories which are told by the elusive "friend of a friend" (Smith 1984) responsible for variation. There is a general and vague reference to oral transmission, but as things stand, the oral existence of legends is usually simply assumed rather than documented by evidence of existing legend-telling events in the same way we speak of storytelling events. Folklorists collect modern urban legends in the United States in two ways. One method (and I myself am quite guilty of this) is to ask students to collect legends as a class assignment. Thus, we learned about adolescent ritual legend telling—the legend trip—and its content and meaning through the written papers of our students, or from our own recording from volunteer informants; we were not really in the field, observing the oral telling event (Dégh 1980; Baker 1982; Ellis 1983).

The majority of legends come from the cross-section of America that may be regarded as a virtually functioning legend-breeding community, but not in the more traditional sense of folklore communication. The bulk of contemporary legends were reported not from oral informants but from the media. Newspaper clippings, television and radio reports are the sources, either secondhand reports of assumed legend-telling events or the recounting of a certain unnamed person, lacking the data accuracy which as a rule authenticates folkloristic recordings. As Brunvand writes: "folk tradition even hitchhikes along with technological advances . . . we hear urban legends now on radio and television, see them dramatized in film, read them in newspapers, and transmit them to others via the mail, computer or telephone" (1986:10). The oral telling in each case was the secondhand reaction to the reading of a legend, which makes the informant remember another. In this case, we must speak of non-oral folklore variants which, as Brunvand tells us, we should collect, organize, and try to explain.

If we do not try to find out how legends spontaneously manifest themselves in interpersonal communication, the vacuum-cleaner style of collection may result in no more than an increase in the corpus of legends by the clipping of media variants from printed matter and newswire releases, or the taping of television and radio programs by volunteer collaborators. Interpretive commentaries appended to such collections cannot yield more than cautious statements of the obvious, such as: the legend "reveals society's broader fears of people . . . " (Brunvand 1981:11); they "explain unusual and supernatural happenings in the natural world" and "appeal to our morbid curiosity and satisfy our sensation-seeking mind" (Brunvand 1981:12; 13), "reflect or articulate many of the hopes, fears, anxieties and submerged desires of our time" (Nicolaisen 1984b:170) and "are stories told as true which circulate by word of mouth in contemporary society and exhibit traditional variation" (Buchan 1981:2). Most of the recent researchers, however, avoid generalization and limit interpretation to smaller legend categories. Of course, it is easy to criticize, and the task is enormous. But it is worth trying.

Concluding Remarks

What can we do to improve our tools for researching folklore in a world whose abrupt changes we cannot predict on the basis of our traditional expectations? At the end of this sketchy survey of the variant's behavior in the two fundamental narrative genres on opposite ends of a continuum from the fictional to the realistic, bridged by transitory narrative forms, only modest suggestions can be made.

One thing is certain: the variant is a more important manifestation of the type than we thought before. Dealing with modern society—mass society—in rapid transformation, we must realize that the variant and variability are the key signs of life, securing the continuity of tradition and absorbing the shock of inevitable change. To pursue the avenues of variation is more difficult in mass society than ever before. We are unable to follow cross-cultural comparison of texts without first subjecting our local and regional types and variables to close scrutiny on the basis of the realities of social life from which they have emerged. This kind of identification of types may be more laborsome and less spectacular, but it would furnish materials for a more dependable classification system. Regarding the development and general function of folklore as a response to social reality, we have to rethink our earlier concepts of the relationship between type and variant.

With consideration of variants appearing in all communicative media, the registration of the basic stories humans tell may be possible. Would it come as a surprise that an all-inclusive basic narrative index would still be limited as much as human imagination and human choices of careers are limited by sociobiological factors? An all-inclusive typology may prove the vaildity of the *einfache Formen* theory or prove that the *homo narrans* mirrors the human need to express and creatively magnify everyday experiences. There is no new story under the sun, but old stories are repeatable in innumerable ways.

The variant should not be defined only by its plot content but by the consideration of all possible contributing factors both typologically and generically, to find out if formal surface similarities also mean internal identity. Not only full narrative texts, but also ingredients lacking the narrative core, as well as texts manifested in forms other than oral telling or literary fixation, need to be considered in order to understand the rules of story formation. With all contributing factors—oral, literary, personal, communal, and electronic mass manipulation of traditional materials, we may come closer to the mystery of the continuity of folklore. These were the questions raised by the pioneers of folk narrative study, Axel Olrik, Antti Aarne, Kaarle Krohn, Walter Anderson, C. W. von Sydow and Albert Wesselski. Among the answerers who contributed with insightful ideas are the authors of the Festschrift for

Hans Moser (Bausinger and Brückner 1969) and most importantly, Gyula Ortutay, whose affinity theory (Ortutay 1959) gains new impetus when applied to tale variation in industrial society.

As to the definition of folk narrative, indeed of folklore in general, the qualifier "oral" needs to be replaced with the more fitting term "variable" with reference to the diversity of mass media participation in the transmission of folklore. We can no longer limit our concept of folklore to "purely oral" utterances. Variants of the same items from any source, folk or elite, professional or lay, spoken, written, broadcast, taped, projected visually or through audio or in body language, need to be assembled and analyzed together as equally important links in the chain of transmission. Any attempt at a more realistic description of a tale or legend type, subtype, oikotype, redaction, or variant must include accessible items circulated by any communicative vehicle in interactional relationship with any other. Is there any other way to distinguish the rules of oral composition and variation than by measuring modification by comparison to nonoral variants?

The following chapters of this book will sample from the multitude of appearances of folklore in and around the mass media. They will illustrate how folklore continues to manifest its traditional ideas, beliefs, attitudes, and meanings in modern industrial society. By its ability to adjust to new vehicles of communication and exploit their potential to reach out to a much larger audience than ever before, folklore appears to increase its effectiveness both in sustaining tradition and reforming folk groups. The sample presented will be modest, compared to the epoch-making contribution of mass communication to social transformation, but hopefully sufficient to open the door for the exploration of folklore in our time.

2

Magic for Sale

Märchen and Legend in TV Advertising

Television as a Narrative Conduit

THE MÄRCHEN, the classical oral prose narrative of Old World peasantry, barely survived the cultural upheaval caused by industrialization.[1] Nineteenth-century pioneers in folklore noted the decline of the Märchen due to the termination of the isolation of the self-sufficient village. Their early twentieth-century followers reported that the Märchen was losing its central position as adult entertainment and survived primarily in the memory of old, marginal people and among women restricted to the audience of their nurseries. No wonder that European peasant immigrants to America imported little if any of their tale treasury.[2] If they did, new industrial work conditions soon rendered storytelling obsolete and substituted for its enjoyment more easily available forms of recreation. Modern West European folklorists, examining current social conditions of narration, unanimously state that the Märchen "disappeared from tradition with the dissolution of peasant society" (Klintberg 1976:269). As Hermann Bausinger summarized his observation in West Germany, there is "practically no living Märchen tradition left. The rise of rationality has pushed the Märchen into the world of children, and there they have been standardized for educational use" (Bausinger *Volkskunde*, 145; see also Röhrich 1974).

Evidently, when conditions favorable for its continuance ceased to exist, the tale, with its entertaining function depending on primary communication, became dispensable, often unnecessary, and in most cases impossible. The people of our time, city dwellers in particular, have practically yielded control over their free time, indeed, of their thoughts (including folkloristic reminiscences) to the ever-present mass media. As concisely expressed by McLuhan and Fiore, the media "leave no part of us untouched, unaffected, unaltered. The medium is the message" (1967:26). The messages of the traditional folktale, estranged from their proper setting, have become less and less audible in the overall hubbub of mass media.

Even though it is true that the media, most prominently television, supplanted the tale as traditional social entertainment, it does not necessarily

34

follow that the media were an apt replacement in every respect. If television were the perfect equivalent of the tale, the alternative "Märchen or TV" would also be feasible. In accordance with this logic, one would be led to believe that the tale came into existence only because humankind was tardy in inventing television. Of course, we would be as reluctant to accept such reasoning as we would the claim, for example, that human beings acquired the habit of fruit-consumption early in their evolution because vitamin pills were not yet available. The alternative certainly is not "Märchen or TV" but rather "TV or traditional storytelling." To be sure, television might force the tale into obsolescence, without being a satisfactory substitute for it, unless the television borrows from the tale, relies on it, or places its new propositions under the protection of ancient tale conventions. Approximations, however, amount not to substitution but rather to expansion, which is a mere technicality, not affecting the deep substances of the Märchen.

The tale has not only technical determinants, however. The inherent, inimitable, and irreplaceable essence of the tale lies in its magic worldview, which we will discriminate from the magic, the irrationality of the legend, later in this discussion.[3] The peculiar magic expressed by the Märchen finds its way in both the declining peasant world, and the developing industrial society.

With reference to the conventional model (Jakobson 1964), it should be remarked that the dispersion of folklore material does not come about by a sender (addressor) by his or her own volition transmitting a text randomly to someone who happens to be present and who by this act becomes an unexpectedly and arbitrarily elected receiver (addressee). It is true that the word "receiver" (and even more so "addressee," also in terms of the vocabulary of the United States Postal Service and its clientele), suggests a certain passivity. Nevertheless, in folklore communication the role of the receiver might be considered almost as active as that of the sender. The receivers expect and count on the message appealing to them; this relationship between innumerable senders and receivers extends to worldwide proportions. Thus, the pretension of receivers turns into social expectation, and communicative sequences of folklore materials, including tales, turn into separate conduits that follow their own destinations in society (Dégh and Vázsonyi 1975:211–214). To borrow this time from the language of commerce, the folklore receiver can be compared to the consumer who made out the order for the merchandise delivered to his or her address.

The tale consumer of today will find "real" tales in which form, content, and other defining features fit the traditional scheme only with difficulty. After all, the most traditional and persistent of Märchen attributes is its remarkable surface flexibility, which facilitates its transmission and at the same time protects the immutability of its essence: the peculiar magic worldview.

Magic is merchandise of prime necessity. Magic is in demand. People who travel by airplanes still cannot do without the magic carpet. Let us see where the magic carpet is for sale.

Generic Properties of the TV Advertisement

"The folklore of industrial man, . . . so much of which stems from the laboratory, the studio, and the advertising agencies" (McLuhan 1951:v), cannot be severed from the folklore of pre-industrial man. The magic carpet might be torn, shredded, faded, and misshapen, but its driving energy, magic, is as powerful as ever before. It might sound strange to those early theorists of folklore, but television (which at the time of the quotation above did not yet have as much impact on everyday life as it does today) is the main dispenser of certain forms of folklore, including the tale. "I suggest," says Dorson, "that the American folklorist consider the relationship between mass culture and folklore patterns" (1971:46).

We do not want to talk here about the currency of certain tales that appear on television. It is a known fact that several traditional folktales have been presented in inventive but unfaithful recasts prepared in the workshop of Walt Disney and other animators, and that several other children's programs also regularly utilize tale elements and their analogies. One can easily find themes, episodes, motifs, structures, indeed the naive morality[4] and *Weltanschauung* of the Märchen in television plays, Westerns, adventures, docudramas, science fiction, and social dramas "taken from real life," quite often with a primitiveness provoking a smile. One also can find a wealth of stylistic turns, similes, metaphors, and formulaic repetitions in both verbal and nonverbal forms that allude, sometimes quite awkwardly, to the world of the Märchen. Be that as it may, none of these features can be attributed specifically to television, nor can they be considered as exclusively American phenomena. I do not believe that they deserve too much attention from the folklore analyst. Instead of gleaning them from the daily TV programs for an inventory, as literary folklorists did from classic authors for almost a century, it will be more rewarding to consider television's most characteristic, though by definition least fantastic and most conspicuously earthbound genre: the dramatized commercial. This remarkable modern art form evokes most frequently and obviously the Märchen, its constituent elements—that is, its ad libitum variants—and, what is even more significant, its view of the world.

Giants, dwarves, fairies, witches, mermaids, anthropomorphic objects, and personified principles appear on the television screen to enlighten the viewer on the value of certain commodities as often as the clowning of comedians, the horror of suspense dramas, and even sports stop to allow room for an "important message" from the sponsor. The viewer might hardly be surprised by the presence of a magico-animistic worldview, parodistic and anachronistic, as related to coffee, constipation, bad breath, or the cleanliness of dishes. As already noted, the dramatized commercial advertisement is a genre in its own right. It is characteristically American, like television itself along with almost all of its genres. There are commercials on European television (Kübler 1975:148–162), but because of smaller quantity and relative novelty, their sociocultural impact is not comparable to that of their American counterparts. In the words of George Gordon, "Advertising has occupied a peculiar corner of American culture for a long time, because it is the subject of widely ambivalent emotional and cognitive dispositions" (1971:130). Commercials have their distinctive features and specific properties, and in many instances they resemble the Märchen in ideology, in application of paraphernalia, and even in structure.

In one study of folklore as presented on television, Tom Burns, with *TV Guide* in hand, sat in front of the screen from early morning until late at night on 15 May 1969 (Burns 1969). He watched programs chosen from the four main networks and a local station in order to compile a representative sample of folklore on American television. During his nineteen-hour vigil, Burns did not pay special attention to any particular genre (such as the folktale) or to one kind of TV show (such as commercials), but indiscriminately recorded every bit of folkloric material. He reported a total of 101 "traditional items and themes" which he qualified as "true" folklore. This count indicates that in every hour of TV broadcasting, an average of at least five "traditional" folklore items appeared.

To ensure accuracy, the survey had to determine its subject matter and the principles of selection. Burns stated that "true folklore" was the target of his search. Thus, as consistently as possible, he adhered to the criteria of the "traditional." It should be considered, though, that the traditions in question came to us from a cultural epoch whose transformation was facilitated radically by television itself. In the course of its fifty years' existence, television has created new traditions and, along with other media, has contributed effectively to the need to update the definition of folklore. Priscilla Denby, another examiner of folklore on television, also doubted that all criteria of traditionality in the old sense could be found simultaneously in single items (Denby 1971:114).

Burns ordered the "traditional" folklore material that he found into twelve categories. Although he did not indicate numerical distribution, he remarked that "folk belief themes," including "traditional supernatural beliefs," were "utilised extensively in advertising" (Burns 1969:98, 103). The word "extensive" is appropriate. If as a television viewer one does not stick to the traditional interpretation of the term "traditional" and only remembers how many times commercials evoke allusions to Märchen in one's mind, it is not difficult to realize that magic—the only traditional but still viable Märchen trait—has found its refuge in TV commercials.

Ostensive Use of Märchen Elements

Advertisements can be divided into categories by their way of applying Märchen magic. The simplest and most conspicuously tale-like commercials invite such magic openly, simply by inserting tale formulas, actors, actions, and situations. Now and then, in order to hit the right chord and lull the viewer into the Märchen mood, the commercial explicitly begins with the phrase "Once upon a time," as in the story of the gentleman whose bewitched touch wrinkled everything with the exception of his bedsheet. This could not be harmed because it was a genuine Stevens-Utica No-Iron Sheet which never wrinkles (Burns 1969:99). In another commercial, Cinderella scrubs the floor with ammonia while her sisters, dressed in fine garb, leave for the dance. She scrubs and scrubs, then waxes and rewaxes, until her Fairy Godmother comes to her rescue. She hands her a bottle of "Mr. Clean," an effective floor polish which shines the floor without waxing. This hard task completed, Cinderella can follow her sisters to the ball; but she chooses to go bowling instead.

Mr. Clean himself also appears in a leading role, without Cinderella. This benevolent genie with shaven head and gold earrings, brought to life by the advertisers of potent dirt removers, looks as if he had been summoned somewhere from the peripheries of the Arabian Nights. Sleeping Beauty is also a popular consumer persuader; in one ad she prompts the viewer to buy the softest bedding and lingerie ever produced. In another commercial, Prince Charming is unable to kiss Snow White awake until clean-shaven and emanating the right fragrance of Palmolive Rapid Shave. The talking mirror of the Wicked Stepmother is also utilized; it reveals the name of the moisture cream that made Snow White's beauty superior to hers.

In a commercial set in an industrial plant, a worker suffers from a stomach upset. Suddenly a sweet old lady steps from behind a machine. "Who are you?" asks the astonished victim of heartburn. "Mother Tums," replies the lady with the matter-of-factness of supernatural helpers in folktales, and she indeed appears to be a kind of good fairy. "Can you help, Mother Tums?" asks the worker with fearful hope, whereupon she chants her formula: "Tums for the tummy." The worker wants more assurance that it will cure his pain: "Is it strong?" "Tums is strong medicine," asserts the old lady. "Strong" is one of the most emphasized adjectives in TV advertisements, as if medicines, detergents, deodorants, and nutrients are agents to fight evil powers whose only aim is to destroy mankind. Obviously, strength is also an indispensable virtue of folktale heroes and their helpers.

According to the elf who dwells in the Hollow Tree, the secret of Mr. Keebler's Golden Pecan Sandies is that they are baked by elves. Mr. Keebler's firm seems to be in closer cooperation with miraculous beings. Currently it advertises a pastry named Elfwitch. Elves are at the disposal of other advertisers as well: they are covering De-Luxe Grahams with fudge.

A group of workers in soiled overalls is on the screen. They hear a sudden tramping of hooves, and a white-armored medieval knight on a white steed gallops by with his spear aimed at them. A sudden spark from the spear causes momentary alarm, but then they look at each other and discover that their dirty overalls have been turned sparkling white, and they are filled with delight. Their joy is underscored by a massive masculine choir declaring in a strong and victorious tune that "Ajax laundry detergent is stronger than dirt." (Here we again have strength, with reference to the mystic duel between contrary principles.) Who can tell why this folktale hero with his characteristic medieval props assumed the name of the Greek warrior? Tom E. Sullenberger explores the etymology and the probable symbols of the name (1974:54–56).

A homemaker is in trouble with wrapping; she cannot get a decent plastic bag. But she need not despair. Out of the blue, here comes the Man from Glad on a heavenly chariot, dressed in white, almost the color of his light blond hair, and hands her a box of first-rate plastic bags. Another kitchen, another housewife. "I need help," she whispers with a sigh, and not in vain. Lo and behold, a mysterious hand with a face on its palm grows out of the middle of the kitchen cabinet, offering a good cue for punning: the helping hand hands over Hamburger Helper to help make hamburgers.

The FTD Florist Company's trademark turns itself into a living being with a bouquet in his hand. We recognize the mythological Hermes, messenger of the gods, in winged hat and footwear. If the gods could entrust their valuables to his care, we also can trust him to deliver our flowers anywhere in the world speedily. Another remarkable transformation story is introduced and framed by an invisible announcer who claims (and proves) that there is a monster in all of us—a cross between a werewolf and a vampire. In this commercial, a man whose bad mood turns him into a monster leaves his comfortable average home and drives to a breakfast place. As soon as he finishes the first cup of coffee, his fangs disappear and his beastly hairy snout turns into a cheerful, clean-shaven, handsome face.

The Jolly Green Giant, trademark of a big canning company, mythical helper, guardian of vegetable production and packing, and supernatural guarantor of quality, is depicted towering, hands on hips, over the valley named after him. Otherwise he does not play much of a role. His deep voice sounds benevolent. As a symbol his meaning is not altogether clear, but this does not distort his image. One thing is clear: he is strong. Strong champions are what we need in this wicked world full of ill-will and intrigue—strong like Ajax, and the others we already know. Calgonite is no weakling either. This power for automatic dishwashers destroys the treacherous Spotmakers who hide between the dishes and whose goal is to keep plates and cups dirty.

An example of the defeat of malignancy is the story of Mr. Cholesterol. This relatively pleasant little podgy fellow enters the kitchen of a model homemaker who is surrounded by compassionate neighbor ladies. His symbolic character can be read off the apron he is wearing with his name on it: Mr. Cholesterol. He did not come as a casual visitor. He has a mission: he brings rich, enticing junk food and offers it to the ladies who are preparing healthy food and sitting down to eat. Although they patiently listen to the praise of the harmful meal, their scornful smiles tell us how determined they are to resist Mr. Cholesterol's temptation. They display a package of Fleischmann's natural margarine, and he staggers backwards with great consternation. Then, almost in tears, he collapses. Cupping his head in his hand, Mr. Cholesterol complains: "It has no cholesterol! Zero!" As a matter of fact, the desire of the stocky little man to fill the world with cholesterol is rather repulsive, but his defeat is so quick and complete, his grief so sincere, that the viewer, who, after all, likes some cholesterol-containing delicacies, almost pities him.

For sure, humanity is surrounded by vicious enemies. Intentionalism is an attribute of tales. Pests are featured as deliberate antagonists in TV commercials: an army of anthropomorphic bugs are destroyed by Raid, and hordes of maliciously sneering bathroom germs are devastated by Lysol. But if there are such enemies, there are also adequate helpers. They come not only in the shape of fairies, mysterious envoys from a commercial fairyland, but sometimes also as objects—especially foodstuffs—that come to life to spell out the magic truth about what is good and useful, and to educate ignorant consumers with their incantations. Various animated beings voluntarily offer even themselves for consumption. A large baking potato sits up on a plate between a neighboring sirloin steak and tasty toasted roll to praise its nutritional value and vitamin richness. With vivid gestures, he admonishes the onlooker to eat more potatoes. After concluding his speech, the potato withdraws and resumes its place among other foods ready for consumption. Two loaves of Wonder Bread introduce themselves: "We are the fresh guys." "If we are not fresh, we are out of business."

A tiny cook-manikin made from dough is a cute advocate for Pillsbury's products. He stands on the table next to the pastry tray. One of the guests pokes his round belly gently with his finger, whereupon the manikin closes his dough eyes with a giggle. Mrs. Butterworth's story is not that clear, but nevertheless acceptable in the specific language of the commercial genre. She is a bottle containing syrup. Standing on the table, she narrates in a kind motherly tone the advantages of her thick brown contents to a little girl, who, after tasting her, exclaims: "Mrs. Butterworth, I love you!" with innocent sincerity. The good lady timidly turns away her transparent head on top of her bottle neck: "Oh . . ."

Another self-sacrificing benefactor is Charlie the tuna fish who wants us to know how nutritious, appetizing and good for our health it is to eat more Starkist canned tuna. Likewise, the mermaid urges us to taste her tuna kin from the Chicken-of-the-Sea canning company. Which is the most delicious chicken stuffing? This question is discussed on screen by a group of hens. They decide—and who are more qualified to judge?—that Uncle Ben's is the best. Sacrificial selflessness on the part of those ready to be eaten, cannibalistic residue on the part of those ready to do the eating.

Magic Is in Demand

Giants, dwarves, fairies, goblins, mermaids, talking animals and objects, miraculous beings flying in the air, emerging from earth, water, or nothingness, strong heroes and their allies, helpless maidens in distress saved at the right time, disappearances, transformations—where do they belong, if not in the world of the Märchen? Folklore scholars, in order to understand the place of TV commercials in human culture, can easily assign the appropriate type and motif parallels for a comparative diffusion study; they can etymologize the words, interpret symbolic meanings,[5] or identify surviving relics of myths in commercial advertising, and they can apply depth-psychological hypotheses in search of interpretation.

The structuralist could also resourcefully match most components of the commercial genre with the morphological description of the folktale (Propp 1968; 1984: 67–99). In the first place, lack appears as the initial disposition even more conspicuously and with more obvious manifestation than is the case in most folktales. The hero is evidently the consumer (symbolized by the central character), who in his or her struggle (for a better spot remover, more potent deodorant, crunchier cracker, better-absorbing paper towel, or other treasures without which life is not worth living) is assisted by magical agents and helpers, with the aid of magical objects and with magical certainty. After the victory is achieved, we can say that the liquidation of lack could not have been more successful.[6]

In sum, many television commercials exhibit not only overt but indeed ostensive analogies with the best-known and most characteristic traditional tale motifs. These motifs frequently play an active role in the brief plots. If the Man From Glad had not furnished the helpless homemaker with tough plastic bags at the right moment, she might still be in need of wrappers. Had white-armored Ajax not ridden along the street, dirt would never have disappeared from the work clothing. Who knows how much the heartburn victim would have suffered without the appearance of Mother Tums? And who knows what would happen to green peas, lima beans, cabbage, and broccoli if the Green Giant did not watch over them?

In his witty article, Tom Sullenberger identifies the Giant "as a twentieth century holdover of fertility symbols and vegetal spirits" classified by Fraser. He also examines the symbolism of elves on a comparative basis. In reference to the Axion laundry detergent suddenly emerging from the washing machine, Sullenberger compares this action to Excalibur in the Arthurian legend cycle. He views Ajax's upcast spear—in one of the current fashions in folkloristics—as a phallic symbol (Sullenberger 1974). Such interpretations, no matter how inventive, are always somewhat suspect as reflective of the arbitrary and personal associations of the authors. We might have the same suspicion, in this case, if the story in any of its parts could be conceived of as a spontaneous creation. But there is little if any spontaneity in commercials. They are, as a rule, the inventions of sophisticated and experienced specialists based on penetrating public opinion research. Sullenberger is probably correct in asserting that "In the case of the White Knight, the intended association seems apparent" (1974:58), inasmuch as he is probably also right in suspecting calculated deliberateness, even in seemingly accidental allusions.

According to Priscilla Denby, "Madison Avenue"—the metonymy referring to the center of all these sophisticated, scientifically-educated practices— converts folklore into "folklure" (1971:114). Viewers can never be certain whether what they perceive as genuine tradition, folk belief, surviving myth debris, or archetypes innocently projected on the television screen by the collective unconscious is or is not the well-tailored product created by Madison Avenue experts on the basis of computerized research results (Mayer 1958; Packard 1957). Instead of folkloristic, sociological, or psychological analysis, one could find out the routine of production from the source, by telephone. Indeed, this would be a modern, fast, simple, but unfortunately seldom applicable method of learning the secrets hidden at the roots of human civilization.

From the vast number of folklore-fakelore-folklure materials discernible in television commercials, wherever they were taken from, inferences can be drawn which otherwise could be learned only with more difficulty and less authenticity. The advertising industry, even though it serves gigantic interests and works with enormously large budgets and personnel, never loses touch with the masses. In all its moves, it consults public opinion, which sensitively and immediately reacts to advertising strategies. We can be certain that commercials that are kept running for a longer period of time on television correspond to the taste of the masses and satisfy public demand, whereby they achieve the expected goal: to popularize a good slogan and promote the product in question. TV, after all, is an "actual participating member of North American families. . . . For a large proportion of the roughly 50 million U.S. families, television—the one-eyed monster resident in every well-furnished living room—controls both *time* and *space*" (Key 1973:65–66). It is interesting to learn, as George Gordon concludes, that "quite a number of intelligent people in contemporary Western society enjoy advertisements" (Gordon 1971:126). Similarly, Fairfax M. Cone estimates that "about two thirds of the viewing public seems not to mind commercials . . . two out of three people show favorable attitudes towards television commercials" (Cone 1968:265).

The programming of TV commercials can be regarded as the result of an ongoing uninterrupted poll. This poll seems to indicate that Märchen-like enchantment is in fashion, that magic is in demand. The industrialization that relegated the tale to the background seems to have provided compensation for the losses.[7] Television, which terminated the occasions for traditional storytelling, now helps the Märchen to survive on the basis of entirely new traditions. The Märchen has become a built-in part of everyday life. "[The Märchen] will replace irrational moments of life that have fallen by the wayside in the world of technology" (Röhrich 1974:iii). Average Americans, for whom television advertisements are intended and who might not be willing to open their doors to a traveling salesperson, are eager to welcome into their homes the salesperson's substitute: the fairy and goblin impersonators. This arrangement is more convenient; the salesperson might arrive at the wrong time, whereas the supernatural messenger offers his improved toilet bowl deodorant always when it is most needed.

It might sound surprising that the number of Märchen from which commercials usually borrow are rather small in number (Burns 1969:99). A closer look will reveal superficial familiarity with not more than about a dozen tales. As already mentioned, the American folk has a rather modest Märchen repertoire, to which the continued flow from Old World tradition has contributed little. The commonly known popular tales that Americans cherish as part of their childhood enculturation stem from countless storybooks containing selections from the Grimm Brothers, Hans Christian Andersen, and Andrew Lang, often combined with the arbitrary formulations of storybook illustrations, cartoons, and comic strips.[8] Thus, speaking only about complete Märchen plots, the frame of reference is rather narrow.

As it happens, however, in most cases the tales do not spread in their entirety as finished entities and ossified types. They disseminate rather in the form of disintegrated, atomized units and enter the bloodstream of communication and "manipulated communication" in disjoined particles.[9] What is the tale in the view of typical people? Mostly small incidents remembered at random without the context of a lengthy narrative. A fairy princess appears on the television screen. She is a fairy and she appears; this is the whole tale. Who knows which tale was her original home environment? As a matter of fact, this cannot be known, because the fairy in question—offering margarine, floor wax, hair conditioner, or coffee—originates not from one specific tale but from the tale in general. And whence comes the genie who, released from the plastic bottle that confined him, helps the needy consumer? Like the other irrational figures, creatures, and apparitions who arrive to aid irresolute humankind with sound advice, he too belongs to the Märchen world.

Even if tales are less popular in America than in Europe, and even if the number of the most popular ones can be limited to just a handful, the world of enchantment, composed of the multitude of forgotten or maybe never-heard tales and daydreams (which, by the way, could still be fitted into the classification systems of traditional folkloristics), lives vividly in the human mind. This, at least, is what the continuous "poll" of television commercials indicates.

Symbols of Persuasion

One could raise a question at this point. What is the business of magic personages in this by definition sober, prosaic, causal consumer universe? As it is generally known, the traditional tale is not meant to be believed by its audience; it is a declared "lie" by some narrators and is intended as a creative fantasy (Dégh 1989:86–87). Children in their "magic age" (Piaget 1976) are inclined to believe that everything that happens in the tale is true, whereas normal adults do not. The tale itself suggests with its style, formulae, emphases, and situations that, in the everyday sense of the word, it is not true. The tale does not demand, and indeed does not tolerate credence. This is one of its most important generic characteristics. What the tale demands and stimulates is a more simple act: the temporary suspension of disbelief on the part of the audience, which is the key and condition of artistic enjoyment, and a perfectly rational behavior. Similarly, the advertisement-Märchen neither needs nor tolerates belief. If the viewer could be led to irrationally believe that the tale elements in a television commercial could be taken on their face value, there would be no reason to advertise.

In a popular advertisement, a family sits around the breakfast table. One by one the members taste their toast spread with Imperial Margarine. A fanfare resounds as they chew and imperial crowns appear on their heads. If the viewer could not resolve the metaphor expressed in this scene, telling us that

"Emperors could not have a better feast," the advertisement would lose not only its sense, but also its commercial persuasion value.[10]

The creators of Ajax do not want us to believe that the silver white-armored knight cleans spots with his spear. What we are supposed to understand is that "Ajax cleans as if by the touch of magic." The advertisers of Hamburger Helper do not want the housewife to stay in her kitchen and wait patiently until a hand grows out of the cabinet to present her with the mixture. It is the other way around: all advertisements try to persuade the viewer to hasten to the store and purchase the merchandise offered—somewhat hypersymbolically—as the best of its kind.

Märchen Characters in Disguise as Ordinary People

The magic world of the tale is broader than one would think at first glance. The good fairies and goblins, the helpful genies and dependable giants do not stop at the borderline where manifest miracles end. They just change their costumes. If we suspected up to this point that we are dealing with human fairy impersonators, disguised salespersons, we have good reason now to find supernatural helpers disguised in everyday clothing: human impersonators.

For example, Mrs. Olsen, a kind, middle-aged woman with an alluring smile on her face, goes from home to home—not as a saleswoman but just as a casual visitor, advising everyone to drink Folger's coffee. For some unknown reason, she always has a package with her which she displays or gives away. Either way, one thing is certain: she presents the family with the magic incantation "It's mountain-grown," which, in addition to the magic drink, speedily resolves the tension threatening the harmony of the home. Mrs. Olsen's colleague, another elderly benefactress of coffee drinkers, is committed to Maxwell House coffee, which, she chants, is "good to the last drop!" In fairyland, it seems, there is free competition.

The desk clerk of a motel—middle-aged, reserved but friendly—constantly encounters guests suffering from headaches. He offers them a bottle of "Arthritis Pain Formula." The guests—a traveling salesman or a vacationer—object; arthritis is not their problem, but a headache. It does not matter, says the clerk; it is good for headaches. "It must be strong," remarks the guest. "You bet it's strong," repeats the clerk, and the chant really works. The next morning the guest praises the efficacy of the strong medicine to the clerk, who is not surprised. Mouth odor is the worst enemy of people; it makes them outcasts from society. It is worse than dandruff or flatulence. A pretty girl, for example, is about to join a boating party, but her friends leave her behind on the ramp. A handsome young fellow is about to kiss his sweetheart when she staggers backwards, excusing herself and departing. The career of a promising young executive is threatened because of his bad breath. A good friend rescues the victim and supplies the necessary mouthwash.

A trim professional woman accidentally meets an old friend and complains about her greatest worry, her occasional irregularity. Fortunately, the other woman not only knows the remedy—Ex-Lax pills—but has them in her purse. "It's gentle to the stomach," she chants reassuringly. It is hard to imagine what would have happened to another victim of irregularity, a young bride still in her bridal gown, if her problem had not been resolved before her wedding night. But there is help: the adviser and the medicine are at hand, and the new bride, signaling with a wave of her handkerchief that the problem is resolved, takes off with her new husband down the road to happiness.

A man is coughing in bed so badly that his wife wakes up. She immediately knows what is wrong. Opening the drawer of her husband's night stand, she finds the medicine he has been taking for his cold, against her advice. She then produces some tablets of potent Dristan, which calm his cough. With a seraphic smile on his face, he happily goes back to sleep. True happiness, however, is brought to earth only by Geritol. The short drama in this case does not show the helpless hero and the helper in the process of being enlightened and brought to ultimate bliss. The attractive, invariably happily married couples on the screen are already in the state of enlightenment and success. The fairy has already disappeared and they know what to do. They inform us of the secret of a good marriage: the wife—not the husband—must take Geritol, which contains twice as much iron as any other leading panacea. This is not only the means to perfect health, but also evidence of marital devotion. She takes it for his sake. The husband knows this and expresses his gratitude. He looks lovingly into her eyes, and love will not slacken as long as one single Geritol pill can be found on this earth. "Geritol every day" is the chant.

Variable problems, variable helpers line up in an endless sequence in the framework of the "happy end"-oriented Märchen. It almost seems that if you get used to the rhythm of the interruptions of the television programs, your reward will be the assertion that nobody is alone with personal displeasures; we share them with other people and, like them, we can be helped quickly and easily. Are you bothered by perspiration? There are "extra dry" deodorant sprays, sticks, and soaps. Do your china and glassware look dull, your silverware spotty? Try "new, improved" cleaning powders, and even your mother-in-law will admire your housewifely virtues. Is your skin "dry and flabby"? Here are some excellent oils, creams, and moisturizers with proteins and vitamins. Are you overweight? Take these reducing thirst-quenchers, appetite-spoilers, exercisers with "money-back guarantees." Are your dentures yellow, do your acquaintances call you Mrs. Crabapple because you tighten your lips to cover your shame? This effervescent pill will "give you back your smile." Do you suffer from heartburn, arthritis, back pains, itching, headache? Do your children develop cavities in their teeth too quickly? There is remedy for every plague. One is better than the other because it is "twice as strong" and there is also an "extra ingredient" in it (sometimes concealed in a hard-to-understand formula) of unknown but surely good effect, if it is worthy of being advertised. The Helper who brings relief, gives advice, shows you the right path from which you strayed, arrives not necessarily from a mysterious faraway world, but often from the other room, the neighboring house, or the next office, always at the right time.

To end the list of redeemer fairies concealed as providers of merchandise, we return to smell the coffee with a new type of character replacing the long-lasting Mrs. Olsen: the handsome neighbor gentleman who provides a charming woman in distress with coffee because hers ran out before the guests were satisfied. This episodic TV commercial, escalating from one installment to the next like a novella (or soap opera?), features the romance evolving around Taster's Choice coffee (a magic potion). It capitalizes on the expectation of an international TV audience craving a "happy end"-oriented love story. Public interest in this case has raised the usual anonymity of TV commercial actors into the spotlight of talk-show stardom based on the success of the story plot itself.

From Magic to the Everyday

Some commercials are composed entirely of an almost realistic story. It might happen that a woman expecting her dinner guests at any moment actually discovers an ugly stain on the carpet and a friend accidentally drops in with the remedial spot remover at the right time. A good scriptwriter can even make this believable to us. However, the legion of helpers that appear during the breaks of a prime-time program and behave according to the same predictable formula expose each other. Watching these "realistic" commercials, viewers, even the most tolerant and gullible, will inevitably feel themselves in an unreal world similar to the one presented through the commercials that were obvious Märchen travesties, although the latter were never designed to be credible. Slowly viewers will realize that the acts of the tale characters in civilian clothes are tale motifs, just like those that they encounter in the Märchen-like commercials, but this time twice-travestied.

However, the introduction of Märchen characters is as inessential to the actual messages as the magic concomitants that we have mentioned already in Märchen-like commercials. In the same vein, boyfriends, neighbor ladies, motel clerks, and supermarket salesmen, these pseudo "opinion leaders" in this pseudo "two-step flow of communication" (Lazarsfeld, Berelson and

Gaudet 1948:151), have as small a dramaturgic role in commercials that imitate reality as the magic characters in commercials that imitate Märchen. Their presence does not assist, their removal would not weaken the actual message. For example: "A ring around the collar is disgusting, but can be cleaned" is a realistic statement. The rest of the commercial—children travestying a game, dancing around drying laundry in the yard and singing sarcastically, "Ring around the collar"; the helper, arriving at the right time, the use of Wisk and the housewife's instantaneous relief after trying this liquid cleaner—all this serves only as exaggerated figurative expression and does not add to the essential message. Evidently, the concealed tale elements can as easily be removed in this type of ad as from commercials that openly show off their tale features. The creators of such advertising stories doubtless expect the audience to carry out this editing, since the intent of the commercials is to popularize nonfiction—an assertion posited as "true"—contrary to the fictional tale.

Presumably, some television spectators will judge certain commercial story-frames as superfluous, primitive, awkward, and even in bad taste. Discriminating people should remember, though, that the advertising industry knows what dosage of primitiveness, awkwardness, and bad taste is called for to satisfy public demand. The results of penetrating market and laboratory research vouch for the efficacy of these commercials among the majority of consumers: the result of the "poll" is also highly indicative of mass pretension in logic, sophistication, and taste. Nevertheless, from the vast store of information gleaned from this poll, we still consider of prime importance the observation we already have mentioned, namely, that magic is in demand.[11]

The advertising business, like so many other businesses in our society, seems to have realized that modern man's continual need for magic can be easily exploited for sales puposes. Magic as a vehicle for advertising shows more dependability than sober and objective reasoning. Magic, however, is also a message in itself. There are situations in which the well-known thesis can be paraphrased as: "The message is the medium."

Magic, it seems, can transport us into the world of reality. The unreal elements of the Märchen undergo Märchen-like transformation themselves. Enchantment is converted into features of artistic narration, figurative speech, symbols, and metaphors. Even if our attention is called to certain articles by Märchen characters who try to influence our decision with their sometimes parodistically designed Märchen magic, we viewers feel free to make our own choice. We can take a closer look at the nasal mists, baking powders, sleeping pills, and shampoos in the light of reality, and if we are careful enough to think ahead, we will write down the phone number of a friendly mortician of our own free will.

We might say that with this act we regain our previously violated civil liberties.[12] The helpful fairies, provident elves, benign magicians invade our privacy, after all. How does a supernatural envoy dare to enter our kitchen without knocking on the door? What right does this emphatic masculine voice from behind the camera have to interfere with our business? On what grounds do the various unrealistic or pseudo-unrealistic beings intrude unannounced into our life, only to impose upon us and our family the best floor polish, the highest-protein breakfast cereal, and the most potent deodorant? They probably operate some kind of bugging device. How else could they possibly know when to arrive at the most opportune time? The consumer understands the metaphor. Any minimal, or so to speak subliminal suggestive effect that the playful Märchen personages and situations have on the buying mood of the viewer is probably negligible. We leave the world of Märchen magic behind us.

The Product Itself as Magic

It is a question, though, whether we have left the world of magic altogether behind us.

Let's see. What happened to the pretty blonde who did not have much to look forward to in life because of her yellowish teeth? What a sorry sight—her tortured, hopeless face. Is there no help? Oh yes, there is! Close-Up turns dingy teeth brilliantly white, consequently also drawing men close up. (In Germany, this merchandise is advertised as Ganz-Nahe ["Close-Up"].) Once this product is applied, hopelessness turns to optimism. "I danced all night," she tells her girlfriend, and from her happy smile we can tell that she is going to dance happily, carefree through life. The voice that usually summarizes the ultimate message of television's optimistic commercial stories repeats the girlfriend's advice as a tip for the viewer: "Put your money where your mouth is." The question is whether such slogans actually represent the essential, ultimate message of this and similar stories.

In a striking Cinderella travesty, a homemaker appears in a sorry state, completely absorbed in the endless struggle against dirt on the floor, carpet, dishes, walls, and clothing. Suddenly she kicks off her slippers, takes off her apron, headscarf, and rubber gloves, obviously indicating that she has had about enough, and breaks into song in pop star style: "I'm a-gonna have an Aviance night." While she unbuttons her blouse, her rich dark hair flows down her shoulders seductively, and as she sprays on Aviance perfume, a handsome man, dressed for the evening, appears.

A young man, obviously early in a promising business career, is invited to a party at his boss's house. His joy, however, is marred by the dandruff that dots the shoulder of his dark tuxedo. Both the host and the guests notice it, although they pretend not to look; their exchange of glances em-

barrasses the young man. The picture shifts: the same young man is shown
at another party after the successful use of the shampoo that controls dandruff. With his impeccable tuxedo, he is assured of a brilliant future. The
change of luck of another young man is similar, but his reward is more conspicuous and instantaneous. Although he has short hair (according to the
announcer hidden behind the camera, this is the fashion again), it is not
perfect, and he is made aware of this by his friends. But again, there is help
in the shape of Vitalis hair lotion. As soon as he applies it, girls who perhaps
earlier had turned away from him reappear. They wink at him, snuggle up
to him, sit at his table without an invitation.

A lady complains to Madge, her manicurist, about her dry, rough hands,
caused by dishwashing. With great surprise, she learns that it is Palmolive
dishwashing liquid in which her nails are being soaked for the manicuring.
"It's black magic, it's real magic!" insists Madge. "Magic" is also mentioned
by a health spa masseuse, but, conversely, she offers One-a-Day vitamins to
a customer, insisting: "This is not magic."

We also learn how humiliating it is to wear wrinkled stockings. A youthful grandmother notices the indignation of her grandchildren, but as soon as
she buys L'Eggs pantyhose, which "never wrinkle" but hug her legs
smoothly, her family is satisfied. And we certainly should not forget the remedy that for a long time has been the universal panacea of Americans: Alka
Seltzer! It cures headache, headcold, fever, heartburn, indigestion, hangover,
and who knows how many other discomforts, as we learn from the great
variety of Alka Seltzer commercials on TV.

The sleeping pills, cough drops, nasal mists, hair conditioners, germ kill-
ers, oven and toilet bowl cleaners, paper towels and tissues, and low-calorie
margarines (not to mention the larger needs of life such as cars, homes,
travel, and the like) that we are persuaded to buy cannot all be mentioned
individually here, although the lists are entertaining as well as educational.
We also need not exhibit a selection of commercials in which the receipt and
comprehension of the message is de-emphasized or dropped entirely. These
allude to an existing common knowledge and consensus that the product in
question is "used by most people" or "prescribed by doctors most often,"
that "everybody knows" them, and even that they are "nationally advertised." Such claims absolve, so to speak, the individual who cannot resist
seduction or who is scared off by intimidation[13] from even the least odium
of ignoring fashionable behavior or opposing public opinion.

The enumeration of further examples would obscure our original purpose of dealing with only one kind of television commercial, the one that
exhibits a close relationship to the folk narrative. In our examination of this
type, we have adopted the impressionistic point of view of the TV audience:
the consumers of folklore. We encountered superhuman beings who stepped

out from the world of folktales, messengers of magic powers disguised in human shape, and finally, and perhaps most commonly, we encountered superhuman beings who—regardless of how they acquired their knowledge—know what medicine, fragrance, or nutrient can ensure a long and happy life. The question might be raised: is it justifiable to handle these three rather distinct prototypes together and ascribe to them common folklore characteristics?

Rationality of Märchen vs. Irrationality of Legend

Adorno has called attention to the multilayered structure of television. "Mass media," he writes, "consists of various layers of meanings superimposed on one another, all of which contribute to the effect (Adorno 1972:601). His article concerns television programs in general and not commercials in particular. As we see it, however, the layering of the commercial, this television genre par excellence, is especially manifest. The most prominent layering occurs in the Märchen-like commercial. The top layer is the manifest tale, which we have already ascertained is functionally no more than figurative expression, dramatized metaphor: an ingredient of the advertisement but not the whole of it. In a story, a witch is shown in a characteristic outfit. Her magic wand, which she waves over a lady's hairdo, splits in two. As it turns out, there is no need for the wand because Hidden Magic hair spray does the trick. The idea behind this story is not that there was once a witch whose magic wand broke, but rather that whoever applies the hair spray in question will have no need for any other help.

A genre like the Märchen, which is fiction and by definition cannot be believed, is unfit for the conveyance of belief. The symbol must be understood and the figurative expression decoded in order to reach the second layer, in which the suggested to-be-believed statement is expressed. This statement usually points out the advantages of purchasing the merchandise in question or the disadvantages of contrary behavior and other pertinent circumstances. Its aim is persuasion.

What is being stated in the commercial (and what we have to call the "story," for lack of a better term) is, at least formally, nonfiction: something that is believed by some, doubted by others, but, after all, might also be true. This description fits the legend best. Are there any additional features resembling the legend in such pedestrian accounts, which illustrate that a laxative helped a constipated housewife, that the fragrance of a girl's perfume was alluring to her boyfriend, or that one paper towel proved to be tougher than another? We certainly admit that the question provokes a smile. Anyone would instinctively say that there is nothing legend-like in such triviality. If, however, we maintain that folklore genres, the legend in particular, can be identified only in their contexts, we should not be afraid, even if risking ridicule, to project laxatives, perfumes, paper towels, and similar articles into ideological perspectives within the context of television advertisements.

Why should we not recognize, by the same token, the legend in TV commercials under the Märchen layer? The answer seems evident. Legends and legend-like stories usually concern "supranormal" or "supranatural" events—(we prefer to include both in a larger category characterized by its "extranormal" nature (Dégh and Vázsonyi 1973:48–50)—whereas TV items deal with the most "normal" everyday events; on this count they should be excluded from the class of legends even if defined in the most liberal sense. But is the answer that simple? Normal things require normal emphasis; everyday concerns deserve everyday treatment. Naturally a certain degree of hyperbole is unavoidable and even indispensable. "Advertising by its nature (including even such neutral announcements as those found in classified sections of newspapers), must always be selective, and often, to certain perceptions distortive," writes Gordon (1971:130). All types of advertisement have their generic rules, and certainly none of them is identical with those of naturalism. Advertisement necessarily has to focus on one subject, one problem, and one resolution. This does not contradict the normal treatment of normal concerns and in itself is unsuited to transform normal things into extranormal things.

Television commercials, however, exceed these limitations. A careful examination of any typical show will reveal the actors' intense emotional reactions to banalities—their deep grief, sudden alarm, irritation, or despair when they discover that they have dandruff, their floor does not shine, and their coffee does not have the right flavor. No one in real life would express the bliss, happiness, or relief that spreads over the TV actors' faces at the moment they discover the right solution. The viewer must feel the coercion of a certain monomania that compels some to yield or to obey, others to resist or to sneer. In any case, some paranoid simple-mindedness has directed the spotlight that is due to the important, the extraordinary, and the extranormal, to illuminate simple everyday events.

"Advertising helps to unify taste, to de-individualize it, and thus to make mass production possible," says Ernest van der Haag (1957:511). Mass production needs mass consumption. Therefore, advertising, in a very broad sense of the word, including all instruments of intended persuasion, strives for the development of a consumer culture, not on the grounds of some "conspiracy" (a suspicion that has been voiced now and then), but in its general effect. "Our schools, from kindergarten to professional academy, adjust the young to our way of life and probably succeed better at making them consumers than at teaching reading and spelling" (Gordon 1971:130). We are con-

sumers. Consumers of belief—most of us at least. We are also consumers of
legends: consumers of irrationality.

We have made an attempt in the above to separate the Märchen-simulat-
ing, tale-like part from the legend-like part of commercial advertisements—
that is, to separate the rational from the irrational. The Märchen-like portion
is the rational because the viewer does not have to struggle through strategies
of persuasion[14] and can clearly distinguish fantasy from reality. The legend
portion, on the other hand, is the irrational side in which magic appears,
even if only latently, as a real power in real life. The tale frame, as we have
seen, can be easily peeled off every commercial. (Many do not have such a
frame.) Hence, they are legend-like stories. Their "overt message," to use the
words of Adorno (1972:601), evidently is that the purchase of a particular
product is advantageous, but the "hidden message" is much more general
than that; it suggests that certain everyday situations represent intolerable and
maybe ruinous deficiencies, beside which everything else shrinks into in-
significance, and which can be remedied exclusively by one single solution.
Through the synergism of innumerable repetitions, this message gains ideological meaning and propagates a certain messianic worldview, a peculiar
"cargo cult" (Jarvie 1977) that makes believe that the sought-after goods have
already arrived and stand at cult members' disposal.

If the television commercial cannot be considered the cause, it certainly
is an indirect, unintended promoter of the kind of irrationality that makes
millions of people fanatically use a certain toothpaste and avoid others, or
trust the guidance of their horoscope, join social movements and religious
cults, chase monsters in the woods, summon spirits, exorcise demons, search
for UFOs in the sky, and become well-versed in the legendry of such activities. This view of the world, as in commercials, shrinks the complex problem-
atics to a single isolated problem, only to solve it with a single magic trick.

We live in the world of modern legends, modern magic, modern irratio-
nalism. Anyone who does not like them, should turn off the television.

3

Magic as a Mail-Order Commodity

Marketing Magic

MAGIC IS MERCHANDISE of prime necessity. Magic is in demand. It always was, as a part of the imaginary world that runs parallel to the real world in terms of wishful thinking (Caughey 1984). Magic, manifest in beliefs, symbolic acts, and narratives, is the key to the optimistic worldview of hope that Ernst Bloch describes as the utopian fantasy of humans (Bloch 1959). Modern entrepreneurs, who developed merchandizing into a separate scholarly field and an art of persuasion, recognize this need for fulfillment by magic where rational behavior is insufficient. They do everything to satisfy, indeed, to cause, stimulate, and increase this need. "Bad news," writes McLuhan, "has long been the hard core of the press, indispensable for the moving of the mass of 'good news,' which is advertising" (Key 1973: xviii).

Contemporary authors often express their concern and surprise that traditional belief ("superstition")[1] is alive and well in modern industrial society, and that magic as a coercive power (Winkelman 1982) departs from its collective and authoritative social existence and increasingly fulfills discrete personal needs in mass society (Angst 1972:10–14; Kurth 1976:113–130). Some authors are alarmed by the fact that traditional belief and magical thinking were not eradicated by technological enlightenment, urbanization and education, and that contrary to their expectation, existing forms have proliferated and become cores of mass-based, institutionalized, occult subfields as substitute religions.[2] The "occult explosion," however, does not mean that urban mass society has become more "superstitious," only that mass communication and social stratification have made supernatural belief more visible, more normalized and adaptable. Forms of collective tradition have become increasingly personalized as individuals in mass society have been liberated (and alienated) from their inherited nuclear family values and as they design their own system of protective magic in pursuit of happiness. Modern consumerism has found magic a useful tool for developing selling strategies for the convenience of service companies.

It should be noted that the exploitation of magic to market products is not an entirely new phenomenon. The miraculous effects of wares offered for sale have been advertised in newspapers in the western world since the mid-nineteenth century, the industrial revolution. Nevertheless, a special salesmanship emerged in the United States during the first two decades of the twentieth century. Although for a long time the rough and aggressive Yankee peddling and boosterism seemed repulsive to the dignified patriarchal merchants of Europe, American-style advertising has been adopted by most industrial nations during the last three decades. Indeed, exploitation of magic in the advertisement of products that claim to change the life of the buyer by miracle is common. The currently booming occult markets of West Europe—in particular Germany, Italy, England, Austria, Switzerland, and France[3]—along with the recently liberated market of Eastern European countries, have borrowed the American sales technique; if the ad is not the accurate translation of an American original, selling an internationally merchandized product, good disciples rush to learn the trade in selling home-grown wares.

There are multiple ways to commercially manipulate standard forms of supernatural belief in the interest of marketing and selling merchandise, even to the point of commoditizing magic itself. Magic appears in diverse commercial promotions, generating distinctive and well-structured genres in the broad liminal field between folklore and literature. Fit for the appropriate mass media channels (radio, television, billboards, posters, packaging of products, personal promotion letters, classified columns in daily and weekly papers), magic is featured in dramatic oral and written narrative forms for successful sales. With the addition of operating instructions and exemplifying commentaries, magic is placed into the framework of familiar formulas that belong to the traditional stock of folk beliefs listed in standard encyclopaedic works like the *Handwörterbuch des deutschen Aberglaubens* (Bächtold-Stäubli 1927–42) and the section on "Magic" in the *Motif-Index of Folk Literature* (Thompson 1958).

The plainest and most conspicuous commercial exploitation of magic appears as a metaphor in the offer of products through demonstration rather than through slogans ("It's magic," "Works like wonder"). Supernatural forces perform miracles: with their magic wands, a benevolent witch turns the ineffective hair spray into an approved formula; in front of the stopped-up kitchen sink the frustrated housewife is led to the right product by a heavenly voice that shakes the house; little dwarves in the dishwashing powder gobble up the sneering, evil green germs. These are real miracles. The merchandise metaphor magically comes to life and offers itself for sale. One canned tuna product loses to the other—the mermaid on its label offers her tastier self. So does Mr. Turkey, sliced for convenience, or Mr. Steer, mounted on top of the steakhouse. In the same vein, humanized maple syrup bottles, hot baked potatoes, fresh bread loaves, no-cholesterol margarines, and sparkling deodorized toilet seat covers talk to us, competing for the consumer.

This rather simplistic reference expresses the sales philosophy manifest in more elaborate commercials: people are suffering from the lack of something important. They are in want of a dependable razor blade, a potent mouth deodorant, an effective spot remover, and more generally, luck and happiness. The commercials demonstrate that we, the deprived and unenlightened, can become winners: there is hope—magic can help in a flash and turn unhappiness into happiness. Our fate is in our own hands.

Another common sales promotion strategy also stresses the need for some important substance and the conviction that the greater the distress, the closer is deliverance. In this case, however, help is provided not by fabulous or legendary characters, by magic forces, acts, or events, but by the specific qualities of the product in question. In the foregoing category, a seemingly symbolic magic act expresses the truthful claim that a certain product is better than another. In the second category of commercials, the claim is not dressed in a metaphor but is stated openly and realistically. The promoters of the merchandise are not supernatural personages but friendly neighbors, visiting nephews, expert salespersons or repairmen, or simply a voice in the foreground chanting messages such as: "Bayer works wonders," or "X perfume makes you feel like a queen." Furthermore, in the first category the commercial attributes magic to the merchandise, while in fact its aim is to be taken realistically. In the second, the ever-present magic is wrapped in realistic means of expression. This strategy builds on the common philosophy that people in need do not have to despair, because there is help, if not by magic then by a superb new, or improved old, product that removes the trouble and works like magic. The product bears the essential attributes of magic; it is empowered to act "miraculously," "as if touched by magic." The message instructs the consumer in need that the anomaly may seem a trifle, but it must be taken seriously. Women turn away from men with bad breath, and young executives stigmatized by dandruff will not be eligible for promotion, whereas life will immediately take a turn for the better through magic presented as rational. In this latter case, it is not rationality that assumes formal, irrational, magic tale shape, but magic that appears in rational or almost rational dressing.

Thus the merchandise is nothing less than the key to happiness itself, which is otherwise lacking in this world. Happiness in terms of bare essentials means money (wealth), love, and health, which cannot always be attained through a single gesture or behavior pattern, or the application of a single recipe which is for sale. Sometimes an entire behavioral system has to be adopted: a change of lifestyle, or acceptance of diverse rules and theories, which are sometimes set by rational, seemingly scientific establishments. But even if the rules originate in serious research, the faithful followers display blind, unconditional submission, similar to magic behavior. For example, it might be true that the intake of large doses of vitamin C helps cure a variety of dangerous diseases (as Noble Prize awardee, biochemist Linus Pauling, claims); however, the ardor, devotion, and tenacity of vitamin C fans resemble that of fetish believers. Chemical preservatives may be harmful, while the consumption of organic food is probably healthy; however, recognition of this belief is voiced not only by prudent and sensible individuals but also by groups of mystic worshipers. Believers in magic elevate cautious medical suggestions into the dogma of a cult. Thus, in the service of both rational and magic purposes, sober conviction goes hand in hand with superstitious belief. Sometimes the coincidence is felicitous, because rational aims seldom succeed without magic paraphernalia. I saw this demonstrated by a personal acquaintance—a country physician whose success in making his patients take prescription pills was due to his adaptation of the traditional advice of village quacks: take the pill at midnight, at a crossroad, while making a left turn without looking back.

Many believers do not follow the masters of realistic or seemingly realistic doctrines but rather join sects founded on scientific or pseudo-scientific theories that claim to have been not yet resolved but to hold certain hopes for the future. These believers do not entirely give up the semblance of reality, however. They strive to find proof by calling witnesses and producing photographs and documents certified by public notaries. The readiness to be convinced can be seen on illustrations like the picture of a telephone that rang when a dead relative called, or the burned circle in the cornfield where a UFO landed. However, it is impossible to determine which of the many beliefs, beginning with Alchemy and ending with Zen, have or have not any factual basis and whether there is some similarity among them beyond the fact that all are mystic, esoteric, and unprovable.

Two umbrella features are shared by the followers of all factions: a firm belief in the doctrine, accompanied by an often supercilious demeanor towards life's reality; and perhaps more remarkably, most believers in one mystic system have faith in other unrelated ones as well. They attend meetings of several sects and may hold membership in more than one group. If it can be taken at face value, several believers are eager to acknowledge that they are not selective in their belief. "I believe in everything, you name it," was a typical answer to my question.

Instead of listing merchandise contained in catalogs which cater to the needs of the membership of a single or a few related groups or those that whet the appetite of uncommitted consumers, I will mention only a few to indicate the disparity of the items. Across America, occult bookstores are certainly the most impressive dispensers of materials: educational and advising guidebooks, ceremonial supplies for sectarians, initiates, candidates, and searchers. These stores also function as information centers, reading rooms, and meeting places for experts and novices. Although each occult faction has its headquarters and local chapters, in terms of explicit marketing, the "psychic fairs" are the most characteristic places of trade. These weekend, monthly, or annual events are fairs in the truest sense of the word. Inside a large arena, convention hall, civic club, church, or school building, representatives of diverse occult factions sell their propaganda materials in separate booths. For example, during my last visit to the annual Psychic Fair held in Indianapolis by the largest PSI[4] Inc., in the Midwest, materials were available on the following: astrology, astral body, aura, Buddhism, Ed Cayce's readings, clairvoyance, crystal ball gazing, flying saucers, jujitsu, Kirlian photography, organic gardening, Rosicrucians, numerology, ESP, tarot, water witching, yoga, biorhythms and transcendental meditation. Daily, thousands of visitors paid their entry fee and wandered from booth to booth, obtaining information, picking up fliers, watching demonstrations, listening to addresses of famous masters, and obtaining personal advice for a modest charge.

The fact that anything mysterious, esoteric, and unknown may be marketed at a psychic fair tells us something of the consumer mentality expressed by the participants. Shoppers in the magic market can be characterized as *omnicredent*, a term modeled after the natural history term *omnivorous*. Nevertheless, the list of merchandise at the psychic mart is far from all-inclusive. Eastern mystics and gurus, sorcerers, witches, satanists, and voodoo diviners were missing. Missing too were the representatives of the 2,800 best-known religious sects. Among the absentees were the nine hundred followers of one sect who committed suicide by drinking poison upon the command of their charismatic spiritual leader,[5] and those led by The Two (Bo and Peep) who abandoned all earthly goods to find the place where a UFO—a material object—was waiting to take them to heaven. (Dégh 1977) The disparate religion-like belief systems, which act reinforcingly upon each other, represent the richest and most spectacular merchandise show.

The Magic Supply: Vendors and Customers

So far, magic has not appeared in the vocabulary of marketers and consumers. The suppliers have already offered their products as something that "works like wonder" or "seems magic," or "may activate magic." A slow departure has occurred from the worldview based on causality, from lookalike to explicit magic. In previous categories, magic behavior was cited with reference to cause and effect, even if only superficially, mistakenly, or fraudulently twisted with a shaky logic. But the specific market of openly buying and selling objects to cause magic deals in metaphysics. Salespersons usually limit themselves to a pointless but persuasive rhetoric that substitutes for causality. The promotional statement claims that the product (phenomenon, procedure, or power) is affected by a not yet fully understood but soon-to-be-resolved cause, or that its efficiency can be attributed to its "ancient," "traditional," "oriental," or "Christian" provenience. Those who want to believe find these explanations feasible.

This market is vast and obscure, its dimensions impossible to encompass. The interested public is introduced to it through the pages of special catalogs such as the comprehensive guide to PSI (Regush and Regush 1974), the *Psychic Yellow Pages* (Cocciardi 1977), the magazine *Esotera*, and similar other popular scientific or rather pseudo-scientific periodicals, or simply by leafing through the pages reserved for advertisement in illustrated magazines, weekly or biweekly tabloids, daily and evening newspapers. The advertisements also appear in the publications, newsletters, and communications in the swampy realm of the occult underground press.

The inexperienced reader will find the largest selection of magic in the classified advertisements under these partly specific, partly general titles: Ancient Mysteries, Ancient Rituals and Performance, Astrology, Occult, Prayer Service, Talisman, Wicca, Return to Love, Personals, Unusual Items, Jewelry, and Shopping.[6] In the extremely brief announcements the offers are made in the plainest terms and are limited to mere essentials. The object or the provider of the magic power is named and the areas of competence are listed along with address, phone number, and the amount of remuneration. These ads share a common structural layout and oscillate around a central theme: how to change your destiny by magic manipulation. More elaborate narratives concentrate on the selling of a single product or the expertise of a single person.

The classifieds and the detailed narrative advertisements express the same philosophy: magic alone endows anyone with the necessary luck to fulfill one's heart's desire without working or suffering to deserve it. Contrary to traditional folktale justice (which rewards the poor, the weak, the simpleton), or the Horatio Alger morality of "rags to riches" (Dundes 1971; Dundes and Pagter 1978; Mullen 1978:219), the legend magic of advertisements, offers to confer easy luck upon anyone, regardless of merit, need, or social status.[7]

The ads claim that everyone is in need of something and entitled to obtain the maximum. "Every man, woman, and child is born with one million dollars in credit," reads a headline (*Midnight/Globe*, 20 June 1978) offering a credit card that will "ABSOLUTELY, POSITIVELY grant ALL YOUR WISHES, FULFILL all your hopes and dreams." It sounds sensible to give it a try; the card costs only $5.00 ($3.50 for additional cards). "You owe it to yourself to test the incredible Mystical Forces yourself, in your own life, with this amazing Charge Card." To obtain the "big money," the only requirement is to join the ranks of the lucky by making a small investment: buying magic. Luck is a key that can be purchased in order to turn the born loser into a winner. Just follow the simple rules of magic (instructions included with the purchased symbol of luck), and you obtain (win) the money that is the ultimate key to happiness. It is up to the winner to turn the money into the goods that secure optimal fulfillment. The ideology of buying luck and the prescriptions for manipulating the objectified magic are traditional, following the strict rules of analogic, contagious, and sympathetic magic.

Advertisers, whether honest or fraudulent, fall into two categories: (1) practitioners of magic; and (2) ordinary people who were touched by luck and volunteer to tell about their success to encourage and assist others who are out of luck. The practitioners introduce themselves as experts with a variety of occult vocations. They are referred to as being "internationally famous," "the world's greatest psychic," or "the world's number one healer." Many are "doctors" and "reverends"; many hold "Ph.H., DSG, and AFA degrees"; many call themselves "mother," "sister," "madam," "master," "brother," or "father." The practitioners' names reveal their orientation. There is a "Jesus messenger with God-Given power," a "Dr. Mandrake," a "Dr. Dante," a "root lady," an "Indian Princess," and even a team consisting of a "Salem witch and an Indian Shaman." Men and women are equally represented. On the other hand, those featured as ordinary people touched by luck have plain names—Mrs. Taylor, Bill McCarthy, John Wood, or Jack Smith. They often appear with their addresses, although in other cases only initials or code numbers appear, showing the reader the medium's respect for confidentiality.

The classified ad items, as condensed as they are, contain a fairly complete corpus of magic based on commonly known and culturally inherited beliefs, customs, and practices. The fact that they appear in print gives them a certain credibility in the public eye. Even the skeptic, ready to challenge the believer or half-believer who would view the ads as decisive evidence of what was previously known in family tradition, has to give them some consideration.

Many occultists—"world famous" horoscope chart makers, numerologists, spiritual advisors, prophets, and demonologists—appear as entrepreneurs who market themselves in the classifieds. Gaining access to the name, address, and birthdate of respondents, they offer guidance on the road to happiness through personal correspondence. Their credentials are convincing: Norvell, the World's Number One Astrologer, has helped U.S. presidents, European royalty, and Hollywood stars; Dr. Winfried Noe, Europe's Number One astrologer, has (unspecified) world-famous clients; Marie-Simone, Europe's Number One astrologer (first among the equals?), did the horoscope of Elizabeth Taylor and Steffi Graf. No doubt these advisors will be able to compute the winning lottery number of the customer.

Often, however, the unsuspecting luck-seekers who write to a miracle healer, voodoo witch, or saint, will find that by making contact with one practitioner, they have invited the services of other occultists as well. Using the birthdate as a pawn, several astrologers respond with their offers by private letter or postcard. The narrative is formulaic, containing the same components; only the length differs. Following are the main elements of the letter that arrives, in several copies signed by diverse names, at the home of the customer who answered one classified astrologer's ad:

(1) Apology for writing uninvited;

(2) Miraculous event: While charting the horoscopes of celebrities, the astrologer received "an amazingly vivid reading of your horoscope signs," and lucky numbers for lottery jackpots were revealed to him or her. He or she is conveying the happy news that the constellation of the stars at the birthday date of the seeker promise extraordinary luck;

(3) Instructions: Send $7.00 to receive the lucky numbers, plus a gift—a magic pendant with "your genuine birthstone" and a chain. A winning of $10,000 to $100,000 in the next six months is guaranteed. Promise to donate ten percent of the money to charity;

(4) Further stress on the amazing competence of the astrologer.

It seems the masters are all employees of the same or related luck business enterprises, hungry to exploit the seeker. The return addresses of the astrologers are often remarkably similar, located in the same business.

After making the first step, answering a newspaper ad, the reply arrives in the mail as an intimate personal message, while in fact it has opened the door to an endless chain of magic suppliers who offer other avenues of negotiating magic. Once on the subscriber list, the consumer cannot escape their grip.

The relationship between individual occultists and mail-order chains is hard to discern. A complex network seems to include importers, wholesalers, gift, curio, and tourist souvenir shops, and mail-order retailers who deal with miscellaneous art and craft wares, including magic paraphernalia. Some of the advertising companies (Worldwide Curio House, International Imports, Mercury House, American Consumer Inc., Religious Supply Co., etc.) sell magic objects along with books and imported knickknacks: evil eye beads from Turkey, curse-gesturing fingers and worry beads from Greece, a blessing hand from Egypt, magic horn from Italy, voodoo dolls from Haiti, Jordan water from Israel or who knows from where, because the originals often happen to be copied and mass-produced in Japan, Taiwan, Hong Kong, South Korea, and the Philippines. By calling themselves Psychic Authority, Better Life Inc., or Church of Voodoo, some firms are quite open about the nature of their merchandise.

More aggressive marketing strategies are expressed by firms named after the product they offer: "The Buddha" sells Buddha statuettes whose belly must be rubbed for luck; "King Midas" sells King Midas amulets that turn everything the recipient touches into gold; "House of Fatima" sells the Miraculous Golden Diamond Fatima Medal; and the "Holy Jordan Talisman" offers bottle pendants called Holy Jordan Talisman. One wonders whether these are just special branches of larger firms. A most pretentious sales gimmick is applied by the Good Luck Comprehension Research Project, which distributes luck-bringing jewelry under the claim of experimentation. Buyers who pay a modest $5.00 fee are asked to report on their luck experience, which will be published optionally under their assigned code number. There is a general tendency to hook customers, to make them promoters and associates. Full-page ads include authorization forms for signing: "I promise to testify . . . to let you know as soon as I experience my miracle of THOUSANDS OF DOLLARS."

Everybody knows the great attraction of mail-order shopping in America. Busy professionals or home-bound suburban homemakers, the rich and the poor, the young and the old, the lazy, the thrifty, the miser, and the compulsive shopper, all enjoy buying material goods from printed catalogs, occasional sales lists, and press, radio, and television advertisements that inform about supplies and allow customers to avail themselves of articles they want in the privacy of their homes. For the magic shopper, mail-order service provides not only exposure to a large choice of available magic but also an opportunity to try a variety of objects and advice without embarrassment. It permits the customer to make low-risk purchases with a "money-back guarantee." It also allows for discretion on the part of the doubter, the hesitant, the half-believer. "Do you need a miracle fast?" asks one advertiser. "Have your credit card handy and call our MIRACLE HOT-LINE."

For a long time, we routinely picked up the telephone to order catalog merchandise, taking advantage of free 800 numbers. This gave us the illusion that we got something for nothing—particularly if the merchandise was magic power whose vendors professed shyness about financial gain. Psychics spoke of "donations," or, if the power was in an object, a modest contribution to cover production costs. The idea was that luck is priceless; how could the generous redeemer ever be rewarded by money? Nevertheless, a new sales tactic—the 900 number—now dominates the magic market. The psychic, an attractive, magnetic personality shown in tabloid and popular magazine ads, will help you immediately for a $2.00 to $3.95 per minute fee. "INSTANT PSYCHIC HELP IS ONLY A PHONE CALL AWAY. . . . IMPOSSIBLE WISHES COME TRUE!" is the promise. The personal touch of making voice-to-voice contact is stressed; persons who avail themselves of this service will receive instant power by talking, conducting an intimate conversation through the air, like making a secret confession. Katrina, the founder of a psychic advisor's network, promises she can help, as do the countless others who answer on the mystic airwaves of the 900 payphone.

The auctioneers of magic exploit those rare moments in anyone's life when tragedy hits and rational acts cannot help. Shopping magic preys on people in desperation—the mail appears as the only secret and dependable way to circumvent frustration, to safely suspend disbelief: a harmless way to test one's supernatural experience and psychic capability. In many cases, buying a magic object, following guidance, and adopting suggested behavior leads to the settling of one's belief or disbelief. "No questions asked," "telephone consultation," "send birth dates and initials only," "send no money,"—instructions like these assure complete anonymity.

The common believer, so aptly described by Virtanen (1990), is the largest, invisible contingent in the magic market, the preschool for candidates of occult factions. There is no documented information on the degree of belief among the forty million American tabloid readers who routinely pick up a copy at the grocery store checkout counter; and the degree of belief of those who actually respond to magic promotions is immeasurable, probably divided between strong believers, hesitants, and selective and temporary believers. My own testing of the intensity of supernatural belief in the United States reveals something of the pervasiveness of this interest. Of the several hundred college students who responded to my questionnaire, roughly sixty percent admitted to occasionally following occult guidance, consulting fortune tellers, wearing protective jewelry, amulets, and good luck charms, as well as buying literature on occult themes advertised in the press.

In the narrowest sense, magic (defined in Webster's Third New International Dictionary, 1971) is "the use of means (as ceremonies, charms, spells) that are believed to have supernatural power to cause a supernatural being to produce or prevent a particular result (as rain, death, healing) considered not obtainable by natural means and that also include the arts of divination, incantation, sympathetic magic, and thaumaturgy: control of natural forces by the typically direct action of rites, objects, materials or words considered supernaturally potent." The magic market practices this art accurately, to the letter, through material objects: consumables as embodiments of supernatural power and knowledge. The possession of objects must include instruction to secure proper handling. Early success is guaranteed within the magic numbers of three, seven, or twenty-four hours, overnight, or even "immediately" upon handling, while the money-back guarantee is often extended to months or a whole year in case of absolute failure. The buyer must always "rush" the order because the item is not only precious but also scarce—available in "limited edition" for a "limited time."

The object is also "authentic," which means only that it is a "genuine" reproduction in cheap material of a unique original piece, but by contagion it is mystically empowered with the same secret energy. The statement that a replica of a saint's blood, the Shroud of Christ, the Cross of Magnator, Cheops's Pyramid, or the amulet of the Inca Sun God can be as potent as the original depends on the presumption of the customer's gullibility or momentary mental state. While the object's commercial value is boosted out of proportion, profit is strongly de-emphasized. The dealer in magic often accepts only "donations" based upon the client's appreciation, or a modest, indeed, a symbolic sum—in return for guaranteed lifelong bliss. By stressing the hardship and difficulty involved in acquiring and reproducing the object, the provider appears as a champion of altruism devoted to the salvation of his fellows on earth. According to the claim, the merchandise is not only powerful, rare, and aesthetically attractive, but it is reproduced with great care and craftmanship. Prices do not go beyond the $10 to $30 range ($9.99 to $29.99 rather), and most are well below that amount. C.O.D. and credit card orders are honored. The buyer finds it easy to take a chance and invest such a modest sum.

The purchased object is seen as endowing the customer with power and knowledge, giving him or her supernatural qualities while also turning him or her into an instrument and humble servant of the power. The buyer begins an entirely new life by being instructed in magic and, so to say, embracing magic. With the purchase buyers also learn the history and mystic origin of the object to which they have committed themselves. Although some objects have only limited usefulness (numerology, biorhythm and horoscope charts, which give guidance for conduct only through the calendar year), most of them are characterized by universal applicability. Therefore, in order that the object may be used in unexpected emergencies or when chances of luck occur, it has to be in close physical proximity at all times. Most can be worn on the body as powerful emergizers and protectors from harm, in the shape of jewelry pieces—pins, chains, pendants, or rings—constructed of copper, silver, or gold plate with gemstones and other substances (Golowin 1964: 14–21). Ancient mystic, religious, and Christian symbols, lucky signs and numbers, and legendary luck story references are crafted into talismans, reinforcing traditional belief according to the *similia similibus* rule of sympathetic magic.

A random sample of such jewelry includes: the ESP Pyramid Ring (a replica of the Cheops Pyramid with a set of seven Egyptian good luck symbols); the Mr. Lucky Mayan Symbol; the Miraculous Water of Lourdes (in a bottle pendant); the Gold Hypnotic Eye Amulet; King Solomon's Gold Lucky Hand Amulet; the Miraculous Golden Diamond Fatima Medal; and Aladdin's Magic Lamp. Another category of objects which also must be kept intimately close at hand includes the Money Bag from Jerusalem; the Haitian Voodoo Doll; and the two-and-a-half-foot-long Miracle Cloth. A third category includes a wide variety of written magic: books by famous mystics, clairvoyants, and healers; spells, curses, prayers, incantations, lucky numbers, guides to magic words in the Bible, healing herbs, and magic formulas for all occasions.

As mentioned earlier, the objects are versatile and can be used by people in all walks of life for needs as they arise. Beyond the overall needs within the domain of health, wealth, and love, emergent needs must be immediately remedied; ills must be removed at once. Such help occasionally involves the destruction of the cause—often a perpetrator who is tampering with magic. Although the general intent seems positive (to help, not harm people), black magic is also openly advertised in the market: "Zadok, the Witch, guarantees to hex your enemies in 24 hours. . . . Never fails," reads the classified ad. Another offers "voodoo revenge! Enemies cursed! Anywhere!" Offers are made to "expel witchcraft and devilment," "repel evil, regain love, punish enemies." "I will curse your enemies, known or unknown in 3 hours," promises a witch, who also supplies you with a voodoo doll with "how-to-do-it instructions." A candle-burning ritual is taught for dealing with "enemies, lovers, revenge, wealth," and the offer includes "a kit for forty different spells."

The inexhaustible list tells us that to reach a desired end, both good and evil powers must be summoned. But what is the desired end? First and foremost, it is money. All ills are removable, all desires fulfillable by money. It makes one free, independent and powerful. Money can buy comfort, love, and health.

Money can be obtained by winning, the keyword in the parlance of the ads. Endowed with the power of the object in their possession, the recipients become sure winners of cash. They need only to operate the slot machine, go to the races, play blackjack or roulette, buy a lottery ticket, enter raffles, or purchase bingo cards. Gambling, however, is not always necessary. Gold may be found literally on street pavements, seemingly by accident. Advertisers, like the million-dollar credit card promoter, openly suggest that winning is written in everybody's destiny, and that by acquiring the magic merchandise, one joins the ranks of those among whom goods will be fairly apportioned. There are losers, of course, but the wise, who listen to the call, will become winners.

Thus, the seller of the Midas pendant assures the buyer that "you will unleash the amazing powers of the King Midas legend. Like the Midas touch in the fabled story, King Midas must bring you great fortune, luxurious possessions, and enduring happiness—everything you want in four weeks . . . " Likewise, the Cross of Lourdes will bring "luck into thousands of dollars." Special miracle charms are to be worn for playing bingo or lottery; "I won Bingo for $400. . . . thank you and God bless you for sending Lady Luck,"

writes a grateful winner. Others report similar gains: "I won $1,600 at the tracks by rubbing the belly of Buddha"; "I won $10,000 in a Canadian sweepstakes"; "I am a constant winner at the slots. Once $423, then $290 and now $900."

Through owning the Bethlehem Cross one will acquire "Miracle Money" "to help pay all those bills . . . money to go to a good doctor who can really help you . . . money to finally get your share of all the good things others have . . . money so that you will always be taken care of . . . money so that you will never worry again . . . money to do anything you want."

The rest of the "miracles" advertised in pop publications are more culture-specific, including all the earthly goods middle America considers necessary for having a good life. This relatively limited list includes: "Owning a fine house with a fireplace and a heated swimming pool in a good neighborhood; owning a thriving business or having a top job with a great pay; owning a vacation home and a luxury yacht in the Bahamas; having a happy family life (a successful and affectionate mate and happy children); good health to live long and happily, eating all the good foods without ever being sick again."

Any magic object may also be directed to the removal of obstacles on the road to happiness. For example, six women testify in their "sworn and notarized true stories" how their wishes were fulfilled by the "amazing powers of the Cross of Magnator": "My blood pressure went down, my neuritis is almost gone and I started jogging again," writes Mrs. M., while Miss D. reports winning jackpots in the amounts of $7.50 and $36.00 in Reno. Mrs. L. K. was healed from an affliction by the Portuguese Man-O'-War; C. S., whose husband wanted a divorce, returned to her. Ms. P., a heart patient, was completely cured, just as was Mrs. H. M., who had suffered from allergies for thirty years.

The variety of relief and of gifts obtained through all-purpose magic objects is unlimited. They range from the healing of minor illnesses and the restoration of marriages to winning thousands of dollars. Yet a common factor has to be noted. It seems the winners are well educated in folklore, either by hereditary awareness or by new instruction, refreshment of fading knowledge, from the suppliers. In fact, the boom of the magic market relies on the fact that customers know how magic works. Familiarity with the Midas legend, the Solomon legend, the Aladdin tale, the story of Lucky Hans; and belief in the rule of three wishes, the lifting of buried treasure, and the power of four-leaf clovers, magic wands, and innumerable objects endowed with magic, are maintained and adapted to serve modern consumer society. Folk narrative motifs constitute the building blocks of countless magic object promotional legends, their sales potential founded on traditional familiarity.

Here is a specimen that sounds factual, and may be factual, reconstructed, applied, or cleverly invented:

> Once upon a time, in the reign of Askia the Great, Sultan of Songhai, it is told that a poor camel driver, Ahmed, so displeased the powerful ruler that he was cast out of the oasis to die in the desert. As he lay near death, a Bedouin came seeking to rob him. Ahmed, seeing the dagger raised above him, grasped at the thief's throat and broke therefrom a chain bearing a strangely carved silver Cross. Instantly the Bedouin paled, staggered and fell dead! Praising his luck, Ahmed placed the cross upon his own throat, whereupon the camel of the Bedouin approached and knelt, and bore him to a cave near Agadés. Here Ahmed discovered jewels, spices and gold, looted from a thousand caravans. And from that day forward he and his descendents—for each of whom Ahmed caused a copy of the Cross to be carved—lived in health, riches, and good fortune for all their days!

But why should we be concerned with such an old story? The author also contemplates this question, and then explains:

> In this modern day, such tales are not to be believed. Or are they? It is a fact that in the Republic of Niger, astride the ancient caravan routes across the Sahara, the oasis of Agadés still basks in the sun, little changed from the 16th century, when Askia did indeed control a vast kingdom stretching from the desert to the sea! It is a fact that, since ancient times, certain substances and talismans have been known to millions to have the power to affect the destiny of those who wear them next to their skin—the power to bring the wearer . . .

From here "The Legend of the Amazing Powers of LA CROIX D'AGADES" (*National Enquirer*, 14 Sept. 1976) turns into a sales promotion of a type that we will see more of in what follows.

Legends for Sale

The magic mart that appears in advertisements in the popular press is actually a legend market. More accurately, it is also a legend factory, in which old legends are recreated, modified, and improved, and new ones are created to commoditize magic.

Belief, as the passive but salient agent representing the worldview of a given society, becomes manifest only in dramatic (ritualistic) and narrative forms. Thus, belief in magic is activated through feasible forms, documented by performance, dramatic action, or narrative account. Belief (signified by prescribed behavior) and story symbiotically reinforce and promote each other. Belief in magic, as a referential framework, is the lifeline of the market in which merchants and magicians join forces to propagate their services through documented cases of success in legend form.[8] They want to convince consumers that magic is a realistic force that can be manipulated to their advantage. Newspaper ads exploit all features and attributes of the legend, including its situational context, intellectual atmosphere, and worldview. Content units, motifs, episodes, sequences, whole stories, cycles, conglomerates, and pertinent stylistic conventions are all familiar chunks of traditional knowledge. Although mail-order legends address the reading audience only in printed form, they exhibit great flexibility around stable cores and reflect current conditions of the oral dissemination of magic accounts.

The magic ad business, eager to fill the needs of its broad clientele, greatly depends on oral folklore. It not only acts as a practical mediator of oral tradition but also exerts influence on the actual maintenance and resurgence of traditional expressive forms. Legends sold in the magic market pick up and convey the ideas of a partly invisible, partly visible, and very active audience. These legends are as variable and unfixable in print as the legends that appear in the spontaneous performance of old-time villagers or members of contemporary social gatherings.

In the labyrinth of mail-order marketing, the formulation of narrative is more or less explicit, depending on the degree of elaboration of identical components of a common frame of reference. The classifieds are skeleton-like outlines bearing maximum information stuffed into minimum linguistic codes which, however, may include elements of more than one legend. Each announcement would seem formulaic to the folklorist, like a legend abstract or summary, comprising the ingredients of an implied story that can be varied and extended at will. Here are some illustrative examples:

> Sister Patsy. The vibration of your voice over the phone will tell you your entire future. A message of hope. Sister Patsy is superior to any other Psychic you have talked to. Gives lucky days, lucky numbers. Lifts you out of sorrow and darkness and starts you on the way of success and happiness. You owe it to yourself. Consult this gifted lady. Immediate satisfaction.

> Money Magic. Become rich immediately! Receive millionaire spells, money attraction potion, personal lucky numbers, candle burning wealth ritual, lucky charm collection, full instructions. Quick results. Never fails. Psychic moneymakers.

A somewhat more verbose ad is autobiographical and more explicit in its promises:

> Andreika. "I will cast a spell for you."—I can cast a spell to make one love another, or cause a person to change his mind about a relationship, or bring two people together.

I can do all these things because I have the combined powers of my mother who was a sorceress, and my father, one of the most powerful warlocks who passed on his secrets to me moments before he moved on to a different world.

My magical powers are beyond your imagination. I can cast a spell in your behalf regarding a relationship, your financial situation, future events, or whatever is important to you. I have the power and I use the power.

I am Andreika and I can change the course of destiny. Pay me and I shall cast a spell in your favor. Tell me what it is you want and I shall go about my work. Is it someone or something you desire to have? Do you want wealth or happiness or a mate?

I will cast only one spell at a time. Do not ask for more. My energies must be massed toward one specific target; otherwise, my powers are lessened. Send me your most important desire and I shall work my powers in your favor.

Such rudimentary legends often appear in larger announcements, rounded out in narrative details focusing on selling a single product.

Half- or full-page advertisements, with a picture of the magic object in the center, contain the most complete and elaborate mail-order legends. These remarkably and expertly crafted master legends serve the purpose of selling a product. They initiate a business and at the same time launch a string of other related legends. In most cases, the master story is a proponent, calling for co-proponents (Dégh and Vázsonyi 1973) and supporters. The main story itself is usually autobiographical, a personal career account by an individual who made it from bankruptcy to the top by accidentally gaining access to a miraculous object. The story is moderately consistent and varies only to the extent of introducing different personalities in different situations: easygoing, carefree bachelors, playboys who threw away their inheritance, God-fearing family men haunted by sickness and ill luck, farmers running away before foreclosure. After the desperate situation is adequately dramatized, a detailed account is given of the accidental, serendipitous finding of the object, followed by the fabulous gain of money and the purchases, investments, and the happy life that money has bought. It is important that the narrator always emphasizes that this luck is incredible, he was always a rational person, never believed in miracles or the supernatural, and this experience has convinced him how wrong he was.

At this point the legend itself turns into a sales item. Another legend is introduced in which the compassionate happy raconteur tells how he loaned the object to his underprivileged friends and how they also succeeded. Then a concluding legend explains how the millionaire began his charity business—the promotion of the luck-bringing object—to have everyone share in his luck. He takes the trouble to manufacture replicas of the object, after making sure they are as potent as the original, and lets all people have them for a symbolic fee because "all humans on earth can choose to be the recipient of money, good luck . . . happiness . . . health . . . success." Here the story ends, followed and supported by testimonial mini-legends told by the recipients of luck, strangers who responded to the advertisement and bought the object. These are brief, solicited reports, dry statements of success.

Sometimes the out-of-luck person is about to commit suicide and is stopped by a supernatural entity that offers him the object; in other cases, he or she is sent to an exotic country on business before being sacked and tripping over the object in the desert. The protagonist signs his name and address as an endorsement. He may even strengthen his credibility by including snapshots of his explorations and a notarized certificate, thus making the miracle palpable for the reader. Two of the many variants of this legend will give an idea of the main type outline:

(A) Don Jeffries tells his story of how "The Holy Land Cross brought me $60,000—how can I ever say 'Thank You' enough!" (*The Globe*, 30 Oct. 1979). So it begins:

> 6 months ago I was worse than a failure. For years I struggled along, barely making a living. Then, after reading several "get rich" books, I started my own business—but it failed almost immediately.
> Before I knew what hit me I was snowed under by a mountain of bills. I had absolutely no money but that didn't stop the bill collectors. They called at all hours until my family was frantic with worry and my health started to fail. Old friends began to avoid me. Even my family couldn't hide the fact that they thought I was bad luck. At times I prayed that a heart attack would end all my cares and troubles forever.
> Then,—suddenly—everything changed in one day! One morning as I was going out the front door of my in-laws' apartment—where my wife and I have moved to save money—my wife pushed a small brown parcel into my pocket. "Don't look at it," she said, "just forget it's even there." And I did forget almost immediately because of the worries on my mind.

Wherever he went that day he was well received, his debtors offered to help him out, a check came in the mail, he won at the race track . . .

> the neighbors greeted me with new respect even though there was no way they could possibly have known about my good luck.
> Inside the house my wife asked: "Did the Holy Land Cross help you today?"—Suddenly I remembered the brown parcel she had placed in my pocket!

Here follows the description of the mother-of-pearl cross of exquisite beauty that his wife had obtained. It was carved in ancient design: "Over 1,000 strokes were required to create its intricate filigree pattern. Then a secret polishing solution was used to give its remarkable translucent luster that never fades. Finally, as a guarantee of authenticity, the word 'Bethlehem' was permanently hand inscribed. . . . The art required to make it has been jealously guarded by a single family for almost 2,000 years and is handed down from father to son. . . . Anyone who can obtain one is very lucky" because it has "STRANGE and WONDERFUL POWER to bring MONEY and GOOD LUCK to anyone who carried it." Then, the benefits are listed: $60,000 in 60 days and money is still coming; business and health are restored, and "my family life (including my sex life) straightened itself out as if by magic—and my wife and I are passionate again."

He then describes the hardships of obtaining five more crosses. "We had to pay an arm and a leg" for the "talisman to bring my friends good luck too." The wonderful events prompted him to get a large supply to make available to people for $6.95 plus 65c postage and handling.

Here are some of the reports from grateful recipients: "I won a jackpot of $300 at the Fireman's Bingo"; "Within two hours after receiving the cross I attended a business meeting and during it won a drawing of a $100 bill"; "Its first miracle was to bring my family back together."

(B) John Wright's story is quite different. In his letter, addressed to us as "Dear Friend," he urges the reader to take his offer of guidance to THE ROYAL ROAD TO RICHES (*Sun*, 1985). He is not offering us a precious jewel or a mystic talisman of great value. He offers to tell us a secret. A secret that he had obtained and that has changed his life completely. He does not tell us what the secret is, he just narrates his life story. It begins with the usual bankruptcy account. Not too long ago he was "flat broke." His car was repossessed by the bank; he was evicted from his residence and had to take his family to live with relatives. From here he switches to his changed life, leaving the reader in suspense about what instrument made the dramatic turn. But what he tells about his current life gives us an idea of the common daydream of the good life:

> I own four homes in Southern California. The one I'm living in now in Beverly Hills is worth more than one million dollars. I own several cars, among them a brand new Mercedes and a brand new Cadillac. Right now, I have a $1 million dollar line of credit with the banks and have certificates of deposit of $100,000 each in my bank in Beverly Hills.

After telling about his wealth in terms of home and car ownership and money in the bank, John Wright further tells us how life is to be enjoyed, how he is doing, and what he will also be able to do once he gives us the "money secret":

> Best of all, I have time to have fun. To be me. To do what I want. I work about 4 hours a day, the rest of the day, I do things that pleases [*sic*] me. Some days I go swimming and sailing—shopping. Other days, I play racquetball or tennis. Sometimes, frankly, I just lie out under the sun with a good book. I love to take long vacations from—Maui, Hawaii.

Further, he tells us about the condition of letting us have the secret, which is characterized as

> incredibly simple. Anyone can use it. You can get started with practically no money at all and the risk is almost zero. You don't need special training or even a high school education. It doesn't matter how young or old you are and it will work for you at home or even while you are on vacation.

After some other details on how easy it is to make the secret work and the information that it takes two hours to follow the instructions and learn, that it can produce cash "literally overnight," we come to the commercial offer. When the check or money order of $12.95 reaches John's address, he will not cash it for forty-five days, waiting for our report of success. If the secret fails, he will return the check plus $20.00 cash.

Who can pass up such an offer? The next part of the ad legend is entitled "PROOF." This legend salesman knows his customers:

> I know you are skeptical. This simply shows your good business sense. Well, here is proof from people who have put this amazing secret into use and have gotten all the money they ever desired. Their initials have been used in order to protect their privacy, but I have full information and the actual proof of their success in my files.

Twelve mini-legends follow, each reporting a fabulous sum made overnight, in 24 hours, in a week, 30 days, a matter of months, or less than a year. The grateful recipients are exuberant in their gratitude:

> I didn't believe it when you said the secret could produce money the next morning. Boy, was I wrong, and you were right! I purchased your Royal Road to Riches. On the basis of your advice, $9,800 poured in, in less than 24 hours! John, your secret is incredible! (J. K., Laguna Hills, CA).

> "I never believed those success stories," writes C. M. from Los Angeles. "In just 8 months I made over $203,000"; "My banker was amazed at my success," writes Mrs. N. E. from Sterling, Va.; "15,000 in two months! As a 22 year old girl, I never thought that I'd ever be able to make as much money . . . " (Ms E. L.)

More proofs are given by listing the approval of twelve newspapers and magazines: "You'll love . . . the Royal Road to Riches . . . only wish I'd known about it years ago" (*The Tolucan*); "We've all got to start somewhere . . . the Royal Road to Riches is the first step in the right direction" (*Los Angeles Herald Examiner*). Finally, Wright's accountant also testifies about his more than $1 million assets.

One would like to ask: what is the business of Mr. Wright? Or is selling the money secret his full-time occupation? Maybe the secret is a reasonable investment tip designed by shrewd professionals and promoted by a reputable firm under the fictitious name of John Wright, and the legendary packaging is a successful sales strategy borrowed from the scheme of talisman vendors? We cannot know unless we respond to the offer. But even if all this is fiction and the grateful mini-legend authors are sales agents or imaginary, the formula is rooted in the traditional folk belief system that permeates the imagination of modern people. The legend, marketed by Don Jeffries, John Wright, and innumerable other real or fictitious token salesmen, is based on social expectation and conventional belief in miracles. Therefore, the mini-legends, representing audience response, are aggressively solicited, often in a separately framed section of the ad page showing a tantalizing bundle of $100 bills. Legend telling is encouraged by this more or less standardized text:

> We want you to report the miracle that blesses your life. . . . We want you to tell us about the Money you receive . . . about the Healing your body and mind experience . . . about the Happiness and Joy you feel. . . . List for us some of your many, many blessings and you will be eligible to receive $100 cash. Naturally we ask you to sign the statement that certifies that you have worn the Talisman and have truly received all the miracles you list. And we ask that you have the statement notarized so that even the most skeptical will believe it.

This recruitment tirade offers proof of the unprovable, wards off cheaters, and promises to reward the true legend tellers. The call to join the legend-telling community, though, is ostensibly not for financial gain. The $100 is only a token awarded to those who volunteer to help do a good deed and enlighten unbelievers, increasing the number of recipients of happiness and extending the membership of the legend-telling circuit.

In the mail-order network of legend exchange, the dialectic, polyphonic nature of legend (Dégh and Vázsonyi 1973) appears particularly significant, countering a society divided between believers and doubters. Reference to eyewitnesses and time and place of occurrence is commonly contained in the text of the legends, and is also fleshed out in the promotional material in newspapers and personal letters. The unnamed but anticipated opponent opinion is attacked when a growing number of legend tellers testify that they have experienced incredible miracles. The master legends stress a general rationality, doubt, and initial common sense; conviction comes as a surprise, a shocking discovery of hidden dimensions. All secondary contributors and co-proponents also express their reluctance to believe at first, a hesitancy to make their conversion—making their conviction by direct experience all the more credible.

The lucky winners relate their cases, mostly in the first person singular. Mrs. McGinnis, for example, was never able to win a decent sum playing bingo, and now she has hit the $500 jackpot. Mrs. Schow won $2,308.05, and others were also lucky. On the basis of the numbers obtained through their horoscopes, several people made a small or large fortune and achieved happiness thereby. A man who spent lots of money throwing big parties was always short of cash until he availed himself of the "Witch's Money Jar," which was never drained; "all he has to do is dip in, for it brings him an endless flow of cash!" Evelyn, a good-hearted waitress, lent money to her friends and was always broke because they never paid her back. When she used the "Money Magnet Spell," dozens of people who owed her rushed to pay their debts. Ruth L., a widow, executed the necessary ritual and instantly became the owner of a dream house, and Andy's gallstones were permanently dissolved by Witchcraft.

A buyer of "The ancient symbol of Lady Luck, created over 500 years ago" reports, "I won a car worth $4,995 and a $50 lottery prize." Another grateful client writes that she was always unlucky until she experienced that "Lady Luck works like magic." Another woman who was separated from her husband says, "I can't believe it. My husband came back to me saying he loved me." Another woman had even greater luck: "I won and got a Model S-6000 Super DeLuxe Stretch Sewing Machine with cams." Many accounts are also reported of the power of "Cross of Magnator." A 45-year-old woman whose elbows and knees were failing could not get out of bed. The doctors had given up on her. But her son presented her with the Cross of Magnator and in a few days, she could get up without help. This happened in France, the "home of Lourdes," which makes the account sound even more plausible.

Mail-order magic supply serves a society hungry for miracles that seldom happen without daydreams and fantasy. Traditional solutions continue and persist, refueled by current experience to serve the circulation of consumer goods. No rational act can succeed without irrational means.

4

Beauty, Wealth, and Power

Career Choices for Women in Folktales, Fairy Tales, and Modern Media

Life History as a Folklore Genre

PEOPLE'S LIVES—courses of the life cycle from cradle to grave as well as single sections within the cycle—have become the target of intensive research by scholars in a number of disciplines over the last three decades. Related fields in the social sciences and the humanities have begun to look at human documents, voluntary and elicited testimonies and projections of individuals about their own lives. True to their traditions, professional goals, and research techniques, the various disciplines have applied diverse methods of inquiry yielding diverse types of life histories, stressing some aspects and subordinating others. One reason for this interest as well as this tendentiousness is the insight that individuals, as eyewitnesses of events and as representatives of their society, can indirectly furnish valuable information on lived-through events otherwise not easily obtainable by an outsider. Another reason is that "personhood ethnographies" can be elicited by studying lives containing the subsequent phases and events individuals pass through (Marcus and Fischer 1986:68). Subjects telling their own life experiences do not limit themselves to bare biographical facts but frame these with subjective-evaluative commentaries, illuminating the facts from more than one perspective and revealing thus far unknown dimensions of their mentality.

Although collecting autobiographies has been an ethnographic technique for monographic, thematic, and community studies for decades (for bibliographic summaries of the "Life-History method" see Gottschalk, Kluckhohn and Angell 1945; Langness 1981; Langness and Frank 1988; Dégh 1975; Lehmann 1983; Brednich, Lixfeld, Moser and Röhrich 1982; Bertaux 1981), "life history" seems to have become a "new paradigm" as demonstrated by a booming book market, although there is "nothing substantially new" in it (Bausinger 1988:478). On the other hand, human documents (personal reflections and voluntary, solicited, or analytically acquired self-revelations) presented by modernist anthropologists of the 1980s (Marcus and Fischer

1986:45–73) offer interesting experiments in intercultural discourse analysis while they fall short as life histories. The attempt of field anthropologists to overcome their cultural distance from the object they study does not go so far as to cause them to abandon their intrusive and manipulative interviewing technique. Instead of focusing on the individual's performance and minimizing their own influence, they portray the text as a cooperative construct of collector and "informant" based on their cultural conflict. Becoming increasingly aware of the hopelessness of bridging the gap between the Western elitist scholar and the native, anthropologists now target the subjectively conceived "us" and "them," that is, the description of the self and the other.

For the anthropologist, the life history story has served as a vehicle for studying the culture at large; "it is consistent with the usual research motive in anthropology of describing a larger cultural context rather than making sense out of an individual's personal experience" (Watson and Watson-Franke 1985:169). Only folklorists have developed an interest in the life history as narrative performance for its own sake. This interest is relatively recent because for a long time the folklore text was regarded as a collective rather than a personal product of individuals. Performers of folklore were at best regarded as bearers of tradition, mere receptacles and blind vehicles of heritage. As soon as folklorists realized that the singer of songs, the teller of tales, or the carver of Easter eggs was a conscious agent, recognized by his or her own community, they had to ask questions about personality features and their role in the renewal and dissemination of tradition as a contributing factor to the continuity of folklore in the world (Dégh 1985b). Thus, the life of important folklore performers in their own autobiographical recital became a useful source to append to their repertoire for a fuller evaluation of their art (Pentikäinen 1980).

Folkloristic interest in life history as a genre, as a creative product of individuals, as a matter of fact, from any kind of person, talented or untalented, either eyewitness to great events that shook the world, or simple participants of eventless everydays, resulted from a new interest in what is called the personal experience story (Bausinger 1958, 1977; Dobos 1978, 1986; Dolby-Stahl 1989; Dégh 1985b; Jahner 1985). This interest followed the apparent decline of the classical genres that had been the original targets of folklore study and remained the subject of interest for generations of scholars. More recent ethnographic fieldwork by folklorists has resulted in the discovery that people have the natural skill (and need) of formulating coherent stories from what they experience and that such stories abound out of proportion, compared to the limited numbers classifiable according to the blueprint of traditional prose narrative genres. However, the recognition of the human being as "homo narrans" (Ranke 1967) and that "narrative represents a universal medium of human consciousness" (König 1976), "that pervades virtually every genre and medium of human discourse" (Lucaites and Condit 1985:90), caused alarm and confusion among folklorists. The empirical discovery of new kinds of "nontraditional" stories is a daily sensation for fieldworkers but does not amount to more than the assignment of more descriptive titles—miner stories, firefighter stories, family experience narratives, disaster stories, occupational narratives, commercial fishermen stories, birthing mother stories, and so on. Charles Keil characterized the situation in cynical terms: "There is an academic imperialist tendency at work here, a mystification that turns every group's expressive life and every individual's 'personal experience narrative' into grist for the folklorist's mill. Even if we calculate just one personal experience narrative per person, the planet's proven narrative reserves are staggering, and the folklore empire will never suffer a scarcity of resources" (1979:209). It is true that "in a way, all people perpetually narrate themselves, . . . all people perpetually conceive or conceptualize themselves; life history can be looked at as continually revised, not necessarily verbalized . . . dynamic, emergent . . . " (Bausinger 1988: 482).

Any personal narrative is autobiographical by its very nature. Basically, "the actions and sufferings of life can be viewed as a process of telling ourselves stories, listening to those stories, and acting them out or living them through" (Carr 1986:61). Life history is egocentric: the teller presents it embedded in the current of his or her own life, and the facts of this life are biased by his or her views. This condition, as well as the universality of the sociobiological givens of life history, may be useful to consider in finding an adequate classification system capable of guiding us through this body of everyday narration, which is as luxuriant as the vegetation of a tropical rain forest. Except for practical thematic categories, or distinctions according to the permanent, transitory, or ad hoc social groups to whom the teller relates his or her story, no attempt has yet been made at creating some analytical order. Some thoughts concerning a possible solution will follow.

What is a life history? A narrative—a text that may be told orally as solicited by direct, systematic questioning or open-ended interviewing, or structured by a prepared questionnaire or field guide. It may also be the product of an intensive analytical conversation between researcher and respondent. It can also come close to spontaneous narration in which the researchers minimize their influence on the natural social context (Dégh 1975), allowing the speakers maximum liberty to express themselves—a situation preferable to the folklorist, who focuses on human creativity. It also can be a literary product in print or manuscript form. By extension, the life history need not be a formal narrative, told or written, at all. Individuals may embody their autobiographic testimony in other symbolic forms: photography, painting, handicraft, cookery, gardening, or any other personal endeavor at creativity (Kirshenblatt-Gimblett 1989).

Life history is a much broader universal than one may realize (Hofer and Niedermüller 1988). It may be more or less explicit behind elaborate symbolic forms like folktales. The schematic and trivial story of real life and its most spectacular and obvious fictitious parallel, the magic tale, are both career stories in the true sense of human career, composed of a series of successes and failures unfolding in a temporal sequence. These stages of life, as expressed in the life history, correspond remarkably to the "age pyramid" from cradle to grave as portrayed in pictorial representations since the Middle Ages (Bringeus 1982:59–60).

Life histories, just like folktales, present only fragments of the full course of life; they are incomplete stories. They concentrate on career: ascent, not descent; success, not failure. The common life history, just like the folktale, focuses on highlights—positive or negative actions and their consequences. As biographies, both are incomplete. They end as soon as career goals are accomplished and motivation for action no longer prevails. This is also true of stories of bad luck, strings of tragic turns that end in the temporary interruption or complete abandonment of original goals and their replacement with others. The narrator of life looks back and reflects. He or she selects the most memorable events for recounting, from the most frivolous feat featuring an absurd situation, to crucial acts decisive of one's fate and favorable self-representation. The folktale never informs us what happened after the prince married the little goose-girl and the two became king and queen; only sophisticated cartoonists show them as a quarreling couple with varicose veins twenty-five years later. Likewise, the life history also stops in midlife. The self-made oil magnate and the immigrant tobacco farmer both limit their narratives to struggle and victory and do not inform about their later business investments and lives of luxury. Once the goal of the career marked out by authority (the folk group) is accomplished, life loses its reportability and enters the domain of privacy. It is clear that life history is as much fictitious, subject to personal and communal manipulation, as the folktale. Both forms are shaped and polished by repetition, re-living in thought and in words over time. The incompleteness follows the logic of the arch of the age pyramid, which sets middle age on the top between ascending (active) and descending (inactive) states.

If life history follows the biological trajectory of life, which is also ritualized by the cyclic celebration of passage (Turner 1969), and if, as I would like to propose, this story as a whole or in rudiments is inherent in any story humans tell, it can be regarded as a structural universal. Human experience is the primary source of the ingredients used to construct a story; the objective would make sense only through human interpretation, symbolic or otherwise. The basic experience materializes when individuals create their own variables through the localizing process of bringing together suggestions offered by tradition (the conventional), the narrator (innovator), and the audience (conformist). The creative process in which life stories are transmitted, repeated, corrected, multiplied, spread, varied, and, in turn, stabilized by these three agents establishes their *Normalformen* or oikotypes, subtypes, performative etiquettes, vocabulary, style, and constructional techniques. Once the variants of this 'nontraditional' genre are subjected to an analysis as exacting as folk narrative specialists have used to examine the traditionally sanctioned narratives licensed by international and national type- and motif-indexes, life history narratives will be studied with more scientific rigor.

The life history is an ambiguous piece of art. It is an intimate confession of an individual, a disclosure of feelings and views about oneself, deeply personal, sensitive, and sincere. At the same time, it is a prepared and rehearsed statement for the public. It more or less deviates from sober reality in order to reach its goal: the staging of the image by which the person would like to be identified by others. Thus, life history construction follows the same behavioral course as public performance (Goffman 1959, 1967, 1971). The narrative text is an admixture of fact and fiction, ideal and real elements: life as it is and as it should be. Furthermore, behind each utterance of a life history there is a model, designated by society and sanctioned by tradition. Virtually each member of society is the recipient of a career projection, a script, a guideline to follow and realize. Individuals strive to follow it as closely as they can to fulfill social expectations, but the realization of the script is necessarily as multifarious as human mentality. Therefore, each life history telling can be conceived as a unique event: a variant of a type. The type (model) is constructed by the social group, which has projected the careers of its membership.

Although career stories appear in much greater number and variety than the transparently biographic, 'one-dimensional' (Lüthi 1981:8–12) magic tale types, their natural limitation is imposed by the possible numbers of careers people can have. Careers are determined by the place of individuals in the web of the social network. Clearly, the positions, roles, and relationships of people determine behavioral patterns necessary to fulfill the expected career model, as Bertaux and Wiame convincingly describe with reference to life stories from the baker's trade 1981; these conditions furnish the motivic ingredients for the script. Of course, the fact that each person holds membership simultaneously in diverse groups further extends the limits of the career narrative corpus, the number of types in a virtual index. Beyond kinship, age, gender, occupations, political and religious group memberships, the plethora of voluntary, recreational, hobby, philanthropic, educational, and other associations may also be the focus of life histories. They may fuel total histories, or just parts; they may appear related to certain parts of the life-cycle, offering a more or less coordinated diachronic sequence. Each group's model (the type) regulates and normalizes material life, the performance of prescribed actions. Tradition, convention, and identity formulation belong to the symbolic-ideological sphere of life, which mythologizes and folklorizes behavior and serves to maintain, secure, and necessarily transform material life. So projected, life histories are models representing the status quo of society striving for survival.

The Family as Career Training Center: Assignment of Gender Careers

While progress is inevitable and social transformation follows the generational change, the career model is founded on conservative principles. Society at large tends to maintain values and norms inherited from and believed to have been useful for previous generations. To link the present to a past, to venerate the ancestry that has established unique values, gives a feeling of security and promises future survival and the maintenance of social order. Such ideological schemes unite population groups within nations and professions, while the transfer of norms from generation to generation is carried out in the smallest social unit, the nuclear family. The planning of careers occurs among parents and children, in the family training center "that concerns itself with the reproduction of human characteristics" (Horkheimer 1936). Parents enculturate and socialize their offspring according to a value system that conforms to that of the larger society (König 1976:9–12) quite anachronistically. Life histories, then, are ideological guides to conduct, ensuring loyalty to tradition, projected by the parent generation. They are examples to help individuals conform to their assigned (not freely chosen) roles and careers, gilded and canonized by patriotic and religious rhetoric. A sense of respect, loyalty, indeed awe for tradition persists while the world changes. This respect for sacred ancestral values helps maintain continuity in career projections. These appear in adjusted and reinterpreted forms, as time passes, to fit new ideologies.

As an illustration of the foregoing, I will attempt an outline of the female career script in terms of its most stable elements that continue to exist in modern rural and urban societies. Without tracing evolutionary precedence or arguing for the universality of biological factors in the shaping of the image of the woman, I will concentrate on the career script that has evolved during the last two centuries in Europe and America and is manifested in the folktale and its modern equivalents.

Many radical changes have affected the status of women during this period. Responding to economic and political pressures, women took action to "break out of their homebody role" (Harris 1981:92); and today, more than ever, they are participating in the drive that promises equal rights and the collapse of "the marital and procreative imperative" (Harris 1981:92). Throughout the world, the feminist movement has risen in the favorable political climate of other movements for political transformation in the post–World War II era. It became a powerful force in the political arena, arguing for the rewriting of human history that traditionally marginalized women and was constructed "as if men's experience were normative, as if being human meant being male" (*Personal Narrative Group* 1989:3). The struggle for the recognition of equal rights entered the ideological field: feminist scholars in the humanities and the social sciences undertook the dual task of "deconstructing predominantly male paradigms and reconstructing a female perspective and experience in an effort to change the tradition that has silenced and marginalized" women (Greene and Kahn 1985:1, quoted in Babcock 1987:391). Arguing for women's life histories that represent the informant's subjective viewpoint, Watson and Watson-Franke point out that anthropologists have featured women "as male-defined beings," accepting women who "fit" the conventional norms of society, emphasizing the data that support a male-oriented view of women, and ignoring contrary data. The result of these procedures is that a woman's life emerges only in reference to men, and the full subjectivity of her life is lost (1985:183).

Feminist folklore scholars[1] joined forces with representatives of other fields relatively late to start a "collective revisionary enterprise . . . contributing to destabilizing and gendering dominant discourse, dismantling male bias, and writing women up and into folklore scholarship" (Babcock 1987:391). Contributions to knowledge include showing how bias against women is reflected in folklore genres; how folklore depicts their images, sex roles, and stereotypes; and how women fight against or conform to male dominance in the symbolic language of folklore.

The script of the life of the woman, developed in traditional patriarchal society and conceived in traditional values, has not changed overnight in response to the emancipatory struggle. Although modern technological society offers more choices, the submissive and obedient 'happy housewife heroine' model (Friedan 1963) persists. The constituent elements and related beliefs are matters of commonplace parlance reinforced by folkloric, journalistic, scholarly, and literary works conveyed through media performances. Traditional folktales, normalized children's fairy tales, personal testimonies, memoirs, short stories, romances (in book and magazine editions), movies, theater, television and radio shows, commercials, cartoons, and other products contribute to the variability of the scripts. Each in its own terms conveys an ideological message that confirms the old-fashioned social and economic system of the division of labor, rights, and power between male and female. Even a superficial survey of sources would exceed the confines of this discussion, so I will limit myself to two quite extreme examples: the biography of the woman as dependent homemaker in folktales (along with their rewrit-ten literary version, known as the fairy tale, educating and socializing the young), and in illustrated magazines for women: two subtypes of the same career.

The separation of the sexes and the projection of gender distinction be-gin immediately after the birth of children. The scripts of the life-roles that males and females are expected to play (Sanday 1981:15–51) are written in re-lation to each other, as two parts of one whole procreative system. Successful performances of the two roles guarantee survival. Because diverse social sys-tems require diverse interpretations of these roles, historically there is con-siderable variation. Yet there is also remarkable consistency, particularly in the ideological domain. Although the foundation of the patriarchal family system originated in the Bible and gained Christian reinforcement in medi-eval Europe, feudal elements in gender roles have survived in modern society to this day (Weber-Kellermann 1975, 1983).

This system assigns a leading role to the man, who is the husband, the father, the breadwinner, the provider of material goods, and thus the absolute authority in the family. To fill this role, he must be competent, strong, enter-prising, active, aggressive, and independent. As representative of the family, he engages in public affairs, politics, and warfare, to conquer and defend. His activities often keep him away from the household (Rosaldo and Lam-phere 1974:27), and sexual disloyalty to his wife is considered pardonable. Masculinity is an attribute of prestige, containing superior and authoritative virtues (Warner 1961:120).

The woman's role, although more complex, is centered around three re-sponsibilities: church, kitchen, and children.[2] The woman is the homemaker whose full-time duties tie her to the household except for spiritual reinforce-ment in the church. She is the pillar of the family; she makes the home a safe haven, a miniature universe in itself. She bears, nurses, and educates young children of both sexes, giving them moral values, while the husband watches at a distance. She prepares and serves food and fosters related ritual and social forms of consumption. As representative of her husband, she main-tains domestic family relations (Epstein 1971:40). Although she generates enormous power, the woman is dependent on her husband. "In marriage, as in the economy, woman's position is essentially subservient and supportive" (Gornick-Moran 1971:xxi) to the man who "bought her" and "owns her" (the financial sacrifice involved is apparent, for example, in the Hungarian term for bridegroom: 'völegény' [the buyer-fellow].) The maiden is taken, "swept away," or "rescued" by the husband, and because she is so helpless and un-able to fend for herself, he protects her in the home. She owes him absolute loyalty, body and soul, enduring his "animal-like sexuality" as he is "using her" (Szenti 1985:394).

Although marriage (and consequently, bearing children) is the ultimate fulfillment of true womanhood,[3] she cannot openly market herself. During courtship, traditional rural and urban women must show bashfulness and passivity, industry and good looks without pretense. "Femininity" means subordination and inferiority, except when a father or husband's position gives status to the woman (Warner 1961:120). In a 1959 international survey of boys, *Seventeen* (March 1959:100, 156) reported responses that a girl should be "conservative," "more modest," and "dress well but conservatively." The way to "snare a man" is body language: alluring clothing, makeup, perfume, jewelry. Covert seductive tricks are as important as practical and spiritual qualities. While a man is left to find his partner on his own, a whole chain of businesses specializes in preparing a woman for the "mating game," as one can judge from the limitless number of advertisements focusing on feminine sex appeal.[4]

Essential features of the female career script in opposition to the male—which I have outlined from elements skimmed from ethnographic literature, the current media, and personal experience, too trivial and numerous to list—may be incomplete and biased, but they are remarkably consistent. They are structured around female dependency versus male independence. It seems logical that there should be, as there is, a fundamental division of domains between the sexes, and that this division is interdependent and existentially indispensable. In this symbiotic relationship, however, the man's domain is public and thus seemingly more important, the woman's private, that is, domestic and secondary; indeed, "in every human culture, women are in some way subordinate to men" (Rosaldo and Lamphere 1974:17). No matter how valuable her contributions, the woman's sphere is consistently underrated; overstepping her boundaries provokes criticism from both the male and the female world. Thus, the status quo is reinforced again and again through the channels mentioned that contribute to the projection of separate personality development for men and women. No nature versus culture dichotomy between women and men—it is role-training and indoctrination that is at work here: "Personalities of the two sexes are socially produced" (Mead 1935:226 and 198–209; Ortner 1974; Dowling 1981:4).

Two-year-old Peter and his mother were my houseguests one summer. Since his birth, I had repeatedly been assured that Peter was "all boy." Now I had the opportunity to experience what that meant: the mother's (and the adult world's) agreement that boys need encouragement in their temper tantrums, demanding constant attention and service to develop a distinctive masculine identity "in terms of aggressive, self-determining individuation" (Ruitenbeek 1967:26–27;); encouragement to "act out their aggressions" and express hostility toward women.[5] "Mothers treat their sons differently; it is usually by emphasizing his masculinity in opposition to herself and pushing him to assume . . . a sexually toned male role relation to her," writes Nancy Chodorow (1974:48). This is the initiation for a baby to become a boy, within the mother's authority.

Later, when the boy can swing a baseball bat and go to the ballgame, his father will assume his education, distancing him from feminine authority. In kindergarten, he has to continue his aggressive attack on the world; otherwise he will be called a "sissy"—what a shame. In school, he will draw monsters, cars, trucks, and airplanes, the toys he will play with. "Give it to them!" "Give them hell!" will be the jovial encouragement by father and coach. At this point his further enculturation is transferred to the male world, even with an absentee father too busy to liberate his son from the domestic feminine environment that rejects him and forces him to assume independence following the paternal model (Chodorow 1974:66). The books the boy will be given to read are science fiction, mystery, and adventure. Until maturity, he will not care for feminine charm, kindness, tenderness, or other features of femininity, attributes of the "weaker sex." American teenage boys begin courtship when they get their driver's license and can take their dates to a haunted place at Halloween. The scared girl will find shelter "in the strong protective arms" of the new initiate to manhood.[6]

Girls, on the other hand, must develop opposite faculties. Femininity is the keyword, including "personal warmth and empathy, sensitivity, emotionalism, grace, charm, compliance, dependence and deference" (Epstein 1971:20). Mothers react differently to daughters than to sons; thus, young girls follow their mother's footsteps and become "little women." As Chodorow explains, girls learn to deal with the interpersonal demands of the family, and feminine personality comes to be founded on relation and connection to other people, in contrast to the masculine personality (Chodorow 1974:8). Girls must be pretty, like dolls, obedient, and subdued. For the patriarchal family it always was a disappointment if the socioculturally inferior girl was born instead of a boy, the preserver of the family name. In dismal details, legends and tales dramatize the shame of bearing a female child—a curse, or a crime with cruel punishment.

For the young mother, a baby girl means an extension of childhood, permission to play, to dress and cuddle a doll, the primary toy given to girls to prepare them for their mothering role. While baby boys also get their initial training from the mother, the relationship weakens as they grow, while girls remain attached. The games they learn prepare them for adult responsibilities; playful imitations of adult women's domestic chores—cooking, housecleaning, child-rearing. Small girls like to imitate adult women as they see them every day in the domestic environment. They dress up, put makeup on, play at going to parties and conducting conversations on adult concerns that they have overheard, exhibiting an awakening consciousness of the importance of sex appeal. Girls draw flowers, birds, and butterflies; they are discouraged from aggressive behavior or from playing boyish games. If they do, they are called "tomboy." Mothers read Märchen to their little girls, who later continue reading tales, romances, and equivalents published serially for young girls (such as the Babysitter series, an American best-seller for 8-to-12-year-olds), to educate and entertain the next generation of homemakers. Feminist fiction writer Carolyn See found in a class of high school students that all girls could list the titles of several folktales, while none of the boys could remember any (Dégh 1983b). Kay Stone reported that in her experiment, no males of any age were able to recall tales (Stone 1985:130).

Projecting their own mothering role, little girls play with dolls: their babies to swaddle. Thirty-two years ago, Ruth Handler created Barbie. "Suddenly," she said, children "had a chance to play with a doll that could be them in seven or eight years. They could project their dreams of the future onto her and also learn to deal with the adult world around them" (*Sky*, April 1989: 33). The catchword with Barbie is glamour. For American (and lately worldwide) preteens, the Barbie doll is the fulfillment of their desires. She is a young, sexual being, with the ideal slim figure, alluring clothing, makeup, and jewelry, a candidate for the Miss America pageant. Her life and marriage to boyfriend Ken is the promise of a blissful, conflictless happy end, and subject to "acting out" play (Hohmann 1985). Barbie is the model for "feminine behaviour": "I want to be a Barbie doll when I grow up," said a little girl of seven (Motz 1983:122). Today, Barbie has many competitors on the market, whether feminist critics like it or not. Replicas of top supermodels are sold to children because "every little girl should be able to fantasize for a few hours that she's a model going on a glamorous assignment" (*Glamour*, May 1990).

The Folktale Heroine Script

Traditional folktales reveal much about how society wants to see itself, how it wants to maintain its order and safeguard its continuation. Scholars have long known this and have invested much work in the study of these seemingly simple, naive, schematic texts. Assuming that the stories on the surface speak an artistic metaphoric language that covers a deeper meaning, they undertook the task of finding out what the tales really tell to their bearers, what kind of behavior or action they solicit. Some investigators were driven by practical goals. Generations of child educators, students of mental health, and behavioral sociologists, experiencing the popularity of feminine storytelling in the nursery, have debated whether the tales are helpful or harmful for children (the unisex Märchen-age under ten), but they have failed to realize two things. First of all, the fixed (printed) stories they analyzed were not representative of the countless variants spreading in society. There is no umbrella meaning but diverse ones for diverse people at diverse occasions (Röhrich 1985, 1988; Holbek 1987). Furthermore, the tales are told (created) not by children but by adults, for adults. Therefore, although they may contain childhood residues, they are not the perfect test materials to reveal early childhood fantasies.

In traditional societies, storytelling is an adult pastime not open for children. In Europe, the hotbed of the magic, or more generally of the so-called ordinary tale (AaTh 300–1199), the longest prose epic form was traditionally the domain of itinerant workingmen who imported them to the villages for mixed adult audiences (Dégh 1979, 1984). This type of tale became fashionable in elite society for its charming simplicity characterized as *childlike* (but not for children) by both Perrault and the Grimm brothers. For centuries, literary adaptation was motivated by nostalgia for rustic naivité (folklorism is not a novel phenomenon!), and a part of this nostalgia was the fiction that the simple tales were told by plain old women: mothers, grandmothers, and wet nurses. It is well known that when the Grimms did not succeed in selling their tale collection as a serious scholarly endeavor, more explicit rewriting, a dedication to women and their children, and an emphasis on its "educational" nature turned it into an international best-seller (Weber-Kellermann 1975:33). Thus the *Kinder- und Hausmärchen* became an '*Erziehungsbuch*' by accident and established the genre of the literary fairy tale, devoid of any implications the petty bourgeois morality would not tolerate.

Characteristically, the Grimm tale model has exercised a devastating influence on the retelling of tales by modern professional and amateur storytellers ever since. Although serving the socialization of all children—the Grimms' tales provided models for girls as well as for boys (Zipes 1979/80; Bottigheimer 1987; Tatar 1987)—female hero tales became more popular. This is understandable because as already noted, the intellectual education of boys after a certain age was taken over by the father. The career script of women in tales gained particular prominence (Zipes 1982) and kept its appeal as a charter for feminine behavior in the modern post-Märchen era, particularly because collectors followed the editorial policy of the Grimms. Tale archives and publications are full of distorted texts giving the impression that folktales were totally devoid of sex, obscenity, and rough language. Had modern collectors not gone to the field, we would have accepted the romantic suggestion of many venerable folklorists that the village folk were pure and innocent, not lewd and promiscuous like townspeople.

The folktale as a biographical narrative features an individual's ascent from anonymity to recognition, from poverty to wealth, from ugliness to beauty, from singlehood to marriage, and from nothingness to power. It recounts a series of events; an uninterrupted sequence of acts is placed into a temporal frame from birth through childhood and adolescence to maturity. It is an adventure story of travel, with obstacles of trials and tests. The central hero can be male or female; some tales occur with either male or female protagonists (like AaTh 510, 531, 327, and 400); but there are clear differences between those with male and those with female central characters. Of course, the folktale, as a biographical narrative describing the protagonist's adventure and rise to glory, contains suffering and humiliation, in equal measure. "Fairy-tale heroines have no monopoly on victimization. Male and female figures seem to suffer in equal parts" (Tatar 1987:75).

It is the nature of the genre that the folktale hero, male or female, is passive, deprived, and oppressed and undergoes a miraculous transformation during the voyage to success (Panttaja 1988). But in the male career, the protagonist's goal and fulfillment mean acquisition of power and the winning of a wife, with the two often interdependent. In this scheme the heroine is the prize, although she is far from idly waiting. She manipulates the hero, tests his endurance, skill, and wit, humiliates and embarrasses him, until she submits herself to his desires. She shows herself in conflicting colors: she is enchanted, mistreated, abused, and must be rescued, freed, and disenchanted. She is a seductress, a pitiless "belle dame sans merci," a witch, an adultress, a trickster, who must be outwitted and tamed to enable her to conform to her feminine role: church, kitchen, children, homemaker, queen in the household of a powerful king.

The heroine tale is, in essence, similar to the hero tale; only the goal makes it an entirely different enterprise. Here, the voyage from deprivation to fulfillment through sufferings and tests ends in the safe haven of marriage to the mighty ruler. She succeeds because she has the proper feminine virtues that make her so deserving. She is beautiful, chaste, generous, loyal, compassionate, religious, and hard-working.

While the hero makes mistakes, is delayed on the road by his own folly, and falls victim to temptations, he has more ambition. Often he has a profession, trade, or special skill; he negotiates his pay when he is hired; and most prominently, he displays the political ambition to dethrone the king and take his place. The heroine, on the other hand, has no learned or inherited skill; her characterization is that she is beautiful and in distress. Her competence is limited to domestic chores—spinning, weaving, cooking, geese herding, sewing, and child rearing. In many versions she is helpless, waiting for awakening, disenchantment, and rescue. This essentially passive and troubled folktale heroine image remains a consistent surface feature even when, in the course of the story, she has to gather strength and act.

The heroine does not seek adventure like the male hero, she does not travel in search of a husband; if she undertakes a voyage, she is driven by misfortune, escaping from an incestuous father, an envious mother, or jealous siblings. She is often innocently accused, slandered, banished, and destroyed. Even in tales about unjustly expelled wives who temporarily assume male identities (AaTh 880–884) and prove themselves to be superior to their husbands (the warrior girl defeats the invading army and rescues her husband), the females act only in the hope of regaining their place in the household as loyal wives and mothers. The Clever Peasant Girl (AaTh 922) becomes queen because of her wit but must promise not to interfere with her husband's judgment. But she does so because the king makes a fool of himself, and when she is sent back to her father for breach of agreement, she is allowed to take what she likes best. She drugs and takes the sleeping king—she does not give up her serfdom. The conflict of male and female roles in the Märchen is well depicted in the Cupid and Psyche tale (AaTh 425) as subdued power defeating hereditary dominance (Dégh 1990).

In addition to the title role of heroine, other female figures are featured in folktales. They elaborate the ingredients of the woman's career model in a broader sense, by complementing the young heroine's history with a glimpse into the future. There is the heroine's mother, whose love and concern for her daughter extends beyond the grave, as in Cinderella (Aath 510 A); the mother-in-law who suffers with the heroine when she is banished, and who rescues the golden-haired sons from being drowned in the river in The Three Golden Sons (AaTh 707); and the mother of the Sun, the Moon, and the Evening Star, who protects and guides the girl on her quest for her lost husband, as in Cupid and Psyche.

Besides the allies of the heroine who present later life roles and illustrate proper motherhood, contrasting female figures reinforce the ideal image. The stepmother who substitutes her ugly daughter with the heroine, as in The Three Oranges (AaTh 408); the stepsisters whose self-destruction is caused by their refusal to act like the kind girl in The Spinning Women by the Spring (AaTh 480); the witch, mother of the girl-snatching dragon in The Girl Who Married Animals (AaTh 552); and the offended fairy in Sleeping Beauty (AaTh 410)—all exemplify and warn against improper behavior.

More explicit educational tales, which are rooted in the same traditional social order and support this career script, are simpler constructs. They focus on ridiculing improper female conduct that diminishes the chances of finding and keeping a husband and thus making a living after the parental generation's passing. These warning stories—some of which have counterparts in tales with boy heroes—are humorous and critical of behavior that does not fit the approved career script offered by the Märchen. They are like character comedies. Skilled women raconteurs tell them in dialogues with a minimum of narrative commentaries. They feature girls who are ignorant of their household duties, who do not know how to behave in company, how to talk to the suitor, how to dress. They are lazy, sleepy, and unable to cook, sew, do the laundry, spin, clean the house, milk the cow, feed the pig, weed, wash the dishes, or care for the baby. I believe that fieldworkers in European villages can attest that the repertoire of these educational anecdotes (AaTh 1350–1450) contributes to the model set by the feminine hero tales.

What is remarkable about this career model is that in spite of the modesty of its goal—to be average and earn a living; namely, room and board in exchange for around-the-clock service in the house of a domineering husband—the process to achieve this goal is presented to the public in spectacular sparkling colors. The ascent to fulfillment happens in stages, marking a gradual transformation. The classic Märchen is actually told in terms of sets of transformations, in which the passage of time, growing up, wandering, and struggling with antagonists who block the road to fulfillment, are signaled by an outward change of identity. The transformational episodes structure the story and at the same time set its pace. The transformations are of diverse character; they can cross each other and may switch to different levels. The heroine, a child, ill-fed and ill-clad, is transformed into a beauty. The Swan Maiden (AaTh 400*) loses her feathers, the Orange Maiden (AaTh 408) becomes a princess. She is killed repeatedly by the substitute wife's mother, but returns as a tree, a pot cover, a rosemary, or a dove, from which shape she seven times regains her human shape, as beautiful as she ever was. Beauty and kindness are described in extreme terms, contrasted to ugliness and wickedness. Fleaskin, the unfortunate princess in The Dress of Gold, of Silver, and of Stars (AaTh 510B), has to conceal her beauty in the hide of a fattened flea to escape her incestuous father, but obtains three walnuts with a copper, a silver, and a gold dress inside to show her real identity. Cinderella gets her gold dress from a tree grown on her mother's grave. She has dual identity: she is the ash-girl, impossible to recognize as a princess in the ballroom, just like the overdue pregnant woman who spent seven years in search of her husband, the Snake Prince (AaTh 425C). Similarly, the kitchen maid serving a cake to the prince in which she hides her ring signaling her true identity is a princess, not the Little Goose Girl (AaTh 870A).

The folktale illustrates the validity of the proverb that "Kleider machen Leute" ("clothes make the man,") a truth confirmed and maximally exploited by modern fashion industry: you are what you wear. Tale characters transform themselves or are transformed into animals, objects, plants, natural forces, or supernatural figures easily, and they can reassume their original form as well. Such transformations may be a learning process, the way special knowledge is acquired; or they may be therapeutic, a means of becoming stronger, wiser, younger, and indeed, more beautiful. But the definitive transformation through putting on different attire is the indicator of fulfillment of the career. In many tales, the long-suffering hero and/or heroine reveal their identity by making a public appearance together. The couple change from filthy, smelly clothing into glamorous royal garb. They produce a real show, a victory march, with proper paraphernalia and a cheering crowd as audience. Storytellers who recount the course of events without slowing down the fast-moving series of acts delight in featuring the spectacle in this final scene (Dégh 1989:218–24). First, the hero and the heroine dress up in front of the mirror in red velvet and silk, gold, and silver brocade, known symbols of royal pomp. Then the prince mounts a horse equipped with diamond-studded saddle, spurs, and whip, while his princess rides in a silk-lined gold carriage drawn by six horses. "Who can it be?" whispers the crowd. "It can't be royalty, it must be imperial." This is the final glory for the Märchen princess. The showdown in the palace, the royal wedding, and the assumption of power are the gratification of the hero. The heroine is his property. She can live happily ever after.

Many features of this traditional folktale career model can be found in modern urban narration; some of them live on unaltered. All types of the literary tale, from the closest to the most distant replications of the oral tale, have become prominent among women, both tellers/writers and audiences. The question of the femaleness of the genre came up early, as urban women narrators and authors outnumbered men in France in the seventeenth and eighteenth century (Warner 1990). Later, inspired by the Grimms' example, Victorian English authors adapted a selection of tales, many from the Grimm book, to educate and entertain children (Hand 1963). The so-called fairy tale thus became an instructional device. As Jack Zipes notes, the fairy tale "illustrates the instrumentalization of fantasy, that is to say the setting of products of the imagination in a socio-economic context in order to limit the imagination of the receivers" (Zipes 1980:97–98). Along with the final 1857 version of the *Kinder- und Hausmärchen*, the colored fairytale books by Andrew Lang (Montenyohl 1986), and the *English Fairy Tales* by Joseph Jacobs (1967), the world tale contingent, servicing twentieth-century urban juvenile audiences, was established. These collections, the stylized versions of traditional tales, had a tremendous impact on the continued oral tale tradition (Dégh 1988), while urban society made its own selection for the enculturation of the young.

Storybooks today are beyond number, advised by the pedagogical tradition of expert educators and psychologists. The year-by-year publication of a selected repertoire of stories has resulted in the normalization of fairy tales around the world. Regularly reprinted tales have become extremely popular, and not only through storybooks for mothers to read to children or for teachers to use in the classroom. Convenient electronic devices, slides, records, and cassettes have reached out to the broader public, young and old. More importantly, the most popular tales have been transposed into puppet plays, stage dramas, musicals, movies, poems, and cartoons (Mieder 1979; Röhrich 1988; Uther 1990).

The repetition of a relatively small stock of tales through "technical reproductivity"[7] has caused them to snowball and disintegrate into constituent episodes and motifs. When Schenda talks about the accumulation of a "basic folklore," an "unprinted catchword catalogue," "folklore concentrates," and "folklore residues," he means that the modern culture industry is successful in supplying the smallest elements for consumption through the mass media (Schenda 1992:27–28). But this disintegration—or better, deconstruction of folktales into their essential elements—shows the vitality of and the need for the traditional expressions and imagery of the tale. The metaphorical use of tale images proves that folktales have been absorbed and constitute part of the cultural knowledge of modern society. The familiarity of average people with the image of Cinderella, Snow White, and Little Red Riding Hood, even without knowing the whole story, shows us the importance of these images and explains why media tales reuse them in building happy end-oriented tale equivalents.

Contemplating the gigantic numbers of tale publications for children in the twentieth century (and comments like "the popularity of the *Kinder- und Hausmärchen* is exceeded only by the Bible"), it is time to ask: what is the core material? And who is the target audience? The answer is easy, almost obvious. The core material is extremely small with the following titles essential to any list: Cinderella, Snow White, Rapunzel, Rumpelstiltskin, Sleeping Beauty, The Kind and Unkind Girls, The Seven Ravens, Hansel and Gretel, Little Red Riding Hood, The Frog Prince, The Little Goose Girl, Snow White and Rose Red, and King Thrushbeard: all Grimm tales, to be sure. Nonfeminine stories in the collections include Jack and the Beanstalk, The Bremen City Musicians, Puss-in-Boots, and Doctor Know-All, not counting formula and animal tales for small children; the list is conspicuously small, verifying what we have said before: that boys are not educated to care for tales. There is no question which audience is targeted: young girls and adolescents to be instructed in femininity. The persuasion is successful; urban women, young and old, enjoy the tale heroines' life histories. Heroines of the preferred tales are the ideals, patently convenient for stereotyping gender roles.

Kay Stone explored the American redaction of European folktales and noted an emphasis on the passivity of heroines (1975a). The American repertoire—twenty percent of the Grimm collection—has increased to seventy-five percent in many children's books. "The fairy tale, a male-oriented genre in

Europe," writes Stone, "becomes a female-oriented genre in North American children's literature" (1975b:43–44). Polly Stewart Deemer criticizes Stone for dealing with the surface structure of the tales instead of the "more interesting" deep structure that "mirrors the patriarchal mythic system of the Occident" (1975:103). I feel it is the strength of Stone's essay that it does not enter the slippery soil of speculation but rather prepares the ground for a more ethnographic evaluation of female attitudes to tales.

In another essay (1985), Stone presents field-collected commentaries by male and female informants ages seven to sixty-eight, documenting personal responses to a number of favorite tale heroines. The forty-four women she interviewed confessed to an amazing amount of daydreaming about a prince who will come one day. What strikes one is that the respondents were seriously comparing themselves to tale characters. Stone has also noted that for both modern narrators and listeners, the tale of Cinderella features the whole scale of hopes, anxieties, and possibilities—imagined miracles, fantasy life substituted for real life (1983:79). Discovering the same phenomenon somewhat earlier in France, Simone de Beauvoir was not surprised: "How could the myth of Cinderella not keep all its validity? Everything still encourages the young girl to expect fortune and happiness from some Prince Charming rather than to attempt by herself their difficult and uncertain conquest. In particular, she can hope to rise, thanks to him . . . " (de Beauvoir 1952:126–27). The movie *Pretty Woman* has been severely criticized by feminists for continuing to reinforce the concept of a Prince Charming who comes to the rescue, yet the film has enjoyed enormous popularity. Reading the Grimm version of AaTh 706 (Maiden Without Hands) and 510B (Cap o' Rushes), Elisabeth Panttaja interprets the heroine's achievement as passive resistance and reempowerment countering male disempowerment (1988).

A magazine article by Hildegard Schaufelberger illustrates how the mood of the Märchen appeals to even the most modern of today's youth; to them, the Märchen adventure is wish fulfillment, the arrival home to happiness:

A group of young people sat in a circle. Someone threw in the question: what do they expect from life in store for them? After a brief silence, a girl answered: "Happiness." All nodded. The alternatives, the provocatives, the meditatives. A true Märchen response. In fact, we are always on the road to happiness. In between we err, we stumble, we let ourselves be misled, trapped, we risk a lot, but we never lose the vision of happiness, never. Only that we may learn in time to define happiness differently. . . . Märchen is a literature of symbols: the road of the Märchen is life itself. Märchen is also adventure . . . The lucky can see happiness in dreams . . . In the big tale the hero is almost always a wanderer and his space is this and the other world . . . the Märchen road is our chance. It can be the road home (*Frankfurter Allgemeine Zeitung* 23 July 1989. My translation).

Modern Princesses in the Magazine Dream World

The booming literature that since the sixties has enlightened women about their rights and has encouraged them to take their fate into their own hands does not seem to be winning against the overwhelming propaganda of the feminine mystique, which is supported in equal measure by traditional family norms and the consumer-oriented modern media. To change the comfortable, the customary, means also to attack and destroy the venerable norms of social order and trade them in for an uncertain outcome. Taking responsibility is risky and might fail. A monograph study by Rae André (1981) raises the consciousness of homemakers to the idea that they could make their services a wage-earning profession, recognized like any other job outside the home. But would homemakers give up their role as the mistresses of the household, as powerful mother-figures as well as martyrs, sacrificing themselves on the altar of family equilibrium to satisfy their own professional career ambitions? Would they want to be equals all the way?

The "career woman or housewife" dichotomy has been a recurrent talk show theme. On the Phil Donahue show (to pick one example; I could have mentioned any of the other popular daytime television discussions) I have seen a dentist, a stockbroker, and a lawyer who chose to stay home to raise a family. Career women in starring roles publicly declared their decision to give up their chosen profession for domestic happiness and to serve the careers of their husbands. The press gave front-page publicity to the resignation of Elizabeth Hanford Dole, Secretary of Transportation in the Reagan cabinet. " 'I love my job,' she says. 'I really do.' But her husband, Senator Dole, is running for President and needs her at his side" (*Time*, 21 Sept. 1987). The dilemma of dual careers in the higher echelon is raised: "When husband and wife work, whose ambition comes first?" (*Time*, 16 Nov. 1987). "Did Elizabeth Dole 'give it all up' for a man?" asks Ellen Goodman more pointedly, citing Democratic strategist Ann Lewis: "It gets back to the idea that the job a woman holds is just a little more expendable. How do you put it on your resume, 'left job for husband's sake'? It's something a number of women have had to face" (*Bloomington* [Ind.] *Herald-Times* 18 Sept. 1987).

Scores of other career women followed Dole's example, as the first phase of the feminist momentum came to an end and a new generation of working women reexamined their position. "As women head into the 1990s, are they really so burned out from 'having it all' (i.e., doing it all), so thoroughly exhausted from putting in a full day's work and then another full evening at home, that they dream nostalgically of the 1950s?" asks Claudia Wallis ("Onward, Women!" *Time*, 4 Dec. 1989). She raises the question: "Is the feminist movement . . . truly dead?" as it seems from the attitude of women under thirty. This "Yes, but . . . " generation wants to restore the image of femininity and is turning against the masculine feminist image. Not to forget that one third of women in the United States who stay home and raise children feel that "their status has been depreciated by feminism." Is it true, then, that in the first round the movement has created more confusion than resolution? If the feminist revolution has succeeded in lifting women's status and self-respect, aren't the large masses still unaffected in their subservient homemaking role? Isn't there still a long way to go? "We are responsible for keeping alive the 'He-Tarzan, Me-Jane' ethic, rendering ourselves powerless all over again. But somehow comfortable," writes Mary Anne Dolan ("When Feminism Failed," *The New York Times Magazine* 26 June 1988).

The conflict between vocation and household is genuine even among ambitious professional women, whose achievement orientation is similar to that of men, because traditional values prevail and override attempts at deviation. As reported, however, the great majority of American working women do not pursue an independent career. They take jobs only until they find a husband to support them, or they regard their earning as a supplement to their husband's income. They work in part-time, temporary, or full-time but low-level service occupations, (secreterial, clerical, and sales-factory-, or health-related) which do not necessarily need commitment or make the woman an equal agent, in danger of losing her dependent status and value in the family. The old ideal, the submissive little girl who was trained "never to work for pay" and who leaves her father's custody only at marriage, persists (Harris 1981:87). "Parents still raise their daughters with a view to marriage rather than furthering her personal development. . . . she dooms herself to remain in its [the profession's] lowest level, to be inferior; and the vicious circle is formed; this professional inferiority reinforces her desire to find a husband," writes de Beauvoir (1952:127). The 1987 issue of *Woman's World* goes so far as to blame the Women's Liberation Movement, which "has taken American women out of the home. . . . They lost the protection of the past, such as the long-term, reliable financial security of marriage."

Examining the feminine career script against this background as it is being reshaped from traditional folktale rudiments, we discover persistent frame stories behind formulas altered to fit given socioeconomic conditions. The stock elements—characters, situations, and ideas, as well as the success story frames—are similar but are not always combined into a one-dimensional narrative ending with satisfactory fulfillment. The heroines are models—often from real life, but distant enough from the average householder to be food for fantasy. Most of the time they star in episodes—happy, tragic, or scandalous adventures that remain open-ended—but the audience always can make up a blissful conclusion in daydreams.

The script is further fragmented because it is communicated to the female audience through modern mass media vehicles. Fragmentation is also caused by the fact that the single or multiepisodic stories are told by professional tellers (writers) for diverse purposes. All market the story, addressing the female consumer; but featured stories, short stories, interviews, gossip, news, and commercial advertisements apply different strategies, each stressing a different message, while reinforcing the image of women in remarkably similar ways. For example, in a survey of contemporary American women's magazines, Patricia Rentz asked how "the image of modern women portrayed by the mass media correlates with the modern image of women held by feminists" (1982:227). Her conclusion was that women's magazines present consistent, contradictory messages to their readers:

> Though many magazines claim to be directed at the modern American woman and her new image of being strong, independent, and freethinking, they fall short of this goal since their advertising disclaims and disagrees with their stories . . . advertising portrays women in the traditional role of being weak, passive and dependent . . . for example, shampoo promising silkier, sexier hair or cigarettes, telling the woman 'you've come a long way, baby' (1982:233).

In the same volume, Patricia Hesseltine examined 389 television commercials to adduce a similar traditional sex-role enculturation to housewifedom. "In today's television commercials," she concludes, "even in a time of female liberation, women still cannot extricate themselves from the image of the kitchen and laundry room. This stereotype is being taught every day, through tacit enculturation, to the youngsters of America, as well as to its frustrated housewives" (1982:44).

No wonder that the scenario reinforced by the mass media does not dispel the daydream of women to identify with fairy tale heroines in distress. The young woman waiting for the arrival of a rescuer, Prince Charming on a white steed, is a constant stereotype. Prolonged identification with such figures as Sleeping Beauty, Rapunzel, Snow White, Cinderella, and even Little Red Riding Hood may become pathological (Berne 1972), but in ordinary cases the "Cinderella Complex" (Dowling 1981) seems to be a normal consequence of formal and informal adolescent education in the virtues of femininity. Folktale heroines are metaphors of beauty, wealth, and successful marriage to a glamorous prince, and they keep their market value to this day. Among the dolls regularly advertised in all American women's magazines, the most prominent Grimm heroines play a leading role. For example, picked at random, the *Ladies' Home Journal*, *Redbook*, and *Family Circle* advertised two porcelain Cinderella dolls as she appears at the ball, charming, yet innocently humble. One of these dolls was pink: "the ultimate fairy tale princess comes to life" read the ad. The other Cinderella doll was blue, with one glass slipper in her hand (the Perrault version), promoted in an ad telling us that "Cinderella is a fairy tale come true." The ash-girl is not offered for sale—who would display her among the collectibles? Cinderella's submissiveness to the Prince also means a victory, covert dominance, power being empowered.

That to wait for a prince is the normal behavior not only of average girls is the message when real princesses are featured in magazines. *Das Neue Blatt* (27 July 1988), for example, shows a picture of charming "young ladies who wait for their fairy tale prince who would not court them for their title or money but want them for what they are." Among the eleven princesses are Sophie von Hapsburg, Lady Sarah Armstrong-Jones, and the two daughters of the King of Spain, while a twelfth, the lucky Princess Mathilde von Württenberg, is shown with the "dream man she has already found." "She does not have to wait any longer," we are told—the wedding is set with the attendance of the high nobility of Europe. Fashion designer Diane von Fürstenberg enjoys American's attraction to nobility, saying "I guess people see my life as a fairy tale." The Belgian beauty married an Austrian prince, moved to America, and became an overnight success in business. "But you realize very quickly," she points out, "that if it *were* a fairy tale, the prince would have taken care of me, not sent me out to work" (*Parade*, 30 Aug. 1987).

In her influential book *The Feminine Mystique*, Betty Friedan evaluated the magazine sources which created the image of the woman and which shaped women's lives and mirrored their dreams. She found that the world of the American woman is "confined to her own body and beauty, the charming of men, the bearing of babies, and the physical care and serving of husband, children and home" (1963:31). Although her book appeared thirty years ago, before women activists began their large-scale consciousness raising, the magazine image she described has not undergone any fundamental modifications. Not that there is no mention of working women; nevertheless, the average woman in the magazines (catering to a large contingent of lower-middle-class women) seems to regard employment not as a profession but only as a money-making device, or as a filler between high school or college graduation and marriage. The working woman, as one reads in magazines, keeps up her spirits by daydreaming about liberation through an economically satisfying marriage.

Tabloids and women's magazines like to write about the career of Vanna White, who in 1987 became a star overnight, and whose private life continues to be the topic of press publicity. Lifted out of the TV game show "Wheel of Fortune"—who knows why?—this woman, whose role was limited to smiling, clapping, and waving, became "the most exciting celebrity to win America's heart." Susan Lapinski's article "Vanna! The Woman Behind the

Hype," in the September 1987 issue of *Lady's Circle*, suggests how a woman should feel about herself even if she steps out of the ordinary. The life story of this "girl next door who went to Hollywood" tells that she was about to marry her high school boyfriend after graduation, as was customary for girls in North Myrtle Beach, and start having babies. But her mother's ambition encouraged her to seek a career in show business. All went well; she even met a "handsome young soap opera actor." But tragedy struck: her mother died of cancer, the young man was killed in a plane crash. People said: "Oh, Vanna has a beautiful house, a great job, wonderful clothes." "But that's not everything," she answered. "What makes you happy is having someone to lean on."

How can the popular press, including women's magazines, refrain from promoting women as homemakers, sex objects, and mothers? Without commercial advertisements addressing female consumers, they certainly would go out of business. There in no doubt that advertisers "exploit women's subordination"; "One of a woman's jobs in this society is to be an attractive sexual object, and clothes and make-up are tools of the trade" (Gornick and Moran 1971:662). How can anyone beat the lobby that promises everlasting happiness, love, marriage, and wealth by virtue of beauty? I am sure that companies are powerful enough to keep their consumers brainwashed and enslaved to the belief that clothing, cosmetics, perfume, hairdo, and jewelry are the primary devices for attracting and keeping men. (Remarkably, the gift of jewelry is the most valuable symbol of admiration that men can offer women, as the "diamonds are forever" advertisement and other dramatic and sexy TV commercials suggest: it is a male gesture of love. In an interview, French author Marie Françoise Hans, talking about her new book *Les Femmes et l'Argent*, said: "To give is masculine, to accept is feminine" [*Frankfurter Allgemeine*, 12 Aug. 1988, 34].) Second to these items of personal toilette for attracting males are health aids, discreet methods of staying young and sexually active; third are domestic tips for child care, home decoration, cleaning devices, and kitchen recipes. The rest (the smaller part!) of the magazines comprises articles, short stories, useful advice and juicy gossip on related themes focusing on glamorous women, models to follow. The career script discernible from the magazines does not leave much time for women to work outside the home. To do all that is suggested for self-improvement is in itself a full-time job; even if not stated, the target of these presentations is the homemaker.

In support of the glamour market, illustrated magazines offer ideological assurance for wish-fulfillment stories, the modern versions of traditional folktales. They fill the magazine racks of West European and American shopping centers—the lure in German but lie in American, notes Ernst Bloch—guiding their petty bourgeois readership to absurdly happy solutions. Servant girls marry successful gold miners; a starving typist buys silk stockings on saved calories and then attracts another office worker who turns out to be the boss in disguise—"sounds like magic, doesn't it?" (Bloch 1973:408). The plot runs parallel to traditional Märchen and concludes with the marriage to money and power. The feminine readership never tires of this kind of modern fiction, be it Western, country, or urban style.

Manufacturers of the glamour market join forces to forge a new version of the normalized Cinderella fairy tale in order to sell their products as a wedding package. In fact, their "fairy tale" is the spinoff from the happy end of the traditional tale. Every skilled Märchen teller elaborates the wedding as a showdown where justice is served, reward and punishment are distributed, and the transformation of the ash-girl into princess is staged. The staging itself uses the total arsenal of descriptive devices of pomp accumulated through the ages. As Lüthi notes, the folktale "tends to render things and animate beings in metallic or mineral terms" when displaying extreme contrasts; "among the metals, the folktale prefers the precious and rare: gold, silver, copper" (Lüthi 1981:27). The script of Cinderella's wedding is a modern mercantile tale called "romantic," sketching the story of an average girl who is lifted from the anonymity and boredom of the everyday by a prince (Charming). Her "dream comes true" when she transforms from Cinderella into a "princess" for the blissful moment of wedding. Performing "traditional customs" (wearing something old, something new), being showered with rice by the crowd, and "throwing her bouquet to the next bride-to-be," she performs "tradition" and is guaranteed to live "happily ever after."

This story was outlined and illustrated with clippings from bridal guides and magazines in a term paper by Joshua M. Freedman, a student in my class Folklore and Mass Media at UCLA in the spring of 1992. In preparation for his forthcoming wedding, he was surprised to find the numerous references to fairy tale and Cinderella by vendors of bridal gowns, underwear, shoes, purses, jewelry, makeup, fragrance, hairdo, flowers, china, crystal, bedding, tablewear, and kitchen utensils, and by the institutions that advise future couples and that plan and arrange weddings and receptions. He found the words "Dream" or "Dreams" forty-two times in the May/June issue of *Bridal Guide*, and found advertisers promising weddings to be "fantasy," "royal," "traditional," "classic," and "magical." There is no doubt whatsoever that the addressee is "Cinderella"-in-waiting: full-page pictures of bridal gowns invariably feature the lovely girl with a glass slipper in her hand.

The Walt Disney Company's advertisement encapsulates the story. The text is instructive: "Fairy Tale Weddings. The most important day of your life is also the most magical with a Disney Fairy Tale Wedding. Be Cinderella for a day and reunite your family and friends for a wedding dream come true at the most magical place on earth, the Walt Disney World Resort in Florida." It seems there are families that still want to see their daughters married in the spirit of the fairy tale (and pay the cost of between $20,000 and $100,000). Surveying this absolute concentration on the bride, the bridegroom finds himself in merely a supporting role. His role is buying jewelry: to find out her wedding style by talking to her mom and then to "watch her beam with happiness as she opens her gift box."

The daily news is also a frequent source of instant star making. A pretty woman, accidentally involved in a newsworthy incident, is given the chance to rise to the status of the victimized heroine. Three such Cinderellas have emerged from the news during the 1980s on the margins of national scandals. One is Fawn Hall, secretary of Col. Oliver North and the first and only female hero of the Iran-Contra affair; another is Donna Rice, the part-time actress presumably involved in an illicit love affair with presidential candidate Gary Hart; and finally, Jessica Hahn, church secretary, allegedly sexually assaulted by the charismatic impostor, PTL minister Jim Bakker (PTL = Praise The Lord, parodied as Pay The Lady). All three are beautiful and dependent on a "villain." In the story-making process, each was offered money for telling her story to talk show hosts and magazines, and more money, fame, and wealth for their autobiographies as well as contracts for sex magazine photos and Hollywood movies.

Magazines not only engage professional authors to renew old tales and write up-to-date variants that reinforce the intended type, they also want "real," intimate, personal experiences that are told by common people. Triviality is the catch; readers must feel this could have happened to them. The magazine *Secrets* appeals to readers: "Everyone has a life story to tell! Where do the fine stories in *Secrets* come from? People just like you tell us their true life experiences! Why not share your true story with others?" Another magazine, *True Confessions*, has a similar solicitation: "We want your story! *True Confessions* is your magazine. Every story in it is true and was sent to us by someone just like you. Why don't you share your experiences with other readers, too?"

Nowhere is there a warning that only women's stories are accepted for publication, yet the stories are all written (or signed) by women for an all-female audience. The classified ads offer sexier looks, sex aids, fuller bosoms, education, exercise, weight loss, job opportunities, horoscopes, herbal and magic remedies, tampons, and financial advice. There are many such magazines throughout the Western hemisphere, and the stories in each are similar. They all tell about love affairs and adventures in the pursuit of happiness in the haven of marriage and children. "I want a marriage just like the one Grandma had," tells one of the confessors, revealing the basically conservative, old-fashioned standards of these publications. Some stories tell of true love and happy endings, others of guilt, jealousy, double-crossing, and treacherous girlfriends; but the majority of the stories feature trusting, loving, and sincere women who are abused, betrayed, and destroyed by the men they trusted. A few titles will give an idea of the life histories of these storytellers, who reinforce the basic homemaker life script with due variation on the model: "I always want his arms around me"; "I love him so—but I'm so afraid to trust him"; "Saturday night without a man"; "I lied to make him marry me"; "Because my husband betrayed me, I found my greatest happiness"; "I've got all the romance I need right here"; "The magic love locker"; "A sweet-talking stranger made a mess of my life."

The final question to address concerns the nature of modern heroines. How are the most popular women, whose lives are comparable to those of folktale princesses, presented to the magazine readership? The women celebrated by magazines have some common characteristics. First of all, they are famous because they are said to be famous. The image makers have blown some of their true or manufactured features out of proportion. Also, they are beautiful, and they are wealthy. Finally, they are or were married or otherwise sexually involved with a man. The modern heroine story departs from the folktale in that it does not end with marriage or the reunion of marriage partners separated by the intrigue in the tale plot. The emphasis is on sex-related adventure, following or excluding marriage. But no matter what the story stresses, the life history even in sketches includes the past in the form of hardships in early life. Episodes of a celebrity's life are often highlighted in tabloid headlines as "the untold story of . . . " "the secret tragedy of . . . ", which usually includes a tragic event in her early life, a family disaster, unborn children, or victimization by a man. The magazine stories of current heroines, the ones popularized in the immediate present, center on one episode, while other elements of the life history, though also present (as commonly known) are reduced to minimal reference.

Who qualifies to become a heroine? The celebrities belong to two categories: royalty and movie stars. Their shoe fits the traditional success story as the basic script with deviations and a switch of focus. Although there are numerous stars of the past whose life kept them in the limelight—the Duchess of Windsor, Marilyn Monroe, Brigitte Bardot, and Princess Farah, all of whose remarkable lives and personalities still attract magazine authors, I will mention here only a few of current interest: Lady Diana; Queen Sylvia; Caroline, Princess of Monaco; and actresses Joan Collins and Elizabeth Taylor. In the featuring of their lives through a focus on one shocking, scandalous, blissful, or tragic event, the reader is introduced to a foreign world of wish fulfillment, luxury, enchantment, beauty, and romance Hollywood style. This crystallization, in essence, is similar to the world of the folktale and fairy tale, the sparkling and distant never-never land of fancy for the little people who are limited to the boredom of everyday life in the gray, merciless industrial world.

The departure from the traditional folktale plot consists of three things. First, the heroines are not fictitious but real. The mass media continually inform the public about their affairs in the form of similar, as well as conflicting, accounts. Second, the flow of information about these heroines contributes to the formulation of their model lives. Third, there is a built-in ambiguity in the life story of any of these women because it is composed of both their public roles (how aristocratic women are expected to be; what is the personality of the woman whom an actress portrays in the play that made her famous) and their private identities. The discrepancies between the two are well exploited by magazine authors, but nevertheless it is clear that the stories emphasize the domestic life, virtues, and conflicts of the heroines.

The principal goal of modern heroines is marriage. The wedding is presented as a landmark of Märchen fulfillment no matter how many times the star has previously been married. The *Ladies' Home Journal* recalls the British royal wedding witnessed by the largest audience the world has ever known: "It was a marriage that transformed Diana Spencer, an obscure kindergarten aide, into the world's most recognizable face . . . everyone adored the blushing bride, while the dull and not very dashing Prince Charles was transformed overnight into Prince Charming" (July 1987:99). Likewise, the weekly *Heim und Welt* (31 January 1985) writes about the ordeal overshadowing the marriage of the super-wealthy young duchess Marise Gloria von Thurn und Taxis to one of the wealthiest men in Europe, thirty-four years older than she: "What young woman has not dreamt of a morning being awakened by the kiss of a fairy tale prince? For most, this remains a dream, an illusion. Märchen is always overshadowed by kidnapping and death threats."

"Marry me or we're finished," threatened the live-in girlfriend of talkshow host Johnny Carson, sixty-one, who yielded. As the *National Enquirer* (14 July 1987) reports, the bride expressed herself in traditional terms: "Our love has been like a fairy tale and now we are blissfully happy . . . we are going to be happy forever!" But marriage for modern superstar heroines is troubled by tragic circumstances. For example, the *Bild* (21 December 1984) summarizes the life of "ice princess" Marika Kilius in these words: "The German Grace Kelly on skates fascinated millions . . . she made millions dream." However, her life is described as comprising one love, two failed marriages, difficult births, dramatic kidney stone surgeries, months on crutches after a ski accident, and kidnapping attempts on her daughter. The touching story is topped by the latest event: a love story with a man seventeen years younger.

It is remarkable that the magazines seldom discuss the intellectual or professional achievements of these women; if they do so, it is a superficial treatment. Apart from the fact that media princesses are as schematic and characterless as folktale heroines, magazine authors emphasize their domestic, housewifely virtues. According to the *Weekly World News* (21 July 1987), "Princess Diana's astounding confession—she loves ironing the royal duds while watching TV—exposes her as a housework nut, palace insiders say." Another example: the "sex goddesses" or "sex kittens" are often portrayed in German tabloids as remarkable homemakers and wonderful gourmet cooks (the recipes provide evidence for the readers to test); they temporarily suspend their careers to breast-feed babies and dedicate themselves totally to childcare. Conversely, negligence of motherly duty leads to public scorn, as in the case of "Fergie," the Duchess of York, who left her newborn infant at home and went vacationing with her husband across the ocean. By the same token, the popularity of Diana, Princess of Wales, rose and that of her estranged husband plummeted because she demonstrated undying devotion to her sons, while Prince Charles preferred to play polo instead of rushing to the hospital bedside of his injured son "Wills."

One might wonder whether the model of the life of classic Märchen heroines really fits the model of the life of modern celebrities. Does not their turbulent love life, which usually begins "after the honeymoon is over," radically deviate from the ostensibly passive obedience of sweet Märchen maidens? The fact is, the behavioral pattern of folktale heroines is mostly a sham. Even the most docile and helpess girls are extremely active in manipulating others so that things happen the way they want. They test, lure, and deceive their men (in all types in the category of The Man on a Quest for his Lost Wife); they have their suitors executed if they fail the test (AaTh 851A, The Riddle Princess); they elope with ogres and live with other men: with dwarves, giants, seven ravens, in the robbers' den. The chastity of tale heroines is symbolic, the wishful thinking of naive folklore collectors. The bride in King Thrushbeard (AaTh 900) and related stories pokes fun at men and makes fools of husbands and suitors; The Basil Maiden (AaTh 879) induces the prince to kiss his horse's ass and lures him to bed where she places a sugar puppet instead of herself. The smart peasant girl proves that her husband the mighty king is silly and pompous. In many tales, the heroine, seemingly behind the scenes, monitors events and watches her lover on the road of adventures approaching her.

The outlines of the sweet innocent, the shrew, the temptress, the seductress, the vamp, and the bitch are all there in the folktale heroine model. What unites them is their goal—holy matrimony. These roles are played alternately in order to win the man and be conquered by him. Historically, the stories became more complex in the era of rising capitalism and urbanization, when the education of women was fostered by romantic novels, best represented by those of the German Eugenie Marlitt (1825–1887) and the French Georges Ohnet (1848–1918).

There is no essential difference between these heroines and modern glamour queens whose love affairs are written up in women's magazines and aired by TV's popular Hollywood gossip columnists. Stories of multiple marriages, the search for the real, permanent husband, temporary happiness, disappointment, divorce, and new beginnings are told in many installments about Liz Taylor and Zsa Zsa Gabor, the most notorious of all. But hope remains; "some time my prince will come," Zsa Zsa said recently. Joan Collins's evil character in TV's "Dynasty" impressed West European women so much that no women's magazine could afford to omit reporting on her latest love affair, and in 1987, her scandalous divorce was in all the gossip papers. According to *Abendpost* (1985), her contract stipulates that she cannot remarry but must act her role in real life as Alexis, the beast. On the other hand, her "Dynasty" role also shows tenderness, loyalty to family, devotion to children, and deep despair at not having a man to dominate her. In fact, the Alexis character epitomizes the tragic heroine whose malevolence is the consequence of being deprived of marital happiness.

As a concluding observation, I would like to repeat what I have said at the beginning: the purpose of this discussion was to show life history as a folklore genre, and to illustrate the approach of the folklorist to human creativity in telling a story of life. The original aim I proposed was to develop an approach to this genre by viewing it as a product of life experience which is divided into the roles individuals play when they occupy the places assigned to them in the social network. I also suggested that a system of classification for a more intensive analytical study could be attempted on the basis of the pyramid of human life as generating types of life histories. Furthermore, I stated that career models are projected by society and realized by the nuclear family in socializing children according to their gender roles. As an illustration, I looked at the elements of the family career as designed in folktales, fairy tales, and modern magazine stories. When I considered the two modes of telling autobiographical fiction—folkloric and literary—and took the female script as a target, I realized that (1) both traditional tales and life stories in the mass media reflect and reinforce the same stereotypical role of women; and (2) these accounts of women's lives, no less than oral narratives, are crystallized into a fundamental form of narration.

That the tale is an overwhelmingly persistent model for women's lives is indicated by the fact that feminist critics are much concerned with its revision. Jack Zipes's recent collection of new feminist fairy tales is a recognition that traditional literary and oral tales are powerful social educators, basic to the socialization of children, and therefore *need to be revised* for continued implementation. "To talk about fairy tales today," writes Zipes, "especially feminist fairy tales, one must, in my opinion, talk about power, violence, alienation, social conditions, child-rearing and sex roles. It is no longer possible to ignore the connection between the aesthetic components of the fairy tales, whether they be old or new, and their historical function within a socialisation process which forms taste, mores, values and habits" (1989:2).

This is all well stated, yet in the race between the traditional script supported by the mass media and the feminist rewrite limited to a sophisticated reform-minded elite group, no fast breakthrough can be predicted.

5

Tape-Recording Miracles for Everyday Living

The Ethnography of a Pentecostal Community

An Informal Introduction to Grace Pentecostals

OVER A PERIOD of eight years I have been observing the lives of members of a Pentecostal assembly on the south side of Bloomington, Indiana. The Grace Tabernacle Church is the home of worship for a membership of about two hundred men and women, not counting their participating under-age children. The religion they practice can be defined as "an extension of the people's social relationship beyond the confines of human society" (Horton 1960:211); thus it permeates both the sacred and secular life of in-dividuals. Accordingly, the congregation constitutes a subcultural entity of people whose ideas and acts are guided by their intimate relationship with Jesus to achieve personal salvation. The members of the assembly view them-selves as children united by the love of Jesus in an extended family-like com-munality, only loosely connected with sister congregations despite a good deal of visitation by preachers, gospel-singing groups, youth groups, and in-dividuals. In and out of church, in private and in public, practical and sym-bolic acts of individuals integrate this relationship to construct solid unity and cohesion cemented by brotherly love between the members.

What attracted me to this particular Pentecostal group was not so much the spectacular performance of religious rituals, the ecstatic forms of wor-ship, the sermons of expressive preachers, the sung and instrumental perfor-mance of gospel music, dancing in the spirit, glossolalia (Goodman 1972:86–125; Gardner 1989), and the other characteristic features common to evangelical possession religions.[1] I was more interested in the everyday life of average members, the management of obligations to family, community, and work, in subordination to religion. That is, I wanted to learn how the people live religion and utilize religion to maintain order and accomplish goals in the secular sphere. I sought to observe personal lives, ideas, beliefs, opinions, and interpersonal relationships as represented by individuals because I felt that their ways give a key to understanding the nature of belief, ritual, and narrative in this community. No folkloric phenomena can be understood without the knowledge of their bearers. As Jeff Todd Titon has written in his review of Elaine Lawless's book on Pentecostal women, "I need to know the people as individuals, to know how they talk to each other outside of church, to know how they create a social world" (Titon 1991:121–122). Religion needs to be studied from the point of view of its bearers, as it is lived and interpreted by coreligionists, not as prescribed in the canon of the church or as perceived by the outsider.

The Grace people, as I learned to know them, those who call themselves teasingly by demeaning nicknames coined by outsiders—"Jesus Crazy," "Jesus Freaks," "Holy Rollers"—are happy people. They are also strong, mentally sane people who can make sense of their belief and argue forcefully for their cause.[2] Outside the mainstream, they have developed a cathartic practice of maintaining mental sanity by bridging and balancing altered states of consciousness (Parker 1975) and awareness of the real world. It is my purpose to show how this congregation sustains an upbeat optimistic demeanor by experiencing and reporting everyday miracles, particularly by intensifying folklore communication through the creative application of tape recording. I will suggest that the folklore messages individuals preserve on tapes are more functional reinforcers of tradition than printed matter; their replay calls recent total performances of their own to mind.

During the years of my observation, I sensed an increasing concern with miracles that signaled the Second Coming to the faithful and made them aware that the fulfillment of hopes for a happy afterlife is near. Approaching the end of the century, this congregation prepares for the end of the world. They feel privileged to be given the message "in this end time." As a member explained it:

> God's been talking to us, because of all the prayer that's going on. We had tongues and interpretations last night, and God said, "because of your crying and sighing before me, I am going to answer your prayers".... And the Lord told us in tongues and interpretations—about eight people received the Holy Ghost and six baptized—that we haven't even seen the tip of the iceberg. That there would be so many revivals that Bloomington cannot contain it, and there will be hundreds of revivals started in other— in foreign lands and in other places because of the revival that starts in our church here in the city of Bloomington.

What makes this preparation special is the intensification of miracle experiences. The bonding between the membership is reinforced by turning personally lived-through miracles into communal property by the routine use of the tape recorder. This handy electronic medium helps unite individual testimonies into an integrated whole. The experience, formulated into narrative, repeated by the experiencer in diverse situational contexts, and retold by other members of the congregation inside and outside the group, solidifies legends as testimonies of the underlying religious philosophy. By the simple fact that as recordings these legends can be replayed endlessly, at any time, for personal gratification or for discussion and interpretation, and because they can be alternated with oral retellings, they spread faster and affect their bearers more deeply than folklore without media intervention. These Pentecostals exploit the convenience of recording and the advantages of preserving and re-using precious religious messages. They bring their tape recorders to church, or bring tapes to "run off" passages they particularly like from the recordings of others. This case of mass media technique in folklore transmission instructs folklorists of a conscious, creative application.

The Grace Tabernacle Church is located on an old narrow country road and looks immaculately clean, combining white frame with rustic Indiana limestone; its high tower sports a cross on the top. It is a modern church, with an accommodating auditorium, a sanctuary, prayer room, and rooms for activities, social hours, conferences, meditation, study, charity work, Sunday school, and nursery. It is well equipped acoustically and electronically for amplifying musical performance—solo and choir singing and instrumental gospel music—as well as for running slide and video shows and facilitating tape-recording and copying.

The church leads an active life, with people coming and going day and night. Two or three weekly services begin at half past seven in the evening and end about ten or ten-thirty; the Sunday morning service is from ten o'clock to twelve noon. Additionally, twice a week the church holds a prayer meeting organized by Brother Coffey, the pastor, or his wife Sister Coffey, a remarkable woman who excels in tongues interpretation. Other prayer meetings are called by affiliates at will. Besides prayer lines for a concerted goal, many people just come in ad hoc, sitting or kneeling at a favorite corner to pray for help with family matters or personal problems. Working people come during their lunch break or when they can get away for half an hour, feeling the urge "to talk to God." Praying is extremely important—some evangelists pray three to four hours daily; as someone noted, "We are a praying church."

Although the church has an outreach function, the culmination of all ritual performances is the revival, a consciousness raising of the members. "Revival" is posted on the entrance of the church, and conducted by respected evangelists from other assemblies. "Being in revival" means daily services for an indeterminate time, depending on how long the preacher is able to continue to keep the mood of the congregation running high, with new converts, "tongues" (glossolalia) and interpretations, and baptisms—that is, "depending on how long the evangelist feels the burden for the revival and how long it takes that burden to be lifted . . . all this is the Lord's doing." Revival season is a special time of complete devotion in which experiencing an altered state of consciousness is expected to come forth as a result of the grace of the Holy Spirit. The Grace Church holds four to five revivals annually. "The revival is for the saints, not for the sinners." The visiting preacher brings new testimonies and evidences he has experienced elsewhere to enhance the revival. He also acts as a contact to other assemblies whose members eventually also visit in order to spread the news of new miracles personally encountered, and to help make them happen again. Past revivals are kept in memory, and related miracles are often remembered and retold. According to informants, the longest revival took place in 1959 and lasted more than ten weeks: "It was exhilarating, got better and better," as Tom Banks told me. He thought this was the first indication that the Second Coming is near. Impressed by the exceptionally high number of conversions, he thought it was a sign that God plans to start preparation for the final days in Bloomington, from where it will spread all over the world.

Regular services are structured the same way as in nonevangelical Protestant churches, comprising common singing, prayer, choir, sermon, Bible citation, donation, and blessing, but not necessarily so. The normal sequence of the ritual is often diluted by the degree of audience participation. At any stage the service may prompt attendants to respond with coherent, formulaic speech, inarticulate emotional sounds, gestures, or body movements. Essentially, the sermon or other texts uttered in church and the way in which they are delivered appeal more to emotions than to clear logic; thus their effect on audience response is unpredictable. The service may strike a sensitive chord and inspire individual outbursts, changing states of consciousness, and speaking in tongues, which may modify the course and extend the time of the ritual. The sermon itself may be eliminated for more important manifestations such as tongues and tongues interpretations, reporting of miracles, and loud outpourings of sentiments.

It is also unpredictable how many people will go to the altar to seek spirit possession after the formal part of the service is over. Those who come forward to the altar kneel down and raise their arms to undergo a mentally and physically grueling, emotional exercise to receive the Holy Spirit. A support group of friends and kin assist the candidate with constant encouragement and performance of the choreography of the expected endowment. Imitating the process through singing, clapping, and shouting to the dictum of pulsating gospel music, the supporting congregation members moan, cry, and collapse on the floor with the candidate and burst into speaking in tongues, until the goal is achieved and baptism—deliverance from sin by total immersion—is administered. Of course, not all attempts succeed, but there is always hope for next time.

Entering the church auditorium on an average evening, the stranger is impressed by the informal, family-like atmosphere. People gather in groups

Sister Kim praises the Lord with extended arms, typical of worshipers who seek to receive the Holy Ghost. Photo by Billy Adams.

in the lobby and chat; laughter and relaxed familiarity fill the air, shared by couples, newlyweds, single men and women, widows and widowers, teenagers, and children. The church is the home of the whole family, three and four generations, including newborn infants. This emphasis on family contributes to the noisiness of the service: it is good-naturedly tolerated that teenagers gossip, children run around and play, and babies cry during service. During my fieldwork, church members encouraged me to sit in front, far from snickering youngsters, and on the side, where I could plug my tape recorder into the wall outlet.

No question, the Grace Tabernacle Church is truly the home of the people. They feel more at ease in this "house dedicated to Jesus" than anywhere else; they truly come home when they go to church. Anna, a hotel kitchen supervisor, told me, "Sometimes I feel so tired after work, my eyes burn and

The Rev. Lee Coffman, far right, places a healing hand on the forehead of a sister while other members of the congregation gather at the altar to call down the spirit of the Lord at the conclusion of a church service. Photo by Billy Adams.

my whole body aches. Then, I come here and all aches and pains are gone!" Lisa, a housewife, says: "This is so good! When you get into it, it gets better, and better, and better. I always been a type of person, I get tired of things in the world. . . . And I get a new car, my husband got me a new car for Mother's Day, two years ago. I washed it two-three times a week, it was the greatest thing I ever had. But I'm tired of it now. It's good enough if it gets one bath a week, you know. But Linda, I had the Holy Ghost since I was eleven years old and this is something that . . . it gets better, and better, and better—you never get tired of it."

No one is idle when it comes to church work, and members contribute much to turn it into their home, a real sanctuary. To undertake communal work cements friendship and at the same time enhances creativity. For brothers and sisters whose whole intellectual life is absorbed by the church, the outside world remains distant and alien. The church is their real life, and their church family is their real family. The outside world's harsh realities intrude into their life only when their rebellious children get into trouble and need their help, or when they are distressed by conflicts with relatives, neighbors, and authorities hostile to their faith. Intellectual life is focused on the Bible, which is always at hand for reading, meditation, and interpretation; no other book can compete with it. Other diversions are not condoned; if people watch television (most of the families do not even have one), it is at Christmas or Easter, a religious play about Christ, or the ballgame, the weather, the news on weekends. Movies never; not even a delightful Disney cartoon is permissible for children because of the possibility of preceding announcements of other films full of nudity and violence.

Taking turn in performing community functions, be they ritual, ceremonial, artistic, organizational, promotional, charitable, domestic, or janitorial, church members happily take charge of whatever their ability and talent allows them to do. Painters ornament the social hall with religious paintings, quilters and artists prepare handicrafts for holiday decoration, talented gospel singers, drummers, guitar and piano players, and authors of gospel music and lyrics record their performances on video and cassette tapes. Work, worship, spirituality, and artistry go hand-in-hand; work and pleasure in a morally safe shelter make a happy communality.

The membership of Grace is lower middle class: the men are farmers, factory workers, auto mechanics, construction workers, electricians, truckers, repairmen, salesmen, shop owners, office clerks. The women are mostly homemakers as their main occupation, but they also work as part-time factory workers, telephone operators, kitchen help, nurses' aides, or salespersons; some clean offices, apartments, or private homes. This occupational division also explains why women are more visible in church activities than men, as also noted by Lawless (1988b: 152–56). As Lisa Wells, Sue Gardner, and Ginny Cox, three middle-aged housewives and best friends, explained it to me, the greater visibility of women is not because "women are more spiritual" and have more need to find consolation in religion. Men have the same need, as I have seen them performing in spiritual situations, awaiting spirit baptism. But as primary bread-earners, their jobs often prevent them from being more involved. Tom Wells, a Sunday school superintendent, is a foreman at a factory, responsible for a whole unit, and he comes home often at six or seven o'clock; Mark Cook works on the night shift; and truck driver Bob Sparks has an even more demanding schedule. "Men are under more stress because of their jobs," said Lisa. "They have more responsibilities. A man, say, would not come home until six, or seven, okay? I get up, let's say, anywhere from eight to nine, and I straighten up, go to work to clean house, and go home, you know, I've got more free time than my husband has." As far as women's place is concerned according to the thinking of Grace Pentecostals, they literally follow the Bible's guidance: as Jesus's handmaidens (Lawless 1988b), women are supporters, not leaders. But in support roles they are powerful in Sunday school teaching and prayer-line leading, and they also make outstanding itinerant evangelists, like Sister Potter, Brother Coffey's sister. According to Lisa's estimation, the ratio of participation is sixty percent women, forty percent men.

The Grace congregation is a blue-collar, upwardly mobile working-class community, not a poor people's church that casts its eyes to heaven in the hope of an afterlife to escape poverty. They seek respectability and neatness around them. The women pride themselves on having nice homes with colonial style furnishing, embroidered pillows, quilts, framed china plates in Norman Rockwell style, dried flower baskets, and china cabinets stuffed with knickknacks. They have well-equipped kitchens with up-to-date appliances, and they host Tupperware, Avon, cologne, dried-flower, and wicker basketware parties. When it comes to children's clothing, they want the best; mothers and grandmothers often buy expensive outfits at fine department stores while they also visit garage sales for serendipitous finds. As for themselves, following their minister's version of modest dress, as taken from the Bible— long hair in "French roll" style for women, let down waist-length for girls, cut short and clean shaven for men—they enjoy fashionable dressing. Even if not cut, young women's hair wear is often elaborate, teased and folded, decorated with ribbons—yet nothing like current fashion. Women do not wear jewelry or slacks ("The Bible says, a woman should not look like a man"), but they buy stylish dresses with matching color purses, belts, and high-heeled shoes "to feel good in God's presence." Being clean, neat, and well-groomed makes the community look affluent and respectable.

The Background

Historians of religion have identified the roots of the American Pentecostal movement in the post–Civil War period at the last quarter of the nineteenth century. It was one of several Fundamentalist-Holiness sects[3] that broke away from the mainstream Protestant churches, which had abandoned their original revivalistic, missionary purpose and zeal. Catering no longer to the needs of "poor people," becoming "less emotional and evangelical, and more intellectualized and restrained" (Packard 1959:176), the transformation of the Protestant people's churches at large left the folk out in the cold. "People of limited means began to feel more and more out of place. They yearned to return to a 'heart religion' that would satisfy not only their craving for religious certainty but also their emotional, psychological, and physical needs" (Nichol 1974:30). In time, large denominations gained prestige and political power and became instruments of the establishment, while they also became impersonal hierarchical structures more for routine attendance and display of participation than for deep devotion.

By the beginning of the twentieth century, the void created by the rationalization of elite churches had grown, whereas the need for emotional release of a growing mass, alienated by rapid industrialization and urbanization, had also increased. If the urban poor, the transient farmworker, the racial and ethnic ghetto-dweller were among the underdogs who found consolation in the warm fellowship of fundamentalist denominations back then (Williams 1974), it is also true that approaching the end of the 1990s more and more people, regardless of economic and educational status, are driven to seek expressive spiritual gratification.

> One finds—in the flourishing of evangelicalism, pentecostalism, the "born again" experience, prayer groups, excursus religion and para-religious self-realization activities like est—a movement toward subjectivity and small groups. This means, in our terms, that the structure of establishment religion, and the social identity that has gone with it, is crumbling. Indeed, the spiritual style and meaning that is associated with excursus religion is almost becoming normative (Ellwood 1979:171).

From the vantage point of *homo religiosus* (Kurtz 1986/87: 21), the history of Christianity is the history of struggle for dominance against deviant religions supported by the popular masses. Composed of traditional beliefs, forms of devotion, and legends, these popular religions always opposed and challenged the authoritative canon, which was alienated from the folk. Personal and communal variables of the original Christian belief are composed of learned and inherited elements of spirituality which scatter and reassemble in many ways, like the glass shells in a kaleidoscope, while none of them are discarded. The degree of dissent varies from tacit disagreement within the authority church to a complete cutting of ties and a search for new affiliation. A group exodus can result from learning about visions and miracles of individuals aspiring to sainthood but whose testimony has been rejected by church authorities, or from the attraction to charismatic personalities—evangelists, prophets, gurus—touched by God. Testimonies in narrative form have surrounded both kinds of figures through the ages and are repeated again and again today, attracting millions of pilgrims. As *Die Welt* (16 January 1989) has reported, pilgrimage is in fashion, and young seekers make up the majority.

The models—miracles of accredited saints—have been followed by unauthorized contemporary saint's legends, appearing almost weekly in the popular press with almost carbon-copy similarity. Examples include the bouncing of the sun and the color change of the rosary; children conversing with the Virgin Mary in Medjugorje (Bosnia) "to challenge Lourdes, Fatima and Guadalupe for Roman Catholic Marian devotion" (*Time*, 7 July 1986). A similar vision was experienced at the St. John Neumann Church during the Feast of the Assumption in Lubbock, Texas, in 1988 (*Bloomington Herald-Times*, 16 Aug. 1988). Tears are shed by the altar image of the Madonna in a Chicago church (*Expressions*, 1 March 1987), and by the likeness of St. Nicholas in Tarpon Springs, Florida (*National Inquirer*, Oct. 1975), as did their medieval European counterparts. Visions of saints have appeared in a tree in Eisenberg, Austria,[4] in a picture window in the Bronx, New York (*The Louisville Courier-Journal*, 14 Aug. 1978), and on a tortilla in Lake Arthur, New Mexico (*Newsweek*, 14 Aug. 1978). Even new saints emerge and appear to devotees— for example, Princess Grace of Monaco (*Sun*, 5 Sept. 1989) and Michael Landon (*Weekly World News*, 20 Aug. 1991). The oral spread and media popularization of these modern saint's legends signal critical opposition to canonical religions and set the stage for religious populism (Wuthnow 1978:196–201).

Today Christians are more willing than they once were to move from church to church in search of a satisfying doctrine, as elite churches opt to accommodate an increasingly secular culture and their grip on the supernatural weakens. As W. S. Bainbridge predicts: "Existing conservative denominations and new sects will expand to fill the gap. Originally finding their social base in disadvantaged groups, they can grow into the mainstream of the society" (Bainbridge 1988:22). The contemporary increase of membership in fundamentalist churches, summarily described as the American folk church (Clements 1974), is phenomenal.

Many of my informants said that they had been searching for an accommodating sect that would fit more closely their worship preference. A former Mennonite told me he had joined because singing was forbidden in his old church and he delighted in playing his guitar to praise the Lord. A follower of the Oral Roberts's brand of fundamentalism said he was disillusioned by the businesslike running of the church—he cited Jesus's words when he chased the vendors out of the Jerusalem temple. Many believers, raised in the Baptist and Methodist faiths, were disgusted with stiff formalities and lack of sincerity. Each informant had a remarkable story of disillusionment. Seekers often made their decision after attending services and revivals or listening to television and radio evangelists. For some time, they had wandered from denomination to denomination, chased by uneasiness, praying and turning over the pages of the Bible to find answers to their questions. Most conversion stories include a supernatural experience. Like many Pentecostals, former Catholic Al Gossan had a vision: "Something from another world came over me," he said. "Suddenly I saw the light."[5] Forty-five percent of the Grace Tabernacle Church members grew up in the church, fully twenty percent were converts from other denominations and the rest, according to Lisa, "came off the street" and this church had not been their first choice. Couples seldom converted together; one of the two had gone first, and in numerous cases, only one of the marriage partners was an adherent of Pentecostalism. I heard many stories about conversions that caused family rifts; mothers-in-law often appear as troublemakers, condemning the seduction of their sons or daughters into a deviant religion.

Among the emergent fundamentalist sects, the Pentecostal movement appears to be the most impressive, creative, and viable,[6] but what makes this ideology so attractive is its ritual practice. The doctrine of spirit baptism, glossolalia, prophecy, and healing, as recorded in Acts 1:12–2:4, is the core of Pentecostal ideology. In the exercise of a highly unorthodox, unrestrained form of worship, members feel a liberation from conventions, a true expression of sentiments. Freedom to unburden in the antiphonic responses to preaching and related utterances is the indicator of true submission to God's will. The dialogic dynamic of participation allows, indeed demands, the uninhibited public demonstration of transcendence, a personal spiritual unity with Christ. The cathartic effect of falling in and out of heightened spiritual states related to conversion, spirit baptism, and constant conversation with supernatural agencies turn participants into a family of God, a sacred unity of heaven-bound mortals and the Divine.

Thus it is not surprising that the movement has been described as "the third largest force in Christendom, next to Catholicism and Protestantism" (Goodman 1988:52). It sprouted from American grass roots, based on the popular Biblical tradition of literal interpretation; however, the doctrine was shaped in often radically diverse ways, creating numerous branches of Pentecostalism which never coalesced into a unified, normative Pentecostal denomination. The lay preachers, self-styled evangelists and gifted charismatic leaders who pastored the mushrooming small congregations, created their own versions of spirituality, belief, and style of worship to accommodate local fellowship needs. Spreading to other continents, primarily to Latin America and Europe, Pentecostal churches have demonstrated even more flexibility in adapting to other religio-cultural traditions, heralding a tremendous religious renaissance, a return to emotional modes of religious behavior (Stark and Bainbridge 1985:126–48).

In addition to its main spiritual appeal, I see the attraction of Pentecostalism to the individual in that it opposes everything characteristic of modern urban lifestyle in mass society. It gives a sense of belonging and security to the lonely individual craving a warm, loving, family-style support group with old-fashioned homeliness and lack of sophistication. The sustenance of traditional values concerns, in the main, the sanctity of marriage, the patriarchal division of male and female roles, modesty in clothing, charity, and raising children in the church. Turning inward, opposing liberalism, makes Pentecostals defensively righteous and politically conservative (Wuthnow 1978:78–98).

Yet heterogeneity prevails in the practice of the religion by individual congregations because of the freedom of choice given to them. Based on close and intensive collaboration of leaders and the membership, creative choices are made in the interpretation of the basic tenets of the canon. Personally experienced encounters with the divine power are constantly discussed and analyzed for their affiliation with crucial theses in the Scripture, leading to distinctive interpretations of the following tenets of Pentecostalism: belief in rebaptism by the endowment of the Holy Ghost, and speaking in tongues by the possession of the Holy Ghost, conferring sainthood on those "saved," giving them the ability to heal, to interpret tongues, and to prophesy. Diversity also marks codes of behavior in ritual performance and in private life, because Pentecostals view themselves as Christians in the first place, in constant formal (prayer) and informal conversation with Christ, following his guidance to prepare for the Second Coming and the heavenly home.

Okay Jesus, You Are Using Me . . .

The Grace Tabernacle Church is a "Oneness" assembly, often specified as "Jesus Only," conferring baptism in the name of Jesus, in strict dissociation from Trinitarian Pentecostals who baptize in the name of the Father, the Son, and the Holy Ghost. It follows literally Acts 2:38–39:

"Repent," said Peter, "repent and be baptized, every one of you, in the name of Jesus, the Messiah, for the forgiveness of your sins; and you will receive the gift of the Holy Spirit. For the promise is to you, and to your children, and to all who are far away, everyone whom the Lord our God may call."

Jesus, suffering death for our salvation, is regarded not only as the baptist whose sacrifice purified us from sin, but also as the embodiment of divinity as God and the Holy Ghost in one. The resurrected Jesus as personal savior is the main object of worship for Grace Pentecostals. He is the one to whom people address their prayers, who shows himself in visions and dreams, whose presence fills people with awe and joyous excitation, whose advice is heeded, and who is omnipresent as guide and gentle advisor in all moments of need, amidst a crowd or in solitude, in church or out; Jesus is always there for those who call him. Audience responses to sermons, testimonies, witnessing, and other vocal church acts are accentuated by moans, whispers, or screams of "Jesus-Jesus-Jesus-Jesus" and "Thank you, Jesus," more often than the preacher's "Hallelujah" and "Praise the Lord" are used for structuring and spacing formalized speech, as if the mere mention of Jesus's name would make miracles come forth. As flamboyant evangelist Larry Mitchell sings happily and proudly:

> I'm a one-God apostolic tongue-talkin' holy-roller born-again, heaven-bound believer in the liberatin' power of Jesus's name,
> Well I've been washed in the blood sanctified by the spirit, I believe in holiness and I suggest that you should do the same.
> I was set *free* at a Pentecostal altar on my knees, pardon me if I'm not ashamed
> To be a one-God apostolic tongue-talkin' holy-roller born-again heaven-bound believer in the liberatin' power of Jesus's name.[7]

It is Jesus, who is omnipresent, who sends his messengers—angels—to act for him. The ways his messages are communicated are mysterious and awesome. They are conveyed in a foreign language to the assembly of saints through a selected person, while another is empowered to translate the utterings into common English. Jesus uses the people who are deserving to execute his will. Jesus works his miracles through people, even without their awareness. For the members of the Grace assembly, Jesus is the arbitrator of miracles. Yet he acts only when he is asked, answering the supplication of his people. Day by day, life is maintained by miracles that appear as demonstrations of divine mercy and strengthen and prepare people for eternal heavenly bliss. This relationship with Jesus is the gist of the religious practice of Grace Pentecostals.

The ways of Jesus, and the people's relationship with him, are well illustrated in a poignant testimonial legend about the faith healing (Clements 1974:15–39; 1981) of a blind girl, told to me by Lisa Wells.[8] She recounted the story to me and relived this experience at a time when she was under great strain because of the grave illness of a young man who had returned from California just two weeks earlier with inoperable liver cancer. Lisa was active in the prayer line for him. All her trust in Jesus was focused on the healing of Bob, and the sacrifice she was to offer. Her experience with the healing of Debbie, the blind girl, gave her hope that Jesus would use her again as an answer to her prayers and cure Bob, who, so far as she knew, was not expected to live.

Bob was the best friend and schoolmate of Lisa's sons. Lisa and her husband Tom are devoted Pentecostals but their two sons caused them much sorrow. Neither of them—ages seventeen and twenty-one—were living up to their expectations. They mixed with the wrong crowd, had dropped out of school, and were addicted to dope and alcohol. Both were raised in church and the older boy had been baptized in the spirit, yet they only occasionally came to the services, and Lisa's fervent prayers were not heeded. But the sickness of their friend made the two, and "the whole gang they hang out with," desperate. They sat grief-stricken at Bob's bedside and watched him wither away. Lisa herself visited Bob in the hospital several times to comfort him.

"I was prayin' for him because I knew this was a desperate situation," she told me.

> I knew, this boy's goin' to die. . . . First time I called, I felt inspired by the Holy Ghost to call him. He was in the hospital, and I talked to him for a little while. 'Course, he's never been taught God. He said: "Lisa, I don't know. It is so hard to me being in this condition, I'm trying right now to believe there is a God, you know, when I don't know. It's hard for me to deal with death right now and try to sort out whether there is a God or not." And I sympathized with him, you know, and said: "Bob, there is no incurable cancer, no matter how hard it is, it's no harder for God to heal than a headache," I said. "God is God, you know. Bob, honey, you take care of that part of it, you deal with your getting better right now, and I take care of the spiritual part of it."

Lisa told Debbie's healing miracle to me the day Bob was given twenty-four hours to live. While she was praying and fasting for Bob, she remembered suddenly how she had been used by Jesus just a fortnight ago. How could she forget? Remembering gave her new hope that Bob would be healed through her prayer. What she told me was a testimonial miracle legend, which she had first told in her church at a testimonial service, repeating it later informally among friends and family members whenever she had the opportunity. She told it as a witness, to strengthen the likelihood that another miracle was about to happen to Bob, by the grace of Jesus, moved by prayer. In her narrative, Lisa gives us an idea of how miracles are negotiated between Jesus and true believers, and how the power of prayer can achieve victory.

Lisa was visiting a sister church in Newport, Indiana, to pay respect to its minister, who often served as revival missionary at Grace. At the service, Brother White, the pastor, called her to testify about the miraculous healings in her life. She told the congregation about her supernatural cure from rheumatoid arthritis and a thyroid condition, and about the healing of her son's dislocated hip when he was five months old. Then, she began her story:[9]

"Well, the service was just beautiful that night," she remembered. "There wasn't any preaching because people were just dancing in the spirit, just running around the church, glorifying God."

When it came to praying for Debbie, a very sick girl, she was singled out by Brother White to lead the prayer.

> I glanced up, and saw that brother in the church, just looking straight at me. And it wasn't just like looking at my face. It was . . . I was frightened

because this guy really looked different. And so everybody was quietened down and this brother reached over and took the microphone from Brother White and he said: "The Lord told me to have this sister for whom the Lord did all these miracles, to come over and pray for Debbie." Of course, my heart was beating once a minute because, I said, "Oh God, here, I am nothing oh Lord, and this church is expecting me to pray with Debbie, and something is supposed to happen.

So, Brother Danny motioned to me to come around and Debbie was sitting down. And I had just gotten inside and took hold of her hands. And when I looked down at this girl, I have never seen anybody looking so sick. She was little, and skinny, and frail. Her face looked yellow and ashen, her hair was dead like straw, her eyes had absolutely no shine in them. They looked dead. I mean, it was almost frightening, this girl looked so bad. And I thought: I have never seen anybody in my life look like this. Like dead, it must be how they look. So, I was real nervous. Do you see the goosebumps on my arm as I remember?

'Cause I thought: God, you know, I'm nothing without you. I'm worth nothing.—Then, I put that girl's hand in mine and she was still sitting down. And I was standing up. And I started prayin'. And others started prayin'. And I started telling the Lord, I said: "Lord, I can do nothing. If you have to, work through me, Lord, 'cause I'm nothing without you." And I started praying and others started prayin' around me. You can feel that the spirit of God began to raise and get stronger, and stronger, and stronger. And the people started worshiping God, and voices was raised and different people started to speak in tongues, and I started speakin' in tongues. Because when you get out of this spiritual realm and you get into a . . . or, out of the carnal realm which we are living in, into the spiritual realm, then you just naturally . . . the spirit starts speaking instead of you, you know, he starts speaking in tongues . . .

And as I was doing this, I noticed that I was still speaking and everybody around me quieted down. And I thought: "Okay Jesus, you're using me in tongues"—because the tongues were just coming forth, just forceful. Not just like we would, speaking in tongues, praising God, but it was as getting the message forcefully. Now, when I finished this, a brother started interpreting what God had said. And the Lord said: "*You* say, I will build the church, and *I* will heal the sick, and *I* will raise the dead, and *I* will cause the blinded eye to see. And *I* will cause the deaf to hear." But he said, "Thus said the Lord: *I* will build the church, and *I* will heal the sick, and *I* will raise the dead, and *I* will cause the blinded eye to see, and *I* will open the deaf ears." He was telling us: "You can't do anything but through me, you are my hands and my feet and my mouthpiece, and I will do the work."

Of course, after the tongues interpretation we just started worshiping

God for what he had told us. While I was still holding Debbie's hand and I looked down. And she had kinda raised her face upward a little bit and as I was looking down at her face, Linda, these dead eyes I was telling you about, started twinkling. I mean, you could actually see light, flickering and twinkling at the top part of her eyes. But the bottom part of her eyes was still dull and dead. And as I saw this, just the goosebumps came over me, just like now. I thought like, oh God, you're doing something, I don't know what's wrong with this girl, Lord, but I never seen anything like this before, she was just looking like this. And she was saying: "Jesus! I want to live to see my children raised, and I want to live to see my family." And she was just talkin' to the Lord.

Well, after we finished praying and all, there were two little boys there who received the Holy Ghost during the service. So they have taken them out to a new part of the church they was building, and they baptized them. And I was just standing there . . . and Brother White came around and stood beside of me, and I said: "Brother White, what is wrong with Debbie? I have never seen a sicker-looking girl in my whole life." He said: "Oh sister Lisa," he said, "Debbie has a lot of things wrong with her," he said, "she is a real bad diabetic," and a lot of other things which he mentioned. Then, I justa kinda interrupted: "But Brother White, when we was prayin' for Debbie tonight," I said, "I've never seen anybody that sick and so dead," I said, "and I saw something," I said, "the top part of her eyes started to twinkle, and lights was back and forth in them, but the bottom part of her eyes still had this . . . this dull look, and all." He looked at me just shocked, as if you had slapped him. And he said: "Sister Lisa, didn't you know Debbie is blind?" And the spirit of God just came over me and I said: "I had no idea." I said: "Brother White, God had done something for her tonight."

Lisa ends her story here and tells about how she got a ride a week or so later to visit Brother and Sister White again. "I said sure, I am game with two hours' drive but oh boy, you can do something in that church." Then, she resumes Debbie's story:

The service was really precious, you know. It wasn't like it was the first time I went. But during the service this brother stood up and he was testifying. He said: "I want to thank the Lord for what he did for Debbie the other day when she was in the hospital."

So, after the service was over, I found out that they had been making tapes of the different services every night. And I told Brother White I would like to have some of these tapes. And he said, 'Well, he could have me some run off. And as we was sitting there, I said: "Brother White," I said, "this brother who was testifying tonight," I said, "was that the Debbie we had prayed for he was talking about?" "No," he said, "that was Debbie's sister-in-law," he said, "both of their names was Debbie," he said. "But, nobody told you what happened, have they?" And I said: "No. No one." And he said: "That night, after the service, when we all prayed for Debbie, two weeks ago," he said, "her sister-in-law was taking her home from church," he said. "And Debbie let out one of those most awfulest blood-curdling screams you have ever heard. And her sister-in-law said: 'What is wrong with you, Debbie? What's the matter?' And she said: 'I can see the street lights! I can see the street lights,' she said, 'I can see the lights!' " And he said, "The next church night when nobody knew about this miracle yet because they hadn't yet come back to church, and the next church night, this brother stood up in testimony service and he said: 'The Lord talked to me yesterday night and told me that Debbie was goin' to start seeing men walk as trees.' "

Well, there is a passage in the Bible where Jesus puts his hands on a blind man and prays for him, and he said: "Now, can you see?" And the blind man says: "I can see men walking as trees." And then, the Lord touched his eyes again, and he could see perfect. And he says: "Yes, I can see perfect, you know, I can see fine." So, what the Lord was telling them was that Debbie was in a healing process. First she sees the lights, then she's gonna see men start walking like trees. And then I'm goin' to restore her vision.

And this happened two weeks before I found out about Bob Deckard. And I found that the only reason that God let me do this, that God worked through me and let me be there was to give me faith that God is no respector of persons. That what he did for Debbie, and I didn't even know the girl, he would do for Bob Deckard. I feel, that's the reason. You know, we were praying, we were expecting a miracle, and God gave us one.

The miracle Lisa refers to here is only the second act of the drama to be concluded by the healing of Bob. God let her do the praying and the fasting, and she believes the interim miracle that happened the previous night, the healing of Debbie, is the sign that the healing process has begun. "A prayer line was—we were praying in the church. And were there for six hours. And while prayer was being made, somebody had touched God." The miracle was about to happen. Lisa continues:

The Lord had spoken to me at ten o'clock and told me that at the midnight hour it is goin' to be just like it was in the Bible that Paul and Silas had been beat and put in jail in stocks and bonds with hands and feet . . . And they began to pray and worship God. And at the midnight hour the stocks and bonds fell off, they were free. Their jailhouse doors opened, and they went out. This is all in the Bible.

And at ten o'clock, it was Monday night when I was prayin'. The Lord had spoken to me and he said: "At midnight some things are goin' to happen." So, I was waiting for the jailhouse door to swing open and the stocks and bonds to fall off. And like I said, two other sisters had come into the church. They had been to Brother Davis's that night, and they had come, they had come to my house, 'cause they had heard about Bob, that my church had been praying and fasting for him. They came to my house first and my husband said, "Well, she isn't here." And Sister Minnie said: "I know where she's at." So they go down to the church, and they come in real quiet. They get down on their knees and they start worshiping, praising God. And of course, we had already gone out of prayin' into moaning and groaning and travailing before God, just like it speaks in the Bible. Peter speaks about the moaning and groaning which no man, no one can interpret, it's as when your soul is communicating with God, you know, and power . . . it really gives you power.

And then, I have found out too, Sister Phyllis told me that Saturday God laid three days of fast on her heart. It was very hard on her to forgo two meals. And she said: "I didn't know what for." So when I went to the prayer meeting that night, this other sister came in and I was telling her that now I feel this fast was for Bob. They were prayin' with us and then, you know, when we all quietened down. It was about a quarter till twelve. And they walked over and sat on the front seats of the church. And I was still settin' on the floor. And I had just turned around, and there were big grins on their faces. The spirit of God was just so uplifting. And I said: "Boy!" And Sister Minnie said "Ough, that I never was in a prayer meeting like this in my life." And I told them, I said: "I don't want you to think I am silly, but" . . . and then I told them about Paul and Silas, things that the Lord had reminded me of. And I said: "God gonna do something at midnight." I said, I know what I thought, he told me that something is going to happen at midnight.

So, just a couple of minutes before midnight, as we were just sittin' there and talking, the back door opens to the church. 'Course there is a wall and we can't see who's coming in. And this guy comes in . . . David Berry, that had been working on a house next to the church, to use the restroom there. And he comes in and he goes to the bathroom. Well, I'm settin' from where I can see him. I told them: "This is David Berry, but," I said, "he is not by himself. I can see him lookin' at somebody. He's talkin to some-body."

And all of a sudden, in walks seven young people. Here they are tears rolling down their faces. They passed us right up, and right went on, right unto the altar. And they fell on their knees, and . . . like I said, their bodies were shaking under the power of God, crying. And . . . and I thought: oh, God, you know you've done something but . . . And doubt came onto my mind, just for a second. I thought Bob died, and then, . . . No! it couldn't be that. I don't feel that. I feel victory. And so, and here those other sisters, they just walked down on the floor, praising God, speaking in tongues. Because this is miracle.

Miracle it was. For these seven kids to come in like that. Bunch of hoodlums, one might say, with long hair, one of them on dope, one of them, my youngest drinks to excess . . . These boys all came in and knelt down at the altar. And you could see their bodies jerking for they were crying. These kids, like I say, are on dope, or had been on dope. It wasn't dope that night. An' I got down beside Ronnie, and I said: "Ronnie, what about Bob?" And he said: "Oh Mom, you would not believe," he said, "Bob got up . . . " And of course those other sisters were walking and praising God. And I started: "Sh-Sh-Sh! Listen! Listen what Ronnie's saying." And I said: "Okay Ronnie, what were you saying?" And his tears were running down his face, and he says: "Mom," he said, "Bob was laying up there and he could not talk to anyone, anything, you know. Bob gets up in bed, takes the oxygen off, you know what they have, all these, IV, yeah, goes to the bathroom, comes back, sets down on the chair and starts talkin'." And he said, "Mom, this is the only hope Bob's got, You know, just a miracle."

It's a miracle that I saw with Debbie's eyes. And I feel that the reason I saw half of her eye twinkling, that the Lord was starting the healing process. He had done this much, and I feel it's gonna be like this with Bob. I feel like this is not going to be like the doctor comes in and says, "Hey, you are cured!" This liver is full of cancer and his side is swollen four inches larger than normal. It's not gonna be like this, he has got a new liver. I believe it's gonna be a healing process. Last night, God put strength into Bob, he sat up in bed, he could get up, he could start talking, and I believe God is just going to restore this boy, give his life back to him. 'Cause twelve hours of this twenty-four was already gone, he only has a few hours left, and only God could do something like that.

Lisa and I continued our conversation that Wednesday afternoon for a long time. Lisa enjoyed talking about her deepest concerns, and I felt myself fortunate to hear her competent, insightful explanations. The accounts she gave were accompanied with lively good-humored personal commentaries about basic beliefs. Explaining to me the importance of miracles, she pointed out the connection between these two miracle legends. The experience Lisa related reveals how miracles can be achieved, namely: by prayer—making the request, and by fasting, which means making a sacrifice. Both are key acts, and Jesus himself communicates how much of each he wants in return. Finally, when we parted, we both thought of Bob. "I will call you tomorrow as soon as I find out," she told me before we parted.

Her phone call came in the early afternoon. "Did you see the paper?"

she asked. "No, not yet," I said. "Why, what happened?" "Bob died yesterday evening and the family notice is in there." What a disappointment, I thought; how is she going to interpret it? "I will explain to you what happened," she said, as if she had heard my thought.

Next day she was telling me this:

> It was my mistake, I completely misunderstood the Lord. Bob's time came, he wasn't supposed to live. God gave him his consciousness back: he sat up, pulled the tubes, walked to the bathroom, sat down on a chair and chatted—wasn't that a miracle? But the real miracle was that the seven kids were touched, came back to church and worshiped the Lord at the altar. They were so far gone without God, lived for so long in sin, only a miracle could shake them up. And this is what has happened.

The certainty that miracles can be made to happen keeps Lisa's life happy and future-oriented. She knows her sons will find the right way because she is praying and fasting for them.

A year after this episode, it was revival time again. Brother Clifton's preaching was particularly inspiring; his excitement was so great that "God sent his angels—it is just like a soft wind, you can just feel it . . . you can just feel it," Lisa said. "When he hollered, it was just like a . . . I've never seen anything like it . . . And people spoke in tongues. The spirit of the Lord came over you when the Lord speaks through you, it gushes out through your mouth . . . " Lisa told me how she had felt the urge and had stood up:

> I said, "Lord, send those angels to California and bring my son home." In two weeks' time, and I just talked to him and he was just gonna travel with this . . . There was a group that was called Mafia . . . or Mossi . . . and they were musicians. And this guy, he got his picture in some of these catalogs where he's played music and stuff. And that's what Ron was goin' to do. Travel with them and set up their music equipment. And he just called in two weeks after that and said: "Mom, I'm coming home, you know . . . don't be so happy." . . . you just go nuts! And then, he was here in two weeks' time.

Prayer is negotiation: God wants a request explicitly stated. He knows the need but he helps only if the prayer formally asks. As Lisa explains:

> If we don't ask, we really can't expect him to do anything. He knows our needs but he wants us to ask. People who congregate, bring their requests to the Lord and take it before the Lord, you know . . . And then, by asking, whenever we see this need met, then it gives us faith that we prayed about this, that we took it before God and God answered. But if you don't ask anything, then your faith would never grow because you really would

never see what he is doing. But . . . if there was never a problem, how would you know that God could solve them?"[10]

Prayers are offered to remedy all kinds of ills caused by the supplicants' own weaknesses: quick temper, anger, jealousy, or greed, but more often they ask for the restoration of harmony in the family: to settle conflict between couples and in-laws, to help children find salvation. And miracles occur as answers to the prayers. Lisa's consistent supplication and fasting for her sons moved the Lord to act as her legend attests:

> Oh, I want to tell you something. Uh, last night, uh, Ronnie and his girlfriend came over—it was about eleven o'clock. And . . . they're in the process of moving, which . . . this situation really upsets me because they're just living together. This wasn't the way he was raised . . . that's just the generation. Some will, some won't. But he plans on marrying her, but they've just not done it. But anyway, they came over, and I told you, I'd been watching his three cats? Well, I think, he missed them. He ran over last night after he got off from work. He works at two part-time jobs . . . Chi-Chi's I think is where he was working at last night, so he and his girlfriend came over and my husband had already went to bed. And they were sitting on the staircase, playing with these cats.
>
> And I thought, you know, I need to say something to them about the Lord. But I didn't know how to bring, you know, you just don't blunder into something like that. You have to wait until something's said, because people would never come to visit you. So we were sitting there.
>
> And all of a sudden, this music starts playing: "Joy to the world," [she sings] "the Lord has come, let earth receive her King." You know, and Ronnie looked at me real funny. And Debbie looked at me, and I looked at them, and I thought, I knew what it was, it was—I've got a little snow-man, stuffed snowman, that I put out at Christmas time. And, but you have to punch a little place on his tummy to get him to play. And he is in a box underneath the staircase where I store stuff. And Ronnie said: "What is that? Where's it coming from?" Because he knew what the tune was. You know, it was a spiritual tune. And, so he went upstairs, and he came back down, and his Daddy hollered at him, he heard him in there, so he hollered at him. Ronnie went in the other room.
>
> And Debbie said, "Where did that come from?" And I said, "That thing cannot play unless something touches its tummy, you know, the little button." And I said, "Did you realize what it was playing?" And she said: "Yes." And I looked at her and I said: "Joy to the world, the Lord is come. Let earth receive her King."
>
> And she just started laughing, because I've asked her to go to church before, and so I went over and sat down at the table. And I looked at her

and I said: "Debbie," I said, "Maybe I shouldn't tell you this, but I think I need to let you know, so you can prepare." I said, "The Lord is gonna save you and Ronnie." I said, "The Lord is gonna get hold of both of you and save your souls." And it was like this music kinda set the atmosphere, you know, to say something to her. And she just started giggling. And she said, "You mean you think that I'm not already saved? That I'm not already good?" And I said: "Sure, I think you're just perfect. That's the reason I pray and fast for you all the time, Debbie." 'Cause she knows that I don't approve of the way they're living. But I thought, "God, you are so GOOD!" You know, I've never heard that—that thing cannot go off. It was to be activated by the action of the button. . . . But I thought that, that music going off last night was a shocking—and, and 'course it was so loud because here we was setting right over it. 'Course my, my staircase is carpeted all the way up, and muffled the sound just a little bit. And I thought, "You know, that could have gone off and played Jingle Bells or Frosty the Snowman"—'cause it plays eight songs. And here it plays "Joy to the world, the Lord is come."

Lisa's latest miracle concerns her granddaughter Tiffany's abscessed front tooth. The two-and-a-half-year-old's tooth was to be extracted, and Lisa hated to see her go toothless for four to six years until the permanent one would grow in. "She will be teased by other kids, you know how cruel they are: 'You look like a jack-o'-lantern . . . ' " she complained to me. The dentist was ready to listen and wait two weeks: "Okay, Mrs. Wells, you do your praying, and I do my praying with some antibiotics." The infection must have been stubborn because further visits to the doctor's office showed no relief. Finally, the evening before the last crucial visit, the miracle happened at a prayer meeting. Another woman, Sister Jackie, who was on a forty-day fast for her family, reported to Lisa that Jesus had told her Tiffany was healed. Next day Lisa took the girl to the dentist. She called me to tell the good news and let me know that she was going to testify in church that night. At the service, which I attended at her invitation, Reverend Coffey called for testifying:

> We want to have a time of testifying [. . .] We hope you don't let the service drag, but just one right after another, praising the Lord. And I'd just like to see heaven come down around here. I really appreciate those times that we get to sit at heavenly places and heavenly atmospheres, and I tell you, it can be that tonight . . . so smile, come on now, isn't God good? I said, isn't the Lord good, hallelujah! [applause] . . . We'd like nothing better than to send his blessing, and bless you real good. Sister Sue, come and let 'em testify. Amen. Come right on, all right." [Audience: "Praise the Lord"; "Thank you Jesus"]

Lisa was the third to speak, after the testimony of two men:

Sister Sue, I just want to tell the truth that the Lord has been work-ing . . . in a beautiful way [comments muffled by Brother Coffey's "Thank You Jesus"]. I took Tiffany to the doctor, it's been about four weeks ago, she went to the dentist with an abscess on her tooth. And Dr. Roberts told me, he said, "It's got to come out," he said, "it's dead." And I told him I didn't know, I said, "I don't want it taken out, I want to pray about it." So he sent me home for two weeks, and I went back two weeks later and he told me that the tooth has got to come out, it's dead and it's infected. And I said, "No, I want to pray about it." So, two weeks ago, at prayer meeting, I came in early and I was in the prayer room, and the Lord spoke to me. And he said that if I could have faith, that he was going to show it to me. But the Lord spoke to another sister that had been on a forty-day fast [comments drowned as preacher exclaims: "Oh, Thank you Lord!"] . . . and she came to me and told me that Tiffany had been healed. So I took her to the dentist today, and Dr. Roberts looked at it, and he said, "Well, the infection," he said, "has come to a head." He said, "It's all right there," he said, "but the tooth is dead and it needs to come out." And I told him what happened in the prayer room, and he asked me, he said, "has the Lord ever talked to you like this before?" And I started telling him how the Lord has healed me of thyroid problems, how he had healed my son of a dislocated hip, and he looked at Tiffany and he said, "I'm not going to touch that tooth." He said, "Just give it to the Lord." And I love him for what he's done." [Applause]

In her church testimony, Lisa was nervous and not as elaborate as usual: the pastor was hurrying testifers in order that they not take too much time away from his sermon. She was pleased, though, with my taping and the photo shot from behind, showing her from the back with raised right arm, Tiffany's face, and my silhouette with the tape recorder. In order to make Lisa produce a third variant, my assistant asked her to tell her what happened because she had heard only the church testimony and not the whole story. Lisa was eager to comply, and used the opportunity to formulate the whole experience into narrative shortly after the events, at a time when she could relax and report a happy conclusion.

The transcribed text that follows documents the crystallization of the story built over the weeks of tension. It exhibits the skill of the inspired narrator in setting up the miracle event in the context of everyday life. Lis-tening to the variant I had recorded the previous evening (which is quoted above) gave Lisa the opportunity for a critical review and a new, detailed, epic formulation of the experience. Episodes of her repertory of narratives about miraculous encounters with God, the prayer room experience, and the

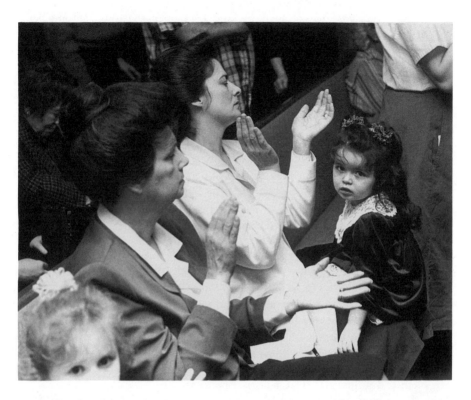

Lisa, center, her best friend Sue at her side and her granddaughter Tiffany on her lap, claps to the music moments before she will stand to testify about the miracle of Tiffany's tooth. Photo by Billy Adams.

efficacy of fasting are recast in this version. Characters—the fasting sister unaware of her blessing, the rationalist doctor acting out his daily routine dealing with patients—are transformed under the impact of the miracle. Lisa herself appears as a catalyst. In her outwardly humble and hesitant but spiritually empowered negotiations with the doctor, she is the winner. In his eyes, the loving grandmother appeals the infallible verdict of the professional, but as the two continue the dialog, their relationship is transformed. The doctor, limited by his learned profession and social position, yields to the believer who stands firm on the grounds of experienced miracles.

Okay. I had her for a week, and she kept going like this [rubbing fingers on teeth]—just rubbing around. And when I brush her teeth, she's always been like this. You have to fight her 'cause little kids don't like to have their teeth brushed. So, anyway, I usually get her out of the bathtub. She's kinda—she's wise to me anymore, and I wrapped the towel around her, drying her off. And I said, "It's brush TEETH time," and so I sat her on the sink, put her feet in the sink, and then I've got this towel around her and I just hold her chin back like this and brush her teeth. Sometimes she throws a fit, sometimes she don't.

But anyway I noticed that she was really fighting me, not wanting her teeth brushed, and I said okay, just let your teeth be nasty then, 'cause I wasn't gonna brush her teeth if she's throwing, you know, a real royal fit. And I noticed she kept going like this [touching gums] even in church, so I brought her home that night. And she was saying, "Hurts." 'Cause I gave her something with salt in it. And I said, "Let Mamaw see," 'cause sometimes her sister gets little kinker sores in her mouth. So I pulled her lip back and when I did, I could see this big abscess, and it—seemed like it was on a holiday. Might have been Labor Day, because that was when? In September?

So anyway, the next day I called Dr. Roberts' office, and he got her in on an emergency call, so I didn't have to wait. And as soon as I went in, he took her in. And he looked at it, and he said: "Let me X-ray that." And so he X-rayed it, and he come back and he said, "That's a shame," he said, "we NEVER have this happen, seldom ever." And he said what had happened, 'course I know what happened—he filed her teeth down—she had what's called "bottlemouth" where they suck on a bottle, and their mother gives them a bottle at night, and milk—sugar in the milk sets on the, the teeth and gums, and then it decays the tooth.

So anyway, he filed her teeth down and was gonna put caps on 'em, but her gums started hemorrhaging. And so I had—she had to wait five weeks before she went back and got the caps put on her teeth. But while they were all filed down, I think they were more susceptible to germs and such.

And anyway, he said something had gotten in one of those teeth, and had just infected in there, and caused the tooth to die, and the poison from the dead tooth had went up into the gum area. So he wanted to take the tooth out, and then I already told you every time he mentioned taking that tooth out, I just felt like bawling. I mean, tears would actually come to my eyes. And I said, "Dr. Roberts," I said, "I don't want her to lose that tooth." I said, "I'll pray about it." So he writes down—he's real smug—so he wrote down, you know, I'm giving Tiffany such and such; grandmother does not want tooth pulled. She is going to P-R-A-Y, and he always, you know, kind of like PRAY as he writes it down.

And so I went back a week later, two weeks later, and he said, "No, that abscess hasn't come to a head." He said, "That has to come to a head." And he said, "We need to get it out of there." And I started tearing up again. I said, "But I don't want her tooth pulled." And he said, "Now, Lisa," he said, "if she was to fall and hurt herself and not get this tooth out," he said, "could you accept that?" And I said, "I could, if it was already out, but," I said, "now that it's in I don't WANT it out." And he said, and 'course I was startin' tearin' up again, and [in sobbing voice] "I don't want her tooth pulled." And I said, "I—want to pray about it. I want to pray about it some more." And he said, "You know, we can't keep going on like this. 'Cause," he said, "if that infection gets over in the other teeth," he said, "you'll have to pull everything that's infected."

So anyway I told him I wanted to pray. That was on a Monday. On Wednesday night is when I went to pray to prayer meeting, and, as I was praying, I prayed once for Tiffany, and then went on praying for other people, and then I prayed again for Tiffany. And, but it seemed like I was just kinda—my prayers was hittin' the wall, you know, like I didn't really feel anything. Well, the third time that I come back to Tiffany, and was praying, in the meantime, just about five minutes before I prayed for her the third time, this sister at our church—she's been in for about probably eight or nine months—but she had been on a forty-day fast, just eatin' at suppertime, so that it wasn't for Tiffany; she was fasting so that her family and her husband would come in to church. But she had come into the prayer room—she didn't even know I was in there—I got to prayer meeting late because I was getting ready for a yard sale, and I wasn't even gonna go, and I thought, "No, Lord, I've got to go—there's too many things my family needs." So, she has come into the prayer room to get some Kleenexes, 'cause the women's prayer room has Kleenexes in it. And she said—I was praying, and so she said, she just thought, "Well, I'll just stay here and pray." So she was walking around praying, and the Lord spoke to her just about the same time he spoke to me. But she said, "Now Lord, if this is just me, I don't want to tell Lisa something and she's going to be hurt later. But if this is you let her mention Tiffany's name."

So anyway, about the same time, the Lord spoke to me, and that time I felt the spirit of the Lord just came in, I mean, you could just feel POWER come into the room. And the Lord spoke to my heart, and he said: "If you could only believe that I am healing Tiffany." And 'course, then I started crying and praying, and it was just beautiful. Well, after we finished praying, I asked her to turn the light on, in the prayer room, 'cause I couldn't find one of my shoes. And I said, "Kathy, you're not going to believe this, but while I was praying," I said, "the spirit of the Lord just came in here and you could just feel it." And I said, "He told me Tiffany—" and when I mentioned Tiffany, she started going [in squealing voice] "OOOoooh! OOOoooh!" like this, and she was just holding her mouth, and she was saying [in high-pitched excited voice] "Oh! I don't know whether to tell you or not!" And I said: "What is it?" She said, what time she was walking back and forth praying, the Lord told her to go over and lay her hand on my shoulder and tell me that the baby is healed. And he said, she said, "I,

I"—she knew that Tiffany was having a problem with her tooth, but she still thought that the Lord meant there was something wrong with the youngest one.

So anyway, this was on Wednesday. I went back to the dentist the following Tuesday. And before he ever got—came into the room to see me, I was telling one of his little helpers about what the Lord has done in prayer meeting and she said, "Oh, that's just beautiful." But she kinda act she didn't know what I was talking about, you know. So he came in, and he had one of the women to go ahead and X-ray her tooth, and he came in ten minutes later and he said, "Well, Lisa," he said, "you know, the tooth is dead, and"—'course I'd already told Linda what had happened in the prayer room and all—and I just, I was just really expecting the dentist to come in and say, "Well, this tooth is no longer dead," you know, and it was just a miracle like that. But he came in and he said, "Well," he said, "I x-rayed it," and he said, "The tooth is dead," he said, "but the poison has all come to a head." He said, "That's good." So he said, "Now we need to get the tooth out," and I said, 'course he sat down and he started writing in his little chart on her, and I said—all at the same I was saying [whispered] "Jesus, Jesus, Jesus," 'cause I—I wanted the Lord help me to tell him what I was gonna tell him, 'cause if he thinks that her teeth are in danger because of this one, I mean, he, he would insist in taking it out— that would be the welfare of her, no matter what I said.

So anyway, he sat down and was writing, and I said, "Dr. Roberts, there's something I've got to tell you." And I said, he had his head down— he wasn't even looking at me—I was standing up holding her. And I told him about being in the prayer room, and I said, "The Lord spoke to me and told me that if only I could believe that Tiffany IS healed"—and he started shaking his head like this. And what I was reading from his shaking his head was "Forget it Mamaw. This tooth is coming out." You know, "I don't care what you say, this tooth is coming out." So he was shaking his head real slow, no. And he was writin' and I said, "Uh, after the Lord spoke to me, he spoke to, uh, another sister that had come into the prayer room, and I—I told him that she had been in church just a short time, and that she had been on a forty-day fast, and I said, "But the fast wasn't for my granddaughter; it was for her family and her husband to be saved." And then he kinda put his head up, and started, you know, listening to what I was saying. And I said, "But the Lord told her three days before prayer meeting that night, to go on a three-day fast with NOTHING to eat." I said she had been on a three-day fast with nothing. And I said, "Then the Lord spoke to her in a prayer room and told her to tell me that Tiffany had been healed—that the baby had been healed." And I said, "She told me later that then, right then, she knew what the three-day fast was for."

Because anytime there is a miracle, there has to be a sacrifice. I had been fasting some for Tiffany, but I've got oh, an ulcer that was caused by Clinoril—it's a medication used for arthritis, and it messed up my stomach up a long time ago, so I couldn't go on a lengthy fast like I normally would, because I was having stomach problems.

But after I told him that, about being on a three-day fast, and how, what God had spoke to her about the same time he spoke to me, he leaned forward and he said, "Has the Lord spoke to you like this before?" And then I had to tell him, you know, yes, he had, I had been healed of arthritis, rheumatoid arthritis, and thyroid problems that my doctor said I'd have for the rest of my life; God healed me of that. And my son was healed of a dislocated hip, and the Lord had just spoke to me about things at different times. And he had this real serious look on his face and he said, "Well," he said, "let's just leave it to the Lord and see what he wants to do with it." And he said, "I'm not just doing this just because of what you're telling me," and I thought [chuckling] "Uh-HUH." He said, "It's just the fact that these things have come about, and I just feel like if we don't HAVE to take out this tooth, and you've had experiences like this before, then we need to kinda wait and see what comes of it." And he stood up and he patted Tiffany on the back, and he said, "You want to come to Dr. Roberts?" And he's never done that before. And he said, "Boy, you sure are lucky to have a Mamaw like this." And I said, "No, it's the LORD, Dr. Roberts. It's all the Lord." And he said, "Well," he said, "call me sometime and make an appointment—she needs her teeth cleaned, and she needs fluoride treatment," and he said, "We'll just let it go from there." So that was, that was just it. That's the WHOLE . . .

But, he did feel sorry for me, even the second time I went in, because he followed me out to the desk; I mean he could see. He told me once that sometimes grandmothers were affected worse than mothers whenever they would bring kids in there with tooths . . . teeth knocked out or something. But he followed me out to the desk and he said, "Now Grandmaw," he said, "Let's keep our fingers crossed about this tooth." And I said, "Dr. Roberts, I don't believe in crossed fingers." He said, "OOOohh, that's all right." He said, "You pray, and I'll cross my fingers."

As we can see from the above, fasting as a form of sacrifice is regarded as a means of making prayer more effective. Lisa explained to me how she handles fasting, while also giving insight into routines in the life of the congregation:

You know any time, let's face it, if you buy any expensive piece of garment, you gonna pay a big price. You will get nothing in this life for nothing, you know. You get what you pay for. Okay? Back in the Old Testament times people used to offer an unblemished sheep and cattle, and dozens of stuff. When God died on the cross he became sacrificed. For us, you know, the only type of sacrifice we do is sacrificing meals. The greatest we can give because it takes nourishment away from the human body and it makes us sick, make our head hurt. But it is a sacrifice, saying: "God, we want you to do more in my life." Usually when we fast, we don't tell anybody we are fasting. 'Cause if you do, then you get the glory from men, and if you don't, you get the glory from God. Oh, these are just all miracles, and I think, more miracles are goin' to happen."

Again, Lisa exemplifies with a miracle. She was on a three-day fast and had done two days before Sunday:

> Sunday morning—and I don't fast on Sunday, because I'm active all day. Sunday school, choir practice, church, and it's hard. But I got up Sunday morning, and the Lord said: "Fast." And I said: "Oh God, I fasted, you know, this week already a couple of days." And it was just like he said: "Fast." So I fasted that day. And I got to church that night and my head started hurting, and I was so sick, but just for a little bit. But while the minister was preaching the word, I just kinda ran my hand under some pages in the Bible, and more or less just kinda fanning myself because I felt funny. And when I flipped these pages over, there must have been three or four hundred of them, 'cause I hadn't turned to the text that was preached that night. And when I turned the pages over, it was underlined with red. It said:
> "This is the fast that I have chosen, to break the bond of wickedness, and let the oppressed go free."
> And Linda, I looked at that, and I thought: Glory be to God.

Considering miracles—experienced, discussed in bits and pieces within the support group during the process of formulation, presented in set form in public as witnessing testimony built into the church service, and repeated to outsiders, like me—we speak of a special category within the genre that folklorists know as legend. I will consider its place in the hierarchy of legends after presenting miracles that appear in the context of sermons, narrated with a more directly didactic goal by religious leaders, ministers, preachers, and evangelists. Told from the pulpit, they are less informal and emotional, but better rehearsed, and therefore more polished and authoritative.

Miracle Legends in Sermon

The *exemplum mirabilis* in the traditional practice of the Christian church since Biblical times was always regarded as a powerful educational tool. Christ's disciples, the Apostles, spread their miracle experiences, and following their example, preachers throughout the Christian world enriched their sermons with didactic narratives taken from existing collections or collected directly from contemporary oral tradition. The exemplum was an important part of the sermon, not only because of its didactic value but also because as a story, it attacted churchgoers who were bored with dry moralizing, and it kept them in attendance (Wesselski 1925; Röhrich 1962; Moser-Rath 1964). But while the majority of these stories concern the lives and miracles of accredited saints of the past, the exempla of fundamentalist sects are contemporaneous, treating wonders that happen to average people in everyday situations, to people they know, to the preacher himself. They may be told in first person as a personal experience, or in third person as the experience of somebody else.

These legends told in the context of the Pentecostal sermon are the more remarkable in that they are a part of flamboyant emotional preaching, appealing more to the senses than to the rational mind. The preacher, deeply involved with the topic he has chosen from the Bible, progressively raises his voice, taking advantage of the capabilities of his vocal cords, shouting, screaming, whispering, sobbing quietly, or crying loudly as the diction of the text requires. Launching his preaching from a Biblical verse, he uses one or more examples to elaborate on the message so the people can identify with it and be moved to join in and together create an atmosphere in which "people would leave the carnal realm and enter the spiritual realm, forget all about carnality." The preacher himself can accomplish this altered state of consciousness and enter a trance-like disposition that invites the presence of God and his angels to break into speaking in tongues. After such a performance by a revival minister or the regular pastor, people would say: "He is just beautiful . . . he just hollered and fell on his knees in humility by the presence of God." Such performance ignites the "saints" in the pews and they break out into speaking in tongues. Here, explains Reverend Clifton, "the Lord takes control as the person feels tongues coming on":

> God is moving your tongue, and you and he does it, until he is ready to stop, and there is an awesome feeling . . . like you could cut it with a knife. And then, somebody else in some place got called in the interpretation. And God does this. Because he lets people know that what is being said is coming from me. So, I'm goin' to give it in tongues and then, I'm goin' to give it in a language that you can understand.

The preacher is judged by his ability to cause this to happen, to lead people to conversion and baptism in the Spirit.

Legends told in sermon are often retold in conversation or replayed from tape-recordings. Here are some texts I recorded myself.

The first legend is told by Reverend Don Deck, who narrated three variants at a revival service in October 1985. The sermon was about the attempts of the Devil to destroy young people attracted to rock music. This legend, formulated and spread through fundamentalist churches, is in general circulation and has generated fear of the seduction of children by hard rock music.[11]

Devil in the Guitar

This boy could not sleep at all. He had a guitar. And his father said, "Where did you get this guitar?" And the boy said, "Well, I got it in a pawnshop." And he said, "And where did the pawnshop get it?" He said: "I don't know, but I will find out," he said. He found out and took it back, and found out that the pawnshop got it from a rock musical group. This particular musical group was known for dedicating their instruments to the devil. They had services, just like . . . this building, I am sure, has been dedicated to God [audience: "Hallelujah, praise the Lord!"]. This musical group dedicated its instruments to the worship of the devil and they had a big time ["oooh Jesus!"]. And this guitar the boy had, had been dedicated to the devil. And that's the reason that he could not sleep at night, that there was an evil presence in the room. And the boy said: "Pastor, what should I do?" And the pastor said, "Well, I read it to you from the Bible," he said. "The graven image of ungodly presence should be burned with fire. It is an abomination, that the Lord, thy Lord commands, in thine house, shall be burned. Because it is a cursed thing." So the boy went home and got the guitar and broke it up in little pieces and took it out into the backyard. Poured gasoline on it and set it on fire. Then, some time later, he came back to the pastor, some days later, and said, "I just want to tell you, sir, before there was a strange, but weird and ugly spirit in my room, and now, there is a strange but very wonderful spirit." He said that everything was just fine. "Thank you," he said. ["Praise the Lord! Thank You Jesus! Amen!"]

Evil Spirit in Boy's Bedroom
[in continuation]
You mean to say, that evil spirits inhabit in all? This pastor in the United Pentecost Church told me this very story. He said, "Yes, you absolutely can use my name if you want to, because every word is true."

One night, my teenage boy was gone from home. He was spendin' the night with some friends and he was, said he was backslidin' and he said he was in with those very things I am talking about. And he said, "My wife and I was retiring for the night, we just got ready to go to bed." And he said, "We heard this loud noise at the other end of the house. It was so loud that it was frightening. I knew," he said, "I was going all way down the hallway. When I got down there, I opened the door to our teenage son's bedroom. And when I did, something came out of the bedroom door, ran across my feet and went straight down the hall and out the front door." He said, "Right down on the floor. It was evil. It was wicked," he said. "It had just a bad spirit, it had just a bad spirit about it," he said. "I went right on in, I turned the light on, and walked into the room. And when the door was closed, right inside the door, there was one of these hideous, demonic-looking pictures, from one of those groups." He said, "Yes, you can tell, I know the evil spiritism is associated with all of that kind of stuff. You can read about it on one of those books in the Christian bookstore. ["Praise the Lord"]

Evil Spirit in the Stereo

One of the famous pastors, his son got involved in this. Went out and bought a rock music record. It had a demonic-looking picture on the front. The boy took it home, and laid the album cover up against the stereo, put the record on, and laid down and began to listen to it. The boy was having an absolutely excruciating earache. He could not even go to school because of them and they could not find out what was wrong. Medical examination turned out nothing at all. A preacher friend came by, and they started talking about it and he said that "this boy's dad sounds to me like it may be the activity of an evil spirit." And the boy's dad said, "Do you think so?" They went upstairs where their boy was and he was laying on the bed, and just wallowing in pain, of this excruciating pain. He started talking to him. He saw this album over there and came to find out where the boy first brought the album home and laid the cover against the stereo and was laying and listening to it. He said himself that "the evil picture in front of the album literally came right off the album, moved right across, and came over right, stood over me while I was laying on the bed." He said, "The thing just stood there and started laughing at me, and," he said, "the pain was so excruciating in my ear," he said, "it never left since. So," he said, "that's what it was." And they destroyed those records that the boy had, and then, the dad and the preacher took authority over and commanded that evil spirit to leave. The power of the thing was broken immediately. The boy's earache went with it when the evil spirit went, and he was never troubled with it again. ["Amen"]

Bob Utterback of Linton, Indiana, is a welcome visiting preacher at Grace Tabernacle. Originally from Bloomington, he is a retired electrician. His stories are different from those of Brother Deck, and very much liked because they tell about everyday episodes of his own life with which people can identify. Also, they appear to be personal experiences, showing him as a searching human being, committing errors and succeeding because God is on his side. He presents mystic supernatural encounters very matter-of-factly, in an almost trivial, down-to-earth style, with a good sense of humor that makes the congregation burst out in laughter. These are modern miracle stories in the best sense of the word. The first was recorded at a revival in 1985:

A Loan of Forty Dollars

I remember one time, I was at the city of Newcastle, I was preaching for a revival at that time. I was driving too the company truck. That company truck broke down and I had two dollars in my pocket. I remember that I made it to the Chevrolet garage, it was a Chevrolet truck, and they said it will take about thirty-five to forty dollars to fix the truck. On a Friday night, the shops were closing. I had to be at a certain place in Greencastle and I called the company in Terre Haute for the work order. They said, no problem, just have it charged to the company. I turned around to the man and I said: "Could I have some credit here?" "Well," he said, "yeah, but your company just bought two new trucks and that exhausted the credit line and the company is now in process of . . . " I forgot now what they called it . . . they could not do it without the meeting of the board, and the board is meeting in four months. Oh my, that's a terrible thing. And I remember walking out on the sidewalk in front of the Chevrolet building. I look up to Heaven, and said: "Lord—you won't believe this—I need forty dollars." I remember, I looked down. And the Lord spoke to me. And he said: "The next car you see to slow down and stop, ask the man for a loan of forty dollars" [laughter]. Praise the Lord [laughter]. I said: "Well, Jesus, come on, let's see if somebody was jumping fast" . . . then I would ask. I would, in Jesus's name. And all right, I tell you something. I obeyed. I stepped up to an oversized van that slowed down at the curb. I said: "Excuse me, mister," and I presented my name, and I said to him, "The Lord said you'd loan me forty dollars." He said, "Oh, he said that?" [laughter] I said, "Yes, he did." He said, "Oh." And he loaned me forty dollars. ["Praise the Lord"] Amen.

At another revival in 1987, Bob Utterback gave an account of his encounter with angels and the help they gave him by the grace of God. It is within the Pentecostal canon that angels are sent by Jesus to act for him. These angels are very different from the traditional Christian concept or the modern guardian angel of the Spiritualist faith (Moore 1977). Generally, the presence of angels may be felt but not visually perceived, as I have heard often from members of Grace Tabernacle; but in the narrative that follows, angels appear in physical form at a church service. Their looking like normal humans beings is so baffling that they must show that they are from "Biblical times" by providing details about conditions in the past that could not have been known from other sources. The second appearance was "a presence felt" at night only, a feeling that drove Bob from bed to walk restlessly through his home; in the third, the angel appears in church, again as an ordinary man, and vanishes after giving advice—indicating that the Lord had directed the loan company to cooperate.

Working in a Supernatural Way

"What my eyes have seen, what my ears have heard, what my heart has felt." ["Praise the Lord!"]

We had three men coming to the Linton Pentecostal church one morning, a beautiful morning it was. If I remember right, it was a cold day and it was very sharp wind a-blowing. And I don't know what the temperature was, but it was quite cold. I remember, we had a hard time, in fact, we could not bring up the building to temperature, and the wind was blowing so hard and so strong. There were three men who came in. They stood on the back row of the church. And as we taught Sunday school, we was teaching about innovations of Elijah and Elisha. And the subject came up from the Bible. Something about different things that happened in those days. I don't remember the names, only that one came back later about twelve years later—I will tell about him a little later on. But he seemed to be the spokesman of the three, and he told us just how exactly, how they done in those days as like he knew. And I can't tell you all the details. But I remember that he told us how they done some of their cooking, just that we know he had been there.

I remember that after church, the men—and if I remember right, they had no overcoats, they had a suit on. Two men got up immediately and left the building, went into the parking lot and stood there for a good thirty minutes. Stood up there in the parking lot with just their suits on them and the temperature was terrible. It was bitter cold that morning. This one man stood behind and he told us a lot of things. And he talked with us. In fact, he played on everything he could get his hands on, in that church. And he did not . . . I'm afraid, I don't mean to insult nobody, but he did not play as he had trouble playing.

My wife became worried about the meatloaf that was in the oven at home. And he brought that up, and said: "Don't worry about the meat, it's all right. And it will not be burned." I said: "What are you doing down here?" He said: "We are down here . . . helping the winter warm. Cut some wood." I said: "Can winter warm itself up?" "No, she needs help. And we want to help her. Amen." That makes lot of sense. You know, those Holy Ghost-filled people that boast of being filled with the Holy Ghost? They would not go across town to cut wood for people. Wouldn't even . . . oh, shouldn't I say it? ["Say it!"] I might as well say it: they wouldn't even cross the town to go to church. ["That's right!"] Amen.

My wife said something about cooking. But she said, "I wish I knew how to cook better." He said, "What do you want to cook?" he said, and told her exactly how to cook. Praise the Lord. She went home and did as he said. She did not burn anything [laughter]. Praise the Lord.

During this thirty-minute talk there was something that was not quite normal. I began to press him to come home with me. He said: "No, but I will be back to see you some day." And he said: "Some day I will go home with you. There will be three, at least three different times."

One night I rose in my bed and I walked through the house about three o'clock in the morning. And I felt the presence of this individual—ghost? And I turned to look and I expected to see him standing there. But he was not. I remember, and I'm going to tell you a little bit about him later on, how he painted the building of the church in which we were worshiping.

But when we were trying to acquire a loan, we was a new church, everyone was trying us, we were strangers in town. We have been in all banks, and the banks said no, and the only way to do it was to put up my property, and that was proper. I was trying to own the church under trustees, under guardians. This is how it had to be done. And suddenly, one night, this same man came into our building. He walked up to me and my wife after church. He said to my wife, he said to her: "Oh . . . you go in and you ask them for a $21,500 loan and you don't even have to fill in an application, it will be ready for you." And he turned, and walked through the door, and we never seen him again.

My wife went to the place, went in there. She said: "I am here to borrow some money." The man said: "How much do you want?" "21,500 dollars." He wrote on a little piece of scrap paper that he had on the desk. He said: "How you gonna pay the money back?" He looked back at her. They grinned to each other. "Oh yes, the same way as you painted the house of the Lord. All right. I can't see a problem why we can't loan you the money." And we borrowed $21,500.

Now, you may laugh at that, and you can snicker, but to me, I feel this was done working in the supernatural way. Praise the Lord. ["Praise the Lord!"] A lot of people don't know these things. [Right!] And you would not know if I hadn't told you. ["Right!"]. Praise the Lord. I said, you would not know. ["Thank you Jesus!"] Amen.

The Importance of Tape-Recording: Maintenance, Perpetuation, and Spread of Miracles

The experience of miracles in and out of the context of the church, the symbolic home of saints, is essential for the community; therefore tape-recording is routinely done. The accumulation of miracle accounts strengthens faith in the infinite love of Jesus; people vividly recall past experiences and occasionally speak about them. Individuals bring their tape recorders to the services—it is unpredictable what is going to happen and they do not want to miss important, spontaneously evolving events. They collect texts to keep and replay for inspiration and for recapturing the experience of having been there when the stories were originally told. They also borrow cassettes from each other for copying memorable recordings—some of my better tapes were also copied. Particularly successful testimonies, sermons, tongues, and interpretations are preserved and thus take an active part in the personal lives of church members. While individuals do their daily chores, clean house, iron, do tedious physical work or other slow jobs that do not need mental concentration, or while they are resting before retiring for the night, or when they are tortured by bad dreams and look for solace on sleepless nights, they replay particularly poignant, prophetic messages.

Unlike the normal intrusion of television into average American homes, the evangelical messages of Pentecostal miracles that took place the previous night condition the minds of the Saints. They recapture, rethink, reinterpret the text, decode hidden meanings while they are alone. It is like meditation; they think loud and converse with Jesus. They ask questions and find the answers. Often it is only an idea, a sentence appealing to the mood of the individual that calls for this kind of meditation. For example, one morning I met Keith Phipps, a young church member, on the street. He was smiling at me, saying that he felt good. What happened? Not much, but he had come back from work yesterday tired and sick of his own weakness, holding a grudge against a relative. Listening to the tape of Sister Potter, the idea "forgive" caught his attention. He prayed that Jesus relieve him from thinking with anger—this is why he felt so good today.

The exposure is so intensive and so customary that there is no feeling of mysticism or awe, but rather a peculiar kind of domesticity in the Pentecostals' encounter with divinity. People are cheerful, self-assured and smiling while reproducing their conversation with "The Lord" in very colloquial, everyday language. They thank Jesus for deliverance from a bad headache or the flu, or they express gratitude for the successful sale of an old car, the good income of a garage sale to benefit the church—just as they later recount the blessing to a friend who has dropped in or just phoned. It is routine to discuss tape-recorded miracles over the phone with co-religionists who missed the event or who were also present but might have had some other thoughts, and this practice intensifies the communality of the religious subculture. More than once have I overheard people ask friends to record a particular preacher's text when they knew they would not be able to attend.

The importance of tape-recording to individual believers is shown by the following account of Lisa. She told it in testimony at a service subsequent to its original occurrence in 1985, and she repeated it to me in 1986. This was an experience that Lisa shared with her best friend, Sue:

I forgot to change my batteries, and they were dead. Anyway, I took the cassette recorder to church, Tuesday night, to tape this evangelist, Brother Clifton. I told Sue, I said: "Sue, my batteries are dead." And she was actually being comical making light of it. Put her hands on it and said, "Jesus" like she was praying for it, but was half-joking . . . Okay, I had dead batteries Sunday night already. And I talked to Sue. I said: "Sue, I had forgotten my batteries today, help me to pray for, that the Lord revive these batteries." But anyway, as we were singing, I see some red light on it . . . And as she starts singing, I just turned it on and waited for the preacher to get up there and . . . I just set it on my lap and I said: "Lord, in the Bible days, in the Valley of Dry Bones you resurrected those dry bones. You put life back in those dry bones. So you put back life in those batteries." And as the evangelist gets up, Brother Clifton, comes to the podium, and he gets up, and he starts for the podium, Sue says: "Oh Lisa, look." And those batteries, the red light flashed on, and Linda, they lived. And they were dead Sunday. I don't feel it was my prayer that did that. And I told Brother Clifton after the service, I said: "Brother Clifton, I don't think it was my prayer." And they were dead Sunday, I mean, *they were dead.* I feel like it was the Holy Ghost that whenever he got up and went to the podium, resurrected those dead batteries. I was amazed. And it was played, the next night, three hours on dead batteries . . . even four hours. . . . [She continued here with another miracle.]

The creation of personal archives for miracle experience is also a concern of the congregation. Churches, as we have seen in the case of the healing service at Newport, Indiana, record their services and make copies upon request as they did for Lisa. But beyond taping and circulating cassettes of their own church activities, gospel music, Nativity plays performed by the members, tongues and tongues interpretation, Grace Pentecostals, like other congregations, also make the sermons of respected evangelists available to the people. These sermons are more topical, dealing with specific concerns—The Temptations of the Devil, The Sign of the Beast, The Second Coming, and the like. The indoctrinational effect and popularity of such tapes in religious practice and education within family circles is shown in a news release about Marilyn Quayle, wife of Vice President Dan Quayle, who grew up listening to the tapes of preacher Colonel Robert G. Thieme Jr. (*Louisville Courier-Journal*, 25 Sept. 1989). As a "dispensational premillenialist," Thieme emphasized Armageddon and the Second Coming of Christ. Mrs. Quayle's sister stated that Thieme's tapes were the background rhythm of daily life in their home. "Mother played them all day, every day" (*Free Inquiry* 9, no. 2, 1989: 10).

Miracle accounts circulated within the religious community follow the rules of the dynamics of oral folklore. Experience is shaped into narrative in front of a participating audience. But by the intervention of the tape recorder, individuals within the community capture and stabilize the oral version of the moment for further oral elaboration and variation. As the miracle story—from the formal sermon or the informal testimonial—arrives on the oral channel to the immediate audience, it incorporates as many oral-folkloric as written-literary antecedents. Conscious technical fixation by the bearers, the attending folk, on the basis of a common frame of reference, leads to a recreation and extension of the folklore process. The tape recording itself, as a repository of folklore, is a valuable document to be recalled and activated at any time to prove a point, to strengthen an argument, or simply to remind the bearer of a significant experience. Often tapes preserve variants of the same story, told in diverse situations and shaped in different ways.

To satisfy my curiosity, Lisa brought me several tapes to illustrate how the sermon-inspired presentation of miracles heightens the mood of the audience and culminates in tongues and tongues interpretation. She chose to show me how her own speaking in tongues occurred when the sermon of one of her favorite evangelists grew into "an unusual service" as he became an instrument of God to communicate His message. Lisa played excerpts of one particular tape she had recorded ("Let's speed it up just a teeny bit. . . . The tape player was clear on the other side of the church, opposite where I was. But it still picked me up pretty loud. . . .") As she played the tape, I also taped her comments which she interjected to explain the interrelationship between the sermon and her speaking in tongues. Thus, my recording contains not only her original taping of the music, the preacher's sermon, Lisa's speaking in tongues, tongues interpretation, and audience response, but also her overlapping comments in the foreground to me as the original recording was played back. In the transcript that follows, her superimposed observations are indicated in italics:

> Brother White: Can I tell you a little story about this? I heard a boy not long ago that I used to run around with. And them folks was absolutely amazed, AMAZED that I could not do all the things I used to do, and still be happy. He said, "Well, don't you miss the old crowd?" And I said, "Well, to be honest with you, sometimes I do miss you folks. I think about you every now and then when I pray." And he said, "Don't—don't you miss the things you used to do?" He said, "I mean, I can't imagine living without, without drinking and smoking and cussing and rockin' rock. I just can't imagine a life without that."[. . . .]*See that was a day that I couldn't imagine. Oh, when I think about what he's done for me.*
> Congregation: Amen!
> Brother White: *When I think about where he reached down and grabbed me up.*
> Congregation: Amen, hallelujah!

[Lisa fast-forwards the tape to the part where the speaker was singing, "Jesus means all the world to me," and then comments:]

Lisa: He starts singing, and what really touched me, "Lord, you've been so good to me." I just, while he was singing that, I got to thinking about all the times the Lord has delivered me out of really serious situations. And it started touching my heart. I think right here—and he also makes the remark that this needs to be an unusual service, with the power of God. And when you talk faith like that, you've kinda set already, you know, what it's going to be.

[I ask, "Did he know it is going to be an unusual service?"]

Lisa: He didn't. He said this needs to be an unusual service by the power of God. You'll hear him say in just a minute.

Brother White: . . . we want to see you Jesus. Ah, I feel like we've been touched by God now. It seems to be an unusual service by the power of God. We have talked to Heaven, got down on our knees, we have brought down the Glory of God.

Congregation: Oh we love ya Lord! Praise the Lord!

Brother White: Thank you, Jesus. Thank you, Jesus.

Congregation: Oh Jesus, we love you, Lord.

Brother White: Well, I want my wife to stand tonight and testify. I ain't done it for a few nights. See, I'm scared to let her go too long without testifying till she gets all powered up, and she . . . the preaching's going to have a new miracle . . .

[Again Lisa fast-forwards the tape, bypassing this testimony but summarizing it, saying it is what led to her speaking in tongues:]

Lisa: Okay, and what she is saying in this testimony is that uh the Lord had changed her life. She said that when they first got married, she didn't want to be an evangelist's wife, because she had two sisters that had married evangelists and they'd go out with a little trailer and she, she's saying that she wanted a life to where she has stability, where she could be with her family and all rather than out traveling in a, in a small trailer evangelizing for the Lord. And, uh, she said, in one part of it, she says, uh, having the condition she has, which she was about eight months pregnant. And she said there's some times that people don't understand her. And she says she'll call her mother or she'll call her sister and she says that they say, "Well, I understand" but she says, do they really understand? But she says: "I'll go to the Lord and then he takes care of all my unhappiness and all my needs and everything like that."

And when she's saying this, it's kinda like I identified with what she's saying. You know, because there's been times when nobody understood my problems but the Lord. But anyway, just a spirit of the Lord came over me so strong, and then I started just cryin', and you'll hear it here. And, I tried to kinda hush it up, because nobody else was doing that, you know. And, it just, you know when the

Lord speaks through in tongues and interpretation, it's a forceful thing. It's not just like, you know, maybe you're praying and speaking in tongues. But it'll just kinda GUSH out by the power of God. And you'll hear here how, you know, it's—it's just real strong. But as soon as she stops testifying, then the Spirit of the Lord came over me, and used me in tongues and interpretation. [she speeds up the tape]

[Lisa (on original tape) speaks in tongues.]

Brother White: Oh Lisa! Hallelujah! Praise the Lord! Praise the Lord!

[Piano playing, Brother White talking softly. People crying out. Lisa continues speaking in tongues loudly. Someone screams; someone whispers: "Jesus, Jesus, Jesus."]

Lisa: This is where Brother White starts interpreting me.

Brother White: Hear me this night, and I will talk to you. Hearken unto my words this day, and ye shall live. [Lisa repeats]. I know your deeds [Lisa: *"I know your deeds"*] and I am your God. [*Lisa: "The eyes of your God"*] You see with eyes of flesh, you see what you want, but I am your God, and I see that which you need most. [From here Lisa repeats every word to me.] If you could see through my eyes, you would know this night my heartbeat, for I have loved you with a great love. And it is my desire to see you grow, and it is my desire to see you be a fulfilled and mature church to the place that souls can walk into your building, and you can minister to them. This night I talk to my people, I compliment you. This night I talk to my home. You are my people and I love you. I see your labor, I see those things which you have done. I have come this night to speak to you to let you know that I am your God and I have not forgotten you. I know who you are! And I know that which you have need of. Yea, I say again, I know that which you have need of.

[Congregation moans.]

Lisa [to me]: You can understand that pretty good. . . . Okay, now I go . . . I've cut a lot of it out because it went on pretty lengthy . . .

[Congregation moaning].

Lisa: How the Lord is full of witness in this place . . . The power of the Lord . . .

[People whimpering, crying, moaning: "Oh Jesus!" After further interpretations:]

Brother White: I never felt like this in all my life. [Lisa repeats]. The touch of the Lord is in this place right now . . . even while you stand in this building God's hand runs in your body and drives out cancers and heals your body right now . . .

Lisa: Now the spirit of God starts building right here. You'll hear him prophesying. Prophesying is where God don't use through tongues and interpreting, but he talks directly through the one that's telling what the Lord's saying. And it's Brother White doing the prophesying in just a minute . . .

Brother White: Your spirit has reached my throne this night. Your speech
has spoken to me face to face. While you stood in this place and ministered
to me, your faith has reached out to me and I have sent my angels among
you this night. Yea, my ministering angels are in this building. I have sent
them here this night to cleanse you. I have sent them here this night to
purge you. Yea, even now they lay their hands upon you . . .
[Loud congregation calling-out.]
Brother White: . . . because in Heaven they know that I am the Lord, I
am the healer! [Lisa repeats every word]
[Loud reaction from congregation: screaming, crying "Jesus, I love you
Lord!"]

This multilayered transcript shows that the tape recorder connects meanings in the total multivocal performance and allows creative interpretations
at repeated replays by the bearers. We can again endorse the observation of
Walter Benjamin that technical reproductivity and accessibility are important
factors in the construction of a new orality, structured by new rules of communication in the epoch of the mass media (1980: 471–77). However, we are
talking here about not a new but a traditional orality, as known to folklorists.
It is carried over and enhanced by the application of electronic devices in the
given traditional setting. The bearers of the tradition select the material for
their own personal archive, for their own use in endless reinterpretation. The
tape recorder does not freeze but, on the contrary, enhances the variation
and dissemination of folklore in an unprecedented way.

An Afterword on Legends in Religion

Over the years I have authored and co-authored several essays on the
legend with the intention of clarifying its main features. Arguing for the
disputability factor as crucial, I excluded legend-like narratives that enforce
belief and that deny the right of disbelief or doubt, narratives that express
majority opinion and are safeguarded by moral taboos from negation and,
what is more, from deviation. These are the so-called religious (Christian,
hagiographic, or saint's) legends, propagated by the Roman Catholic church,
and the patriotic (heroic) legends dispensed through school education by gov-
ernments, confirming citizens in civil religiosity. The reading or telling of
these stories is a part of religious duty and worship, a *cultus duliae* (Dégh
and Vázsonyi 1973:2–11). But what happens when dissident sects establish
their own belief systems in expressive defiance and confrontation with authoritative, canonic religion and its evocative legendry?
The legend dispute, which as I have argued before "resembles strongly
the theological polemics of the Reformation and Counter-Reformation

because of its topic, methods, passion and unreal atmosphere," can be found in every genuine folk legend (Dégh and Vázsonyi 1973:6). Are these miracle legends controversial? Are they amenable to debate? Do they challenge and motivate, do they incite opposition? Yes, they do. Although they stand firmly on the soil of the religious subculture, the experience that demands to be communicated is controversial by its very existence because it is based on the supernatural encounter of each individual. The legends appear as a constant reminder of the presence of miracles, the credibility of the incredible. The ambiguity is built-in but differs in degrees as it is addressed to the sectarian, the hesitant, the skeptic, or the unbeliever. These stories represent a front of minority believers; they are arguments for the acceptability of the sect, addressed to the mainstream. More importantly, and more directly, the personally lived-through miracle targets the unfaithful who were raised as Pentecostals but who have abandoned the faith and are caught in the conflict between two worlds: orthodoxy and freedom of choice. The group of legends generated by prayer for regaining erring souls appears in cycles, marking episodes of visions, precognition, prophecy, and healing.

There is no doubt that the narratives presented in this discussion support loyalty and devotion to Pentecostal ideology, endorsing the literal interpretation of salient Biblical passages. At the same time, they declare liberation from excepted norms of religiosity. They challenge and invite debate on two fronts. First, the legends oppose and attack the theses of mainstream religions, and criticize the secularization of status churches; secondly, they argue against dissenting family members who have become alienated from, or remained unaffected by, Pentecostalism. The stories, repeated by intensive solitary rethinking, cassette-replaying, or social retelling at a variety of occasions within and without the congregation, reaching the larger community of Pentecostals, are legends in the best sense of the word. Their passionate, emotional fervor as the voice of a despised minority belief expresses free opposition to majority religions.

As we have seen, the primary context of these legend narratives is religion. Religion for Pentecostals is the way of living focused on conversations with Jesus. Experiencing a joyous expectation of, and a constant excitement at being possessed by the Spirit of God, they experience miracles as daily events. The miracle of being in touch with Jesus all the time is regarded as evidence that they have made the right choice in turning away from the frivolities of earthly life. The promise of eternal happiness in Heaven has its price: no one knows when they will be called, so a constant readiness must be maintained without indulgence in earthly ("sinful") pleasures. Pentecostals are righteous and conservative in their judgments and intolerant of deviation, while they show tolerance toward the rebellious and scandalous lifestyles of their children. The tolerance is in accord with their humility and piety: prayer will work miracles, and in good time bring the erring children back to the church and endow them with the Holy Spirit.

Both categories of miracle legends presented here—those in sermons, and those in the form of testimonies—are inseparably interwoven with everyday activities; they are as much part of the sacred as the secular life of the Grace Tabernacle congregation, which communicates them as educational, entertaining, and confirming devices at formal or informal occasions, any time, without planning or preparation—they are integral to life and are pillars of the whole religious subculture.

6

Letters to the Dead

Your gentle face and patient smile
With sadness we recall
You had a kindly word for each
And died beloved by all.
The voice is mute and stilled the heart
That loves us well and true.
Oh, bitter was the trial to part
From one so good as you.
You are not forgotten loved one
Nor will you ever be.
As long as life and memory last
We will remember thee.
We miss you now, our hearts are sore.
As time goes by we miss you more.
Your loving smile, your gentle face.
No one can fill your vacant place.

Sadly missed by wife, daughter,
grandchildren and great-grandchildren.

Memoriams in Daily Papers

SINCE 1974 I have been clipping custom-related personal announcements from the classified ad section of Bloomington, Indiana's only local evening newspaper, the *Bloomington Herald-Telephone* (recently converted to a morning paper and renamed the *Bloomington Herald-Times*). Worlds apart from the faculty and student body of Indiana's large and prestigious university which is located there, this typical small town (situated in the midwest "Bible Belt" with an overwhelming Protestant Anglo-Saxon population of about 60,000) has been aptly characterized by the Hollywood film *Breaking Away*. The *Bloomington Herald-Times* is clearly a voice of the community it serves, functioning as a vehicle of social interaction and encouraging the maintenance of traditional forms of communication. In the printing of intimate customary and ritual messages that earlier had circulated among concerned participants on celebratory occasions in oral or handwritten form, designated newspaper columns have considerably increased their publicity.

These traditionally formulated messages, now published and handily accessible in the newspaper, reach beyond the nuclear family and kin to a wider audience and prolong and stress the significance of the pertinent event. Even more importantly, the printing of formulaic occasional poetry related to festive events reinforces conventional patterns and secures continuity of tradition.

People have become accustomed to looking at the classified ad section for information about happenings in the community and neighborhood, thus obtaining news about people they know and upcoming celebratory events. They are also encouraged to clip particularly attractive passages from the examples seen in the paper for adaptation in creating their own piece, if the time should come. Thus related to life cycle events and calendar customs, occasional domestic poetry has left the confines of oral and handwritten lay poetry and entered the print media. There, this poetry continues to bloom and help sustain community norms based on the teachings of the dominant Christian faith: family cohesion, sociability, piety, friendship, love of God and country. Indeed, the pertinent classified ad sections have become useful advisors in social etiquette, as much as Hallmark greeting cards help to fulfill ritual obligations at festive family events.

Although additional newspaper space is provided on special celebratory occasions (for example, Mother's Day, Father's Day, Valentine's Day) for expressions of gratitude to parents and love for sweethearts and friends, the two most important sections in the classified ads that contain ritual well-wishing are the "Happy Ads" and the "In Memoriams," or simply "Memoriams." Both categories celebrate the life cycle stations of family members; while the first addresses the living, the second calls on the dead. The immediate proximity of the two columns emphasizes the contrast: the tone and photos of the first are cheerful, often playfully jocular and teasing; the second is somber, mournful, and sentimental. Memorials display the unity of the entire family (composed of living and dead members) and express resignation to life's transitoriness and brevity; from birth, individuals are travelers, progressing from the living toward their otherworld family, tied to each other by bonds of love, and having obligations to both the living and dead. Birthdays, weddings and anniversaries are cheered in both sections, but memorial remembrances are for those who have completed the total course of the life cycle.

In searching for parallels through a random sampling of classified ad columns elsewhere in Indiana and from other states, I found, predictably, that memoriams are not unique to Bloomington. They are most conspicuous in the small towns across America or in medium-size towns like Charleston, South Carolina, and Batesville, Arkansas, and they are similarly found in Canada.[1] Larger and more cosmopolitan newspapers, ranging from the *Los*

Angeles Times to the *New York Times*, also print memoriams preceding or following death notices, but these seldom contain extensive poetry, only one or two stanzas at best, sandwiched between the introductory and closing formulaic statements. Limited to marking the anniversary of a family member's death, the people remembered in the big city ads are more heterogenous in terms of their religious affiliation and social class, and the texts lack the neighborliness so characteristic of the memoriams of provincial townspeople.

The ads from small-town newspapers show uniformity in the main outline, content, format, and style of the texts, which combine two or four detachable thematic units. The poems reflect uniformity in their religious philosophy and ideology which are deeply rooted in the general American Protestant (not necessarily sectarian) tradition and basic to the worldview supported by working-class fundamentalist believers.

There is a pervasive international literature on customs and beliefs and the poetry surrounding death, "the final stage of growth" (Kübler-Ross 1975). Ethnographic literature is rich in the study of institutional customs and personal performances related to death and the resulting behaviors and expressions that reflect ambiguities toward mortality (Ariès 1978; de Martino 1958; Danforth 1982; Douglass 1969; Huntington and Metcalf 1979). Much has been written by social scientists about coping with the loss of a relative, anxieties about experiencing the same fate, and the creation of an ideology of immortality (Alcock 1979). The ideology includes disposal of the body, bereavement, mourning, lamenting, farewell-taking, the religious belief underlying these practices, and the poetic-artistic expressions related to belief and custom (Mitford 1963; Stannard 1975; Warner 1961; Oring 1982; Moody 1976; Kastenbaum 1977; Benes 1977; Gillon 1972). Yet no study deals with "life after death," the remembering of the dead within a solid bond that keeps cemeteries active and their inhabitants alive as long as family members who knew them survive. "Memory's fond embrace," to cite from a memorial-ad poet, maintains contact after death's separation and incorporates the living into the world of the dead.[2] In terms of eternity, this life span is a limited time. It does not extend beyond a maximum of three or four generations, yet it is more important and lasting than final rites of passage, which focus on the speedy and safe disposal of the dead. Bonding is manifested and a cult of the dead is activated in two ways: graveyard visitation, including decoration of the graves (Gosnell and Gott 1989:218); and annual publication of the memorial poem. The two are similar symbolic acts but with diverse forms of expression. First is the entering into the "memorial garden" for a visit to the "city of the dead," and secondly, the composing of a poem expressing an outpouring of sentiments and experiences of visionary visitation at the cemetery. The cemetery (with its natural beauty—a modest replica of Heaven) is where resurrection is to be expected and is the ultimate home and the future scene of family reunion. The cemetery visit and the memorial poetry are often connected by ritual grave decoration that includes the depositing of the written poem as Bloomington informants have reported.

In what follows, I will describe memoriam poetry as it appears in the *Bloomington Herald-Times*, a representative corpus in its species, expressing the norms and values of provincial Protestant working-class Americans. I will trace its antecedents; identify its roots in tradition, its authors, and its social base; and discuss its current functions and significance for its creators and readers.

Origin and Background of the Genre

The publishing of memorial poems, as practiced today in the United States, has deep roots in history and incorporates many elements of earlier sacred and secular traditions. The poems have nothing in common with the heroic epic songs recited by professional male singers at the funeral vigils of powerful rulers and warriors. It is not like the ballad, lamenting the violent death of a tragic hero, nor like the funeral dirge or complaint of women chanted at rural wakes. Neither does it resemble modern-day death notices in urban newspapers (Bethke 1970; Klymasz 1975; Rihtman-Augustin 1978). The memorial ad is not epic but purely lyrical. It does not introduce the deceased by occupation and status; it is almost completely devoid of facts concerning personal achievements, excellence, cause of death, or practical details about real events. Characterization of the dead and others in the account, descriptions of events leading to the death, pain, mourning, and consolation are all expressed in a highly formulaic, so to speak objective, disengaged language, using traditional symbols and metaphors without many clues to reality.

The poems sometimes conceal violent and ugly stories behind sterile, sentimental commonplaces. One of my informants, when asked for the "real facts" about the people whose memoriams I had clipped from the paper, remarked, "Why cause pain by recalling gory details after so many years?" The ad that I showed her pictured a pretty young woman holding an infant. She had died in her trailer home from natural causes, and her baby had died of starvation by the time they were found a week later. "Why renew remorse and torture for the family?" asked my informant, the wife of a foreman at the RCA plant.

Victims of car wrecks, fires, and crimes; suicides; delinquents; drug addicts; and alcoholics who have caused their own demise are elevated to prescription sainthood by the memoriam's tone of Christian praise-poetry. Horror stories do not fit the genre in which the dead appear as central heroes, models of virtue and innocence, who are "too good for life," whom

"God needed for his choir of angels" because "he takes only the best."[3] Even when no violence was involved, the memory of suffering an extended illness, during which the entire family experienced the nightmares of dying, has faded away by the time the memoriams are due. The sight of bodily decay at the deathbed is suppressed by the peaceful funeral parlor display, and in another year—the first anniversary—the new image of the idealized, deathless loved one can be celebrated. Memoriams exhibit a positive facade from which negative features have been carefully edited. The tragedy of others, which sensation- and horror-loving people enjoy in tabloids, is not accepted within the confines of the family who suffered a loss. The American fetish for the right to privacy as well as the denial and euphemization of death (Becker 1973; Huntington and Metcalf 1979:194-97) are the motivation behind the memorial depiction of dead family members.

While reading the memoriam's simple stanzas, there is a feeling of *déjà vu*. Formulas are liberally borrowed from a stock of poems of didactic, ecclesiastic inspiration, coming from both scholastic and lay poetic tradition. These formulas—mostly similes, metaphors, phrases, cadences, stanzas and techniques, incremental repetition, nature symbols—recall the style of ballads, farewell songs, complaints, and elegies, while remaining separate entities, and are easily detachable from each other and reusable in other configurations.

Many of the phrases, sayings, and stanzas are familiar because they also appear on gravestones, such as: "gone but not forgotten;" "sadly missed but not forgotten;" "the vacant chair;"[4] "beautiful rosebud too sweet for life;" "gone home;" "he is not dead but sleepeth;" "one flower less on earth, one angel more in heaven." Memory cards, handed out after funerals or memorial services, and sympathy cards sent by mail use similar conventional phrases. Closely linked seem to be versions of memorial cards that I found from 1903. A dark card adorned with flowers, sunrays, and the phoenix resurrected from ashes features a photo of the deceased in the center and an eight-line memorial poem underneath. The inscriptions read: "In loving remembrance," and "Gone but not forgotten"; one card gives the deceased's name, rank, and time of birth and death. On another card the printed inscription is covered by this handwritten note: "Mariam Fishback School-mate and friend," concealing the original printed surface.

It is not difficult to trace the poetic props of memoriams to nineteenth-century American consolation literature, so aptly described by Ann Douglas as it emerged and prospered before and after the Civil War, between 1830 and 1880. Douglas defines consolation literature as including "not simply actual mourner's manuals, but also prayer manuals, poetry, hymns, fiction and biographies whose purpose is clearly consolatory, whose authors, in other words, are writing to reach and comfort those suffering bereavement or loss"

(Douglas 1975:48). Memoriams belong to this mass of material as not only poetic but also ideological models recognizable by the same orientation. They are based on the life-after-life idea, with the dead person as the central hero in his or her glorious ascent to Heaven. As a representative of the family, his or her mission is to make room for all loved ones who follow. As examples will demonstrate, the main motive of memoriams is the hope of eternal life in Heaven and restoration of the family unity that was broken by the death of a member.

Themes and Formats

What is a memoriam? It is a personal address to the deceased, an assurance that he or she is remembered. This statement of commitment also contains promise of continued remembering, of renewal of contact by repeated writing and publishing of memorials. In other words, by subsequent repetition, often rewriting, the memorial testimony strengthens the bond between the dead and the living and keeps the dead alive. The most prominent message in the texts concerns memorialization in terms of metaphors, as in the following excerpts:

Memories are treasures no one can steal
*
Memories are keepsakes no one can steal
Death is a wound no one can heal
*
but the memories of you no one can steal
*
The memory of those days we had
are like the sun's bright ray
*
For today in memories [sic] garden
We still walk side by side
*
Remembrance is a golden chain,
death tries to break but all in vain
*
I'll never lose sweet memories
for I loved you so much
*
Softly the leaves of memory fall
gently we gather and cherish them all
*
Planted deep in Memory's Garden
and watered daily with our tears
*
Beautiful memories are all we have left
*
You are not forgotten, loved one

nor will you ever be,
as long as life and memory lasts
we will remember thee
*
Memory has a magic way
of keeping loved ones near
*
I'll live in Memory's Garden dear,
with the happy days we've known
. . . for memory is the only friend
that grief can call its own
*
All the memories you left us
we treasure each day,
your voice, your smile are everywhere
and only a memory away
*
Love and memory will never die
*
Deep in our hearts memories are kept

Memoriams are usually composed of three parts: an introduction and statement of purpose, the main address, and the closing words, complete with the signature of the sender(s). The first and third parts are mostly factual and general, with almost no variation. They may constitute the whole text, particularly for general commemorative patriotic holidays like Memorial Day, when all departed family members are listed in the remembrance notice in the order of their deaths. The memoriam is usually signed by all immediate survivors. For example:

In loving memory of my dear husband XY, who departed this life sixteen years ago today
*
In memory of K. P. who entered into Eternal Rest three years ago, October 3, 1972
*
In memory of our mother Mrs. F. L. who passed away six years ago, February 6

These statements address the general public, mainly announcing the intent of memorializing a certain person who is identified by name, and sometimes adding the birth and death dates.

The most common memorial poem is the personal letter to the departed relative, sometimes beginning with a direct address: "Dear Jay" and signed, "Until then—Love, Kim"; "Dear Mike," signed, "Love you Mike, Aunt Jane." One girl sent a letter marked "Airmail to Heaven," addressed "Dear Dad," and signed "I love you, your daughter Darlene." This letter appears in both 1986 and 1987, but the memorial texts of the poem differ considerably. Another "Dear Dad" letter sent a year after his death remembers the family's difficulty to

> realize after Mom died a part of you
> went with her, and you weren't the same.
> His children ask him,
> Tell her we love her and we understand.
> And we hope and pray we'll see you both in Gloryland.

Another poem utilizes the telephone to make a long-distance call to Heaven to get in touch with a beloved grandfather. Variants of the "Hello Operator" text (1987 and 1988) were addressed to grandfather ("Papaw")[5] and were written by granddaughters "Sherry Lee Meadows" and "Joan Myers," respectively, on the first and second anniversaries of his death. These memoriams follow another memoriam text signed by all family members. The telephone message explicitly "written" by the granddaughters indicates a special relationship between them and their grandfather. However, both are also signed by other grandchildren and great-grandchildren. The texts are identical, but the 1988 version is double the size of the one from 1987. The theme of the first makes contact and gives a message of love, whereas the second elaborates on the happy social life of Papaw in Heaven. According to Sherry Lee, who enjoyed writing poems for her grandfather's birthday or for Christmas, it was natural to her to pick up the phone and make a call in order to chat with him. Saddened by his loss, she liked to imagine that Heaven might be only a phone call away. Similar close proximity is expressed in the letter to "Dear granpa" by granddaughter Kayla:

> Even though I never got to see you I know you can see me from up there in heaven. It's not fair that I never got to see you, but someday I will. We all miss you and love you papaw.

Other signs of domesticity, which is characteristic of this poetry (Welter 1981), appear in some of the letters. Spontaneous, heartfelt recollections appear in the compositions of grandmothers or aunts, mourning the loss of a favorite child:

> Dean, I miss you so much, miss you teasing me, miss your arms around me telling me you love me, and telling me "I am the best-looking nephew you have got." I miss you and Mark playing basketball in my driveway. I look out my kitchen window Dean and think of the time you would pass and then back up to come and see me. . . . Love you Dean, Aunt Barb.

Dean's grandmother also gives an account of their relationship and past life together:

I miss you at church for so many times you came up and hugged me.
We miss you on Saturday coming over many times to carry in the wood or just to help when your papaw was sick.

Among the many expressions of domesticity, a letter written by a daughter to her father displays their joking relationship, underscoring how many ways there are to conceal grief in a memoriam. Asking the Lord to have the angels bake him a white cake with coconut icing despite the danger of cholesterol, the letter assures Dad of a future reunion. Until then, the daughter cannot resist telling a joke she had heard "the other day": "Do you know how they carpool in Kentucky? They meet at work."

The continuation of this joking relationship is apparent in the subsequent 1993 birthday letter: "Happy birthday, Dad, I've asked the angels if they would make a Mississippi Mud cake for you." A postscript follows: "Hey, Dad, do you know how you can tell if a Purdue secretary has been using your computer? There's white-out on the screen."

The closer to reality, the less poetic these reminiscences become. The letter type memorial is, as a rule, in verse, formulaic, and abstract from real life. The main text is considerably longer and more variable than the personal reference framing it, despite strong dependence on two- and four-line formulaic rhymes, sayings, and expressions.

The content of the letter type of memorial poem has a linear structure from separation to reunion. It is built on the former relationship between the addresser and the addressee, the unity that has been disrupted temporarily by death, and the need to have it restored. The underlying Christian mythology rather liberally follows general Protestant conceptions of life on earth, death, Heaven, God's will, and immortality, and provides for a formulaic embroidery of the stages between life and death. I (the living) within this framework, assure you (the dead) that death's separation is only temporary, and reunion is soon to come on a happier plane. The two of us (the dead and living) walk on separate roads—I in the valley of darkness on earth, you on the glorious heavenly path, and until our reunion we are bonded together by memories of a past good life.

Within this frame, the letter begins with reference to the anniversary of the death it commemorates and the pain it called to mind, for example, on a visit to the cemetery:

The rain is softly falling upon your grave today.
Seventeen years ago you left us but we miss you more each day

Then joyful events of life together are recalled, amidst the pain of loss, of being left alone with the "vacant chair" and the "empty place no one can fill."

> A million times we needed you
> a million times we've cried
> *
> Since you have gone away from me
> life is a blue abyss
> *
> You went first, and I remain, to walk the road alone

The next section of the poem features the remembered love one's fine personal features schematically:

> God molded her heart in pure gold
> *
> A heart that was pure gold
> *
> Your loving smile, your gentle face
> no one can fill your vacant place

or

> Your loving smile, your gentle face,
> no one on earth can ever take your place
> *
> Your gentle face and patient smile. . . .
> you had a kindly word for each
> and died beloved by all.

The description of the passing away of the addressee is also schematic: "A golden heart stopped beating"; "God called you away"; "You were called away"; "The voice is mute and stilled the heart"; "Your smiles are gone forever, your hand we cannot touch."

For the passing away of those who died after a long illness, a variety of formulas were used:

> God saw how you were suffering
> and the hill too hard to climb
> He closed your weary eyelids,
> and whispered: peace be thine
> *
> You suffered a lot but showed no pain
> *
> God called you from your pain
> *
> We watched through all your suffering
> and often had to cry,

for we knew that very soon
we'd have to say goodbye
                    *
In tears I saw you sinking
I watched you fade away
my heart was almost breaking,
you fought so hard to stay.
But when I saw you sleeping
so peaceful, far from pain,
I would not wish you back
to suffer that again.

The clichés for those who died unexpectedly and prematurely differ considerably. "Before we knew it, you were gone," is often said, stressing the fact that the family could not say a last farewell, that the death occurred at a place where the family could not be present to help ease the suffering of separation:

You could not say Goodbye
you were gone before I knew it
and only God knows why
                    *
He had little thought when leaving home
he would return no more
                    *
Just when his days seemed brightest
just when his hopes seemed best
                    *
sudden and unexpected
three years ago today
                    *
You went away with no farewell
not a wave of your precious hand.

Jack Hoard used this theme in the memorial poem he wrote for his son Mike, who was killed when he was struck by lightning. In a conversation at his home, the father emphasized the importance of saying goodbye to one's loved ones. Jack reminisced about what a man who had lost a son told him

"Be sure to tell your children goodbye when they walk out of the door because you might not see them again." It wasn't two or three months later, till Mike got killed. And then, later I was telling another man to be sure and tell his children 'bye, because he might not see them, and you know, it wasn't but just a few months before he lost a son. And you know, it was just kind of funny how that was passed down.

For murder or accident victims and servicemen killed in the line of duty, family members have formulated longer complaints calling for witnesses to the tragedy and rhythmically repeating the rhetorical question, Why? The full story, foregrounded by captions under the picture of the deceased, rarely appears: "Killed by a drunken driver"; "killed by a bowling ball"; "Killed in action in Vietnam"; "Rode his Honda into Heaven"; "Killed three years ago today."

In cases of both expected and sudden death, the formula continues with the question, Why? "What purpose could the Saviour have to take the beloved?"; "Why must our loved one die?" But the reason is at hand: God needed the person because he or she was special, "because he only takes the best."

> God picks the best to go first,
> and leaves the rest to mourn
> *
> God picked you as his flower from earth
> and the angels wanted him too
> *
> God took Steve up above
> and planted him in the Garden of Love
> He now sings tenor in the angel choir
> That club of glee to which he will aspire
> *
> God needed a good man to be with him
> so he looked us all over and then chose you
> *
> God needed another angel to worship before his
> throne
> so he looked down from Heaven and called our Steven
> home.

The cemetery garden, the parallel to Heaven's garden, is clear in this symbolism. Humans are seen as flowers to be picked and planted into the Garden of Love (Heaven), there to sing and worship God as the angels do. The dead, freed from the filth of earthly life, deserve eternal life. In the memoriams, the celebrated dead are presented as models of virtue. The theological ambiguity in the distinction between body and soul in Western culture is also clear in this poetic interpretation. The resurrected Christ himself presents the ambiguity between the natural and the spiritual body (1 Corinthians 15:35–53); the body is the shell of the soul, which turns to ashes and dust in the cemetery while the spirit triumphantly enters Heaven. Thousands of witnesses to near-death experiences narrate an identical story wherein their spirit temporarily leaves their body and briefly tastes eternal happiness, guided by the radiant figure of Jesus at the end of a dark tunnel (Moody 1976). In the newspapers, accounts of such experiences are everyday: "A New Harmony woman says she saw Jesus and the gates of Heaven as doctors were working to save her in a hospital operating room. . . . she told her family she had died and seen Jesus" *(Bloomington Herald-Times,* 10 March 1990). Yet homiletic literature supplies the common Western believer with materials to visualize ascendants to Heaven in their mortal bodies—just as they looked in the prime of their lives. In fact, Heaven's population is described as beautiful and youthful. During an episode of "The Phil Donahue Show" that dealt with near-death experiences (July 8, 1988), a woman testified that she had met her brother of whose existence she had been unaware because he died as an infant before her birth. He appeared to her now in Heaven as a young adult because the new body of the dead always remains a young grown-up. Memorial letter writers cast their eyes upward in expectation of a new and a real life in Heaven, surrounded by family members in their beautified shapes.[6]

Repeatedly the memorial letter speaks of death as "going home" to Heaven, a concept propagated by the already-mentioned consolation literature, creating the impression of continuity of earthly life, where families separated by death can reunite in an idyllic tranquility (Oring 1982:70). The models for this concept, designed by clergymen and churchwomen, focused "on the accessibility of the celestial kingdom to earthly intelligence and the similarities between the two worlds which made communication possible. They depicted and emphasized heaven as a continuation and glorification of the domestic sphere" (Douglas 1975:55). The same idea about "Heaven our Home" in modern memoriams was elaborated and exemplified in Elizabeth Stuart Phelps's novel of 1868 (Phelps 1964). Her sacred allegory describes Heaven as an earth-like world, including its landscape, flora and fauna, children's toys, social life, and habitats. "What would be done with the millions who, from the time of Adam, have been gathering there, unless they lived under the conditions of organized society? Organized society involves homes, not unlike the homes of this world."[7]

"There is a hereafter. It is unthinkable that people should just die and that be the end" was the feeling held in common by Middletowners of Muncie, Indiana, as reported by the Lynds (Lynd and Lynd 1937:416). Out of sixty-eight working-class women, thirty-one thought often or every day about the "Heavenly home" waiting for them. Said one:

> My first husband died, leaving me with five children. I'm trying to bring them up to be good Christians, for that's the only way they will ever get to see their father. I just *know* he's up in Heaven now waiting for us! (Lynd and Lynd 1956:324–25)

Indeed, memorial letters speak of death as "going home" to Heaven as a natural course upon the call of God. There is no question about going to Heaven once life's course on earth is completed. The Catholic concept of

Hell and Purgatory is completely missing from this mythology. The departed one enters heaven with glory and will become the spokesman for his or her earthly family members. The departed are not poor souls whose well-being in the hereafter greatly depends on how much the living cultivate their memory, tend their graves, or pay for their masses. As memorials for small children, young people, and virtuous mothers state, Heaven is regarded as the original home from where God lent them to parents for a short time ("You were such a good son, I thank God for lending you to me for 22 years"). A whole origin legend is told in a Mother's Day memoriam about the creation of a mother who was sent to earth by God for a short while:

> He touched her soul, and softly said,
> My earthly pride you'll be,
> and then He placed her on a cloud
> and sent her down to us.

When people die, they are invited "up there":

> The pearly gates were opened
> a gentle voice said "come"

or:

> Heaven's gates were open
> seventeen years today
> goodbyes were left unspoken,
> you suddenly slipped away
> *
> And "the mansion above" was waiting
> in a better place on Heaven's avenue
> *
> Up the pathway to Heaven
> With Jesus the manager and also the guide
> in a place or mansion He planned long ago;
> *
> He rewarded you the door key to your
> "Mansions Upstairs"

and continuing with the mansion metaphor:

> We know that you are happy
> in the mansion of the best,
> Where there is no pain and sorrow,
> In a place of Light and Beauty
> That God has set aside,

a house of many mansions
where His loved ones will abide.[8]

"Safely home in Heaven at last" is another popular formula, followed by a schematic description of Heaven as a "beautiful garden where the flowers are ever-blooming, and where the blessed are living in ever-lasting joy." In the next step, the "Blessed One in Heaven," the memorialized relative who has already arrived at the destination, speaks to the aspiring relative left behind on earth:

Don't cry, I am only sleeping

or:

I am not dead, I am only sleeping

and paraphrasing the words of the resurrected Christ:

Do not stand at my grave and weep
I am not there, I do not sleep

Death is more the beginning of victory than the triumph of tragedy.

At this point the letter type of memoriam changes tone. The pain, sorrow, and earthly drudgery of the past are gone and forgotten. Now for the living comes the promise of "going home" to a happy reunion.[9]

"We will meet again some day" is the recurrent cliché that closes the memorial letter. Those who are left alone, widows in particular, long for this moment of reunion:

You are waiting for me by the river
just across the silent stream
*
I lost a friend and gained a guardian angel
*
If I could take steps out of heartaches
and use my teardrops too,
I would make a stairway to Heaven
and climb it each day just to be with you

It is explicitly stated that the living can count on those who have entered Heaven before them. The cherished parent, child, or spouse is anxiously waiting:

Watching till we come home to him
anxious if we are late,
watching from Heaven's window
leaning from Heaven's gate

*
Angels sing a sweeter song
You walk the hills of glory,
you sit beside God's throne
As you await us at the river
where we will meet some day

and again:

We know you are waiting in God's Mansion far away
and our only desire is to be with you, some glorious day.

The Beloved One is assured of the reunion:

Wait patiently Terry,
We are coming too
When God calls us at last
*
Honey, we'll meet again some day
*
I pray someday to meet you, Jay,
In a beautiful and bright tomorrow

A subvariant of the personal letter type of memorial poem is the "letter to God," which is more reverent and prayer-like. Its central theme is supplication for the Lord to take good care of the beloved since the writer can no longer do so. "Dear Lord" or "Sweet Jesus," "take care of Butch till I get there"; or "Watch over Mike, be his Mom and Dad as we tried to be for 22 years." The author, usually a mother or wife, asks for forgiveness and explains her reasons for asking this favor: "Dear Lord, forgive a selfish tear. . . . But he was ours, we loved him so . . . " Others thank God for sending them the beautiful person for a limited time before taking him/her away, and they are thankful for the pleasure they have in their remaining life with family and friends. The letter then switches back to a more informal style to address the departed, and ends with the usual personal memorialization.

A third type of memorial is the poem written for and dedicated to the departed but only indirectly addressing him or her in the introductory and closing formula. This kind of poem allows room for more originality in formulating feelings. Original lines appear as links between two clichés, two- or four-line stanzas or cadences. Together they are complaints, sentimental reflections about painful memories of tragic life experiences and separations. The main theme is the survivor's loneliness and tortured thoughts as he or she recalls the time of death. The tone is somber, without hope or relief. The complaint is appropriately staged in a cemetery during autumn's decay: fallen leaves, rain, and moonless dark nights. The author sometimes has a title for the poem: "A Broken Heart," "A Humble Preacher," "Together in God," "Golden Thoughts," "Fallen Leaves," or "Loving Memories."

There is great variation within the main type of these complaint poems. The most common variant among them elaborates one of the formulaic themes: remembering the departed, the loneliness caused by the loss, separation, an episode from their past, loving relationship, or detailed description and praise of the superior human qualities and virtues of the deceased. The language is highly inflated and elegiac, rich in homily-like religious references and sometimes quotations from the Bible. Despite this uniformity in style, tone, and theme, and the restriction to a limited stock of expressive motifs, the poems display extreme variability. The poetry, which draws on both the tradition of consolation literature and occasional ritual verse making, uses conventional formulas shared with odes, elegies, hymns, sermons, and obituaries.

The Closing Formula and the Identity of the Author

In observing the closing formula of the memoriam, with several signatures including the author/initiator and the endorsers, all of whom have diverse motivations, it is inevitable to raise the questions: Who writes memorial poems? How does the occasional poetry tradition continue to appear in the pages of newspapers? As several of my informants from Bloomington and other North American towns told me, the daily appearance of memoriams in the newspaper encourages prospective authors to create (or compile) their own poems and fulfill obligations to memorialize dead family members at anniversaries and birthdays.

In a telephone interview on 26 February 1992, Linda Kinsey Adams talked to Leah Leahy, assistant circulation manager of the *Bloomington Herald-Times*, about the customers who place memoriam ads in the newspaper. As an insider and an area native, familiar with the tradition, Leahy was able to give valuable information about local practice. She has been working at the newspaper for five-and-a-half years and could remember a variety of deaths and pertinent memoriams. Although the *Herald-Times* has two booklets of compiled samples which it puts at the disposal of the people, she estimates only twenty percent use the book, while eighty percent make up their own verses. People come in with a poem they have seen and liked and edit it to fit someone else: "One can tell that it was written specifically for that person."

Leahy recalls that memoriam column advertisers have to be handled with extra understanding and care, not as if they are people wanting to sell a car or a washing machine. Sometimes people get "too" personal, wanting to recount murder details or the like, but the newspaper employees advise the customer to use the ad to honor the dead rather than as a vehicle of vengeance; in such cases the customers are helped with style editing. Of course, it is women who do the memoriams. They are more emotional. In the case of a recent death, the death of a child or an accident victim, or the first anniversary or birthday of the deceased, the customers often are in tears and need to be comforted: "It's okay, take your time," they are told; but after two years or so, as time goes on, the placing of the memoriam is less emotional and becomes rather an expression that the survivors still care for their dead relative.

The newspaper keeps a file for the pictures that customers bring in so that they can be reused in the following years. Leahy says that "this is a social thing." When her grandfather passed away, the grandmother wanted the memoriam every year at anniversaries and birthdays, "because that's what other people did, to make people aware of his anniversary, because it's done that way." The newspaper office gets many requests to have the clipping of the memoriam laminated for keeps.

Ms. Leahy allowed us to copy the two booklets the Herald-Times offers to customers. Both contain selections from earlier printings. *In Memoriam* has 114 numbered two-to-eight liners; *Tender Tributes to Those Who Have Gone Before* has 104 somewhat longer texts. Without exception, the items are empty formulas to be personalized for "daughter or wife," "father or brother," "mother or sister," "husband or son," "infants," "military," or "general." I was surprised by the scarcity of familiar stanzas that I found most popular during my data gathering. It seems memoriam authors are more creative and inspired by a much larger body of lyrical clichés than one would believe at first glance.

According to informants, it is usually housewives and mothers who routinely read the ad pages to find the latest memoriams. They enjoy recalling memories of the people they knew and the circumstances of their passing, visiting the funeral home, attending funerals, and so on. They muse over the past while reading the poems, and with a critical eye, judge appropriateness and adequacy. They clip whole pieces or passages that they feel are particularly poignant. It is the women's role to mark family occasions during the calendar year and the life cycle, and they regard it as their privilege, as representatives of the family, to report and publicize joyous and mournful changes in its life by means of the newspaper ad column. The significance of the event is emphasized by the authority of print. Clippings then constitute the models for actualized new versions.

Although writing and placing memoriams in the classified ad column is not an obligation imposed by authority (churches or civic institutions), it is generally felt that it should be done. This is particularly true in small towns where working-class people share neighborhoods, workplaces, and churches;

intermarry; and constitute close-knit communities. In Bloomington and neighboring towns it was easy to find memoriam authors: a glance at the names or the photo on a clipping—informants easily identified others as members of the same network of a family or neighborhood. A whole genealogical chart emerged from our conversations as people placed individuals as personally known or "heard of " to them. Neighbors, friends, and more distant relatives usually approvingly remembered such demonstrations of love and care toward a departed family member: "It means she really was thinking of him; she is a good woman," or "This family is not neglecting their lost son." But they also say that to write a memoriam "is a heartfelt, individual endeavor, letting everyone know whoever reads it, how they loved that person, not a must." "My mother would put in something occasionally," said one informant, "when she really felt [she was] missing her dad, not every year, just when she had a dream of him. She liked to write. She wrote a poem to all of her children, all six of us."

Beyond the religious persuasion of the consolation literature that seems to have influenced working-class American life, custom, and ideology, and endowed lay poets with occasional poetry formulas, another tradition must be taken into consideration. Researching the custom of newspaper memorializing led to the discovery of a lay poetic tradition among women. Full-time homemakers or women who combine their household duties with part- or full-time service as teachers, nurses, or office, factory, or domestic workers, are the authors of this poetry. Contemporary feminist literature has described the artistry of penwomen in nineteenth-century America[10] and traced it to the enculturation of women to their assignee role of "true womanhood" (Welter 1966) which was fostered by pious clerical persuasion (Douglas 1975). However, the feminine lay poetry that sprang from the same ideology has been overlooked. The American idealization of femininity "became interwoven into the defense and promulgation of Christian religion," writes Amanda Porterfield, and "as religion became a matter of family persuasion, women became arbiters of religious life, persuasive, religious authorities as well as exemplars of religious devotion" (Porterfield 1980:78). As pointed out by Welter, the concept of the ideal woman promulgated by women's magazines, gift annuals, and religious literature is identical with that held by the authors of twentieth-century amateur poetry and classified ad memoriams.

These penwomen take full responsibility for the duties conferred upon them in old-fashioned, mostly lower-middle-class patriarchal American households. Included in their role as selfless, devoted partners and representatives of their husbands, they are carrying out the husbands' wishes, nurturing, educating, and enculturating children to become observant Christians. It is their duty also to care for the old and sick, attend funerals, visit graves, and remember the dead. Evidently, in traditional families, these family-supporting roles of women include the organization and execution of ceremonial and festive ritual acts as well as the preparation of materials for the rites of passage for the family. Since these women are the custodians of family values, they compose the texts for occasional poetry, mark and record important family events, initiate family reunions, write diaries, travelogues, family histories, and genealogies, create almanacs, and fill autograph and photograph albums and scrapbooks, mixing and matching self-authored, adapted, and copied pieces of traditional poetry. These writings cultivate tradition and respect for ancestry, particularly for the parental generation.

Doris McDaniel, a farm woman from Martinsville, Indiana, memorialized her father in a 1957 handwritten book.[11] This is a typical example, illustrating the religious hereafter orientation of traditional women's poetry. The book consists of the family history, the genealogy of the McDaniel family, and poems. The history begins with the McDaniels's settlement in the nineteenth century. However, it focuses on the lifetime of her father as Doris recalled episodes from her early childhood. Characteristically, the book is dedicated: "to my mother, who was a constant help mate,/shared all of dad's joys, hardships and sorrows./She helped select materials for this book." The book contains forty-two poems written by eight women—daughters, nieces, and daughters-in-law of Dad. These poems—all occasional, celebratory—belong to the same stock of folk lyrics as the memorial ads. Two of them memorialize the patriarch, and eight others pay tribute to the passing of other male relatives and are strikingly similar to the modern newspaper prints.

The final part of memoriams, the concluding part of the frame of the poem, ends with the farewell note "Sadly missed" and the signature of one or several names. This style of conclusion is indirect enough to address both the deceased relative and the reading audience at large. But who is the author of the poem if there are so many co-signers? In general, all family members sign it with the one closest to the deceased at the top of the list: "Sadly missed by wife Laura," while others are named only in terms of kinship affiliation ("son, daughters, grandchildren, great-grandchildren"; or "Wife Bessie, daughters, grandchildren and in-laws"; or even "Wife, children, brothers, sister, grandchildren, nieces and nephews." In other ads, both names and kin terms are indicated: "Parents, Mr. and Mrs. Edthel Kinser, Sisters Kathryn, Audrey, Reba, Roberta and Shirley, Brother Sheldon and Son Eddy Ray"; or "Parents Dernal and Venta, Brothers Loren, Benjamin, Daniel, Joseph and Samuel, Sisters Beverly, Lois, Leah, Lydia, Patricia and Susan. Also his many relatives and friends." And in still others, only names without affiliation are given: "Jean, Linda, John, Polly, Mike, Chrystal, John D. II and Christopher." It often happens that more than one memoriam—sometimes as many as four to six—address the same person at the same time, signed by parents, siblings, children, grandchildren, and sometimes friends, if the deceased is young.

It seems evident that one of the signers initiated each memoriam and can be regarded as the author. While it would make sense to assume that the author is the first name on the list, it is more likely that the listing follows the order of family relationships. It is the father or the mother, husband or wife whose loss is the greatest and whose name is signed first, followed by sons, daughters, grandchildren, and eventually great-grandchildren. Beyond the straight line of descendants, usually three generations, seldom are aunts and uncles or in-laws included; the names of friends appear even less often. Sometimes a general reference to "relatives" is made, but as a rule more distant relatives and friends would rather write their own memoriams. Commonly, the main memoriam, with a long list of family membership appended, is accompanied by several briefer memoriams signed by siblings, grandchildren, and other relatives, alone or in smaller family units. Thus anyone may compose a memoriam as a gesture of compassion, even if he or she is already included in the ad placed by the larger family unit. Indeed, the identity of the author is hard to guess from the long list of co-signers. For example, Steve Bartlett, killed by a drunk driver, is regularly memorialized twice a year (birthday and anniversary) by his parents, five siblings, relatives, and friends; but only his mother and sister Teri write the poems.

To initiate a memoriam is a matter of choice, a decision which as an elementary folkloric act leads to the composition of a text. The practice of copying or rewriting an earlier version of a text was regarded as authoring, prior to the advent of printing and protection by copyright law. Medieval monks adjusted exempla for their own homiletic practice, thus spreading stories among the folk. Through the centuries, itinerants (soldiers, peddlers, exiles, and emigrants) copied favorite song texts that fitted popular tunes for their own delight and used them for entertainment on social and ceremonial occasions. In many songbooks that I have seen, each item was indiscriminately signed by the compiler as "written by . . . " whether it was written by known or unknown authors. This is also the manner in which authorship is assumed in the case of formulaic memoriams. The author is the one who suggests the ad, and the others endorse it as co-authors, allowing their names to be underwritten. Authorship has to be defined in this case rather liberally, ranging from simple copying to the compilation of floating formulas, borrowing popular stanzas from known and unknown authors and adding one's own. But how do the authors explain their technique of composition?

"Do you clip memoriams?" I asked Mrs. Thelma Crohn. "No, no," was the emphatic answer, "but somebody clips mine. I've seen 'em repeated. I don't copy nobody's memoriams. I don't. They shouldn't. They are free to anybody." "Do you choose your own?" "I might take a few words maybe some of'm that I still like to express to him but word it differently," she said, and continued:

> I always was a person to express my sentiments . . . but I never NEVER copied. Just like that. One song, you know . . . "In this life I was loved by" to figure out what I want to put in it . . . because in this life we were loved by him . . . was on TV. But I probably used one line of it . . . Everything he said fits my husband but I wouldn't use all of it, just a line or two . . . And then, there was one other song: "True love never goes away." And when I put this in there, you know, so it was, if we got true love, it is the same as it was yesterday, it never changes, you know.

Lynne Bruner, mother of little Timothy, admitted writing and copying memoriams for him twice a year since 1973, when he died. She scans out-of-town newspapers for texts appropriate for small children.

Sara Bartlett spoke of a combination of "what I saw, remembered reading and what I also felt. Most of it just done. In the middle of the night, like two or three in the morning when I get up, I just sit down and put it together. And the next day I look at it and rearrange it." She had been composing elaborate texts twice a year since 1987. To the 14 August 1992 anniversary date she added a prayer copied from a prayer book. Her daughter Teri "writes straight from her heart. She does not copy much." However, for the same anniversary, Teri picked her idea "from a card she read."

These three examples reveal the complexity of folk poetry making. Floating lines, traditional formulas multiply and offer more choices for folk poets to create new verses as they are supplied by electronic transmission (TV, radio, video, CD) or printed books, magazines, and greeting cards.

Even if the evidence of my more than a thousand samples did not indicate the fact, it would seem plausible that those who sign first following the "sadly missed" farewell note are mostly women—mothers, sisters, stepmothers, grandmothers, nieces, aunts, daughters, granddaughters, and girlfriends. Eighty to ninety percent of all first signers are women, although only twenty-seven percent of the women claim authorship of the memoriam. For example, in the following item, the author modestly signs her name at the end of the list of family members: "Written in memory of our mother, AVA HACKER, who passed away 13 years ago November 28, 1961. (By daughter Joan)" and after the text: "Sadly missed by husband Clint, son Richard, daughters Mary, Louise and Joan, also grandchildren."

In another example, the statement of authorship follows the poem: "Poem written by Aunt Needy. Sadly missed by Friends, Family and especially by daughter." The poem "Humble Preacher," memorializing Raymond Hughes, is written by Betty Hughes, but no indication is given of where she stands among the endorsing wife and children, while the poem "Broken Heart," for John Hawkins, identifies the author at the end ("By Patricia Beckham, sister"). She is listed later as "sister Patty," third among her siblings.

The author-signed poems range from the most formulaic to the most individualistic. Among the memoriam authors, I found only one well-known professional writer's name: Helen Stein Rice. Her name appears in five instances (three times in Bloomington, and once each in Pampa, Texas, and Charleston, South Carolina). Rice's poetry books are written for the bereaved and are sold in religious accessory and stationery stores. Her poetry contains as many formulaic clichés as those of non-professionals. However, in most cases people do not seem to favor direct copying.

Domesticity and Family Cohesion

Memoriams may also include a picture of the memorialized. Just as photographs on graveyard monuments are popular, so are the pictures for memoriams. About forty percent of my sample include a photograph at the top of the ad, which, as an informant has observed, makes the memoriam look like a bookmark. The families often laminate these memoriams and keep them preserved in a box or a prayer book in the home, along with other cherished belongings of the departed. Most of the photos show a smiling person: a cuddly baby, a pretty child, a cute teenager, a handsome young man or woman, a nice old lady, a beaming grandpa. They probably represent the last good, flattering picture of the deceased taken prior to illness and suffering. The photos actually help to keep the dead alive, fixing not only their ideal image but keeping them magically ageless for eternity, exactly as the family wants to see them in the hereafter.

For this purpose most of the photographs are informal snapshots, more lifelike and realistic than formal or professional photographs that display individuals in their Sunday best. Formal wear in memoriam photographs depicts discomfort and distortion of the normal self. Photos can reveal much more about the social status, class, and cultural background of the deceased and his or her relatives than the text of the memoriams: Jim Smith poses with a dummy of Santa Claus; Gerald Hillenburg wears his bus driver's cap, John Laughlin a sweatshirt and baseball cap, Ray Sylvester a farmer's hat, Doc Boltinghouse, suspenders. Most men wear open-necked shirts without a necktie. "My father never wore a necktie," commented Miriam Altop, who cleans houses and counsels Girl Scouts. "He was a working man and wanted to be buried in his favorite plaid shirt."

Several people are seen posing with their pets, petting them or holding them lovingly on their laps. The latest fashion is apparent among the young:

Adidas T-shirts, jogging outfits, young girls and young men with long straight hair. The printing of photographs of heavily bearded hippies indicates the remarkable tolerance of the conservative families in this subculture. Among these numerous memorials, one written by the sister of Dennis Eads states: "A heavy beard adorned his handsome face / And he wore it so proudly with charm and grace."

There seems to be a taboo against showing the picture of the dead in the company of living family members. When a photo features a young mother with her baby in her arms, two sisters together, a couple, or an entire family, the memoriam commemorates all of them because they died either together in an accident, or separately at different times. Linda Lou Gilliland's 1961 photo, printed annually, was replaced by a picture of her and her brother Sheldon following his death in 1988.

Memoriams with or without photographs are, as a rule, published annually with more or less regularity on the anniversary of the death. Some celebrate only round number anniversaries—the fifth or tenth year, while others are more whimsical. Writing memoriams is done when the author feels like doing it. As a telephone operator told me, it occurs "as they dream of that lost son or daughter; it comes so strongly, as an intuition, a voice, a face, and you feel so guilty to survive!" Or, memoriams are written when "God puts the words into her mind," as a Pentecostal author said. Considering the span of human life and the fact that a solid family unit is usually limited to three generations, the notice for Bobbie Hodges, "who passed away March 3, 1926 on his 8th birthday," the one for Violet Polley who died in 1943, and the one for Henry Siedl, "who left us 62 years ago" are remarkable testimonies to the longevity of family cohesion. Bobbie's succinct memoriam is characteristically formulaic with minimal personal addition:

> The rain is softly falling upon your grave today
> You left us so many years ago, but we miss you more each day.
> We realize God always takes the best.
> We saw you growing weary,
> So He whispered come and rest.
> Fifty-five years ago you left us,
> But your smiling face still lingers with us.
> And your cute little ways are always before us.
> There's no one, Bobbie, that can ever take your place.
>   Loved by all, Mom, Kay & Ann.

Other examples of faithfulness to long-departed loved ones extend as far back as twenty, twenty-two, twenty-five, and thirty years. In my sample, the annual remembrance continues for a period of at least ten years; less commonly it goes beyond that time, up to twenty years.

The length of the poem, its variation, frequency, and tenacity of commemoration are not related. For example, the pretty smiling face of Linda Lou Gilliland, who passed away on January 23, 1961, appeared annually between 1975 and 1989. Until 1979, new poems were written five times, while the following six ads contained only the opening and closing formula. Whalley Ervin's mother, with co-signing family members, wrote personal addresses to her 22-year-old son three, seven, and ten years after his death. Each poem differs from the others. All the different memoriams for white-haired Etta Shields (five of them for anniversaries, and one for Mother's Day) are signed by daughter Theo with only the vague reference "we" used to include other family members. The Shields family of Bloomington seems to have a solid memoriam tradition; diverse poems for father Phillip, mother Ida, and 21-year-old Ricky Scott were published annually and signed by family members. Of the five memoriams for tiny Timothy Bruner ("rosebud," "Angel," "sweetest flower"), two are identical, the rest diverse, with the first being the longest—six stanzas. In the case of 20-year-old Becky Lawson, three different photographs were printed and the four poems dedicated by "mommie and sisters," one by "best friend" and one by "husband and family" are all different, and the occasions also differ. The seven memoriams for Wayne Holtsclaw (three by his wife, three by daughter and family, and one from the grandchildren) include a photograph three times. The picture and poem for Buck Humphrey are identical in the first, third, eighth, and ninth annual memoriams, probably because the memoriam was authored by daughter Cindi, who was the original lone signer.

The variability of the memoriams is controlled by thematic similarity, and like melody and rhythm in the case of lyrical folksongs, variation is slight and contributes to the stabilization of main themes. Variation is caused by many factors: the age and sex of the departed, circumstances of the death, the degree of relationship (blood and affiliation) to the addressor, the number of years since the death, social pressure, and community and personal interest, as well as the capability of initiating, continuing, and creating tradition.

In looking at the family base of the cult of the dead, of which newspaper memorializing is a part, the intensity of this custom is quite noticeable. The family appears as a very strong bond that unites the living and the dead, "spiritually joined and divided by ceremonies for the dead," distinguishing between the profane and the sacred (Warner 1961). The family is the primary group in which individuals are born and die.

> During their brief lives, they are trained by those who precede them and learn how to train others who follow to behave in such a way that, as mortal men, they live in and become part of an "immortal" society. The

"transient" individuals, whose births, lives, and deaths are momentary events in the eternal flow of the life of the species, must learn the morals, values, and beliefs communicated to them by the generations. (Warner 1953:36)

Furthermore,

The family . . . as a paradigm for how kinship relations are to be conducted and to what end, specifies the relations between members of the family as "the loved ones." Love can be translated freely as an enduring diffuse solidarity. The end to which family relations are conducted is the well-being of the family as a whole and of each of its members. (Schneider 1968:50)[12]

The family that cultivates a relationship with its dead members is relatively small, both in temporal and spatial dimension, and mainly consists of three generations closely affiliated by residence. They live together, if not under the same roof then at least in the same neighborhood, town, or region with easy access, and can retain a relative cultural homogeneity.[13] Where the family lives is "home." "To feel at home" is opposed to all other states, which imply a sense of being "alien" (Schneider 1968:45). As long as local cultural and ideological unity as well as physical proximity are maintained, the bond remains solid, as manifest in the brief memoriam for parents Ralph and Elva Carter, who died in 1981 and 1976 respectively:

Mom and Dad we miss you
And think of you each day.
The tears often fall in sorrow,
Since you have gone away.
You can't return unto us,
Your life's begun anew
But through Christ, we have the faith,
That we can come to you.

The memoriam is a confidential family affair. The family negotiates its Christian ideology to keep communication lines open between the living and dead family members. According to my Indiana sample, the general limit for sending memoriams is approximately thirty years. In this subcultural family system, the three-generation unit constitutes a relatively large group. In each generation the families are large, even among the youngest group in spite of the availability of birth control. Families of eight to ten children are no rarity, with five being the average. No wonder the "Heavenly home" is profusely populated with family members from each generation, when earthly kin remain so extensive. The great number of relatives in itself strengthens the women's obligation to write memorials. Although newspaper publication informs acquaintances, memorial poems retain their privacy within the family. The publicity in itself has no status-raising value in society; the modest fee charged by the local newspaper (a minimum of $4.95 for three lines, 66 cents for each additional line—a long poem would not cost more than $15.00 to $20.00; with a photo, the maximum price would not amount to more than $30.00), does not cause a financial hardship even for low-income families whose members are accustomed to donating generously to their churches.

Memorials for Other Occasions

As we have seen, memorializing by poetry writing is primarily a family affair in which the family as a group and its members individually express their devotion to the dead. Women not only have a leading role in this activity, they also are the organizers and maintainers of this ritual relationship. As women tend the grave of departed family members, the "memory garden," the temporary heaven or transitory haven becomes in their interpretation the place where the living can communicate with the dead. The closeness of small graveyards in rural Indiana accommodates frequent visits. Survivors can just drop by at their convenience to unburden themselves if they feel like it by expressing sentiments, recalling happier times, complaining about hardships, or to think, meditate, and "talk" to their dead. The practice of decorating the graves is quite elaborate. Adornment with flowers, birds, reindeer, the American flag, and wrapped presents varies according to the festive occasions, be they the two main days—the anniversary of death and the deceased's birthday—or others, Halloween, Christmas, Flag Day—as Thelma Crohn who does the decoration every calendar day tells us. The memorial poem is a part of grave visitation and decoration. In fact, it is handed over to the deceased by being deposited on the stone, often placed into a greeting card and signed by the visitor or by the whole family. When the Bartlett family had a cookout July 4, 1988, sister Teri took a picture to brother Steve. "Everywhere we were, you were," she wrote in a poem. She folded the picture and poem into a card and took it to the cemetery, her mother said. This poem was not printed. "She did not think it was good enough. She gave it straight to Steve."

Variety in the "poetry of remembering" is apparent when it concerns life cycle and calendar dates and festive seasons other than the anniversary of the death in the family. Memorial Day, as a national holiday, is more a public than a private ritual. It celebrates the life and sacrifice of heroes, uniting the nation as a family (Warner 1953:5–34) in patriotic solemnity. On this occasion, departed members are saluted only in brief ads as part of a large ad-page promoted by the newspaper. Most of these memoriams do not contain poetry

at all, only the introduction and the signature(s), and they address all or several deceased relatives at once. The *Bloomington Herald-Times* invites the public to send memoriams to be featured on a "Special Memorial Page." At the same time, the paper sets the standards of acceptance. Sample texts from previous memoriams are printed with the following instructions: "To those people who choose to write in, please use this form below, and enclose your own verse, or by your request we will furnish one of ours that is appropriate to you."

Mother's Day and Father's Day are inspiring occasions for children to pay tribute to their dead parents, and they also provide an opportunity for widows and widowers left with children to express their appreciation to their departed mates. In addition to the usual themes and sequences of motifs, new clichés praise parental excellence and mourn the loss. Mother's Day memoriams are often signed by husbands, sons, and all family members; however, their tone and style reveal feminine authorship. A much larger contingent of texts—a total of seventy-eight percent—are signed only by daughters who express gratitude for their upbringing and the love and moral education they received from their mothers. From the style of address, the particular mother-daughter intimacy is expressed in statements that are added to the conventional memoriam formulas. Here also, one may recognize feminine authorship. For example, the statement, "She did the best to raise us in a lovely Christian home," is signed by Edith, Lois, Ruby, Edna, Ada, Frances, and Bessie.

Daughters see the ideal of motherhood in their mother, who showed "unselfish love and dedication," "never complained," "took all the blame upon herself," and did not spare her "toil-worn hands"; thus "her life was a long, sweet story." Mother's Day memoriams feature the conservative image of homemaking. Motherhood is perceived as a woman's vocation in which the exclusive aspiration in life is the accomplishment of household chores. Just as their mothers before them followed this pattern, the daughters, in turn, are expected to do the same. The perfect homemaker's life is totally absorbed by the family. The self-sacrificing role of the mother as *imitatio Christi* is explicit in these poems, bearing a remarkable similarity to the ideal that was held up to nineteenth-century women (Welter 1966). Mothers have no individual lives—they live for others and in others; their reward is "going home to Heaven":

There's a place in Heaven that's marked
'reserved' for mothers as she,
Who live life-long devotion to her
husband and family

or expressed differently:

A wonderful mother, woman and aid
one who was better God never made

Perhaps the most captivating among the memorial poems is one mentioned earlier, which narrates the creation of a mother who was sent to earth by God the Creator to help a particular family. The poem begins and ends with the motto, "Every day is Mother's Day." In my sample the motif of "mother sent by God" appears sixteen times.

Although Father's Day memoriams are addressed to Dad, most are women's complaints, elaborating on the tragedy of widowhood. Less room is given to adoration and praise of the father who "never complained," "lived humbly," "was strong in his faith," and

gave many gifts of life
that money cannot buy
the gift of honesty and truth.

The full course of the poetic sequence in Father's Day memoriams, pieced together from ready formulas, contains the following items:

1. the pain due to the loss;
2. the ensuing solitude;

3. the irreplaceability of the dead person;
4. memory as a link between earth and Heaven;
5. happiness in Heaven;
6. looking forward to reunion.

A "Happy Birthday" wish to a dead person sounds bizarre indeed. Yet many memoriams begin with "Happy Birthday, dear," and include which birthday is being marked: "It is your twenty-fourth birthday, Dave," or "On your eightieth, my dear husband." This pretending that the dead one lives and marks his or her birthday is even more explicit in the poem addressed to Frankie Rice, who is seen wearing a T-shirt and smiling at us:

> May God's blessing keep you always
> may your wishes all come true,
> may you always do for others
> and let others do for you.

Here is a three-stanza sonnet ending with the refrain:

> May your heart always be joyful
> May your song be always sung
> and may you stay forever young.

I have found the first stanza of this poem in other textual contexts twice before, inspired probably by Bob Dylan's popular song "Forever Young."

One can even find such small references as: "I love you Daddy and I miss you, so I wrote this little poem just to let you know," or "Happy Birthday Stevie! Although you won't be here with us on your birthday, we love and miss you every day." The latter poem gives the impression of being a birthday letter to a father or brother who left town. However, the euphemization of death does not conceal but dramatizes the fact that the family has to celebrate the birthday without the celebrant. Following this or a similar initial statement, the usual formulaic episodes are pieced together, closing with the usual hope for reunion: "Your birthday will be in Heaven with Jesus, we will all be together someday," or "I'll see you someday, there's no doubt in my mind."

Two formulaic, yet more personal and factual poems suggest that birthdays have a special meaning in family tradition and that on this occasion people need to reminisce about the characteristic features of these individuals and episodes in their lives. A poem signed by Francis Weinstock celebrates the birthday of a father who

> shares with his children the beauties of nature and animal lore . . . whose gentle good humor makes everything right . . . whose honest and ethical teaching of faith . . . in a world full of night . . . steady and gentle, good

natured and fine . . . Though rare is the father who fits the description, I'm grateful that one of those is mine.

If this poem were not signed, "Deeply missed by Wife, Children, and Grand-children," the praise for the father would not seem like a memoriam.

Another poem, with a picture of "our uncle Buck" (who is remembered on his 49th birthday, September 28, 1987), was signed: "We miss you—From all Nieces and Nephews, Mother and Dad, written by Donna B." This poem is a character description in thirteen uneven stanzas with three thematic sections: (1) his character features; (2) his illness and death; (3) his presence with God and his anticipated happy reunion with the family. However, this well-proportioned, formulaic, awkward, and naive poem is uncommon. It reveals many details about the deceased's personality:

> He loved to joke and
> carry on and
> tell about the fights that
> he had won
>
> His favorite thing that he
> liked to do was
> go to reunions and play
> horse shoe
>
> He liked to be around us
> and talk to us all
> Cheering and yelling as
> we played baseball. . . .
> Even though losing a leg
> and a wife
> He had a strong will to
> hang onto his life
> Even sick he'd throw
> you a joke
> as long as you'd give
> him a cigarette to smoke. . . .
> Yes God took him home
> to be with Him
> he would not have to
> lose another limb

If the birthdays of departed family members are special occasions to write memoriams with more concrete characterization, Christmas—the feast of joy, gift exchange, and charity—appears to be a time for heartfelt, collective family tribute to the dead. The Christmas season and the Advent period in general are known as a crisis time, a time when in light of family celebrations, feasting, and good cheer, people feel guilty, remembering those deprived of Christmas blessings (Samuelson 1982). Personal vulnerability increases during this season (feelings of loneliness, deprivation, proverty, ill-success), bringing to mind the fragility and futility of life. This "Christmas malaise" contributes to the increase of suicides during the season. Remembrance of the dead at "Christmas time," "this Christmas season" or when "the Holiday Season [is] approaching," reflects the survivors' feelings of sorrow and guilt. One memoriam reads:

> Christmas joy is everywhere
> Christmas carols fill the air
> friends are sharing warmest greetings
> Families join in happy meetings.

Another memoriam more explicitly states the loss and is inserted in a prayerful letter to God, lamenting that it is "our fifth Christmas without him":

> We can't say, "Merry Christmas, Dear"
> The way we used to do,
> With trees and presents;
> Those joys were buried with you
> And eternity's not measured
> On earth's finite scale of years.
> But here on our heart's calendar
> Today's ever ringed with tears.

The departed loved one is assured that all the fun of Christmas is gone with her passing, and what remains for the survivors is only a mournful recall of the time when they could celebrate together:

> Never a Merry Christmas, Marilyn dear
> You came last Christmas with a heart full of glee
> Because you knew you had gifts for me . . .
>   *
> The time of year that we miss you most of all
> your love and holiday season happiness. . . .
> Christmas comes and Christmas goes,
> each one we miss you more.

Memoriams may also be sent at Easter or on wedding anniversaries, but those occasions do not seem special and do not add new elements to the texts.

Some Conclusions

In this survey of classified ad memoriams, I did not specifically analyze the poetics of the verses. Nevertheless, I hope the selection of texts gives a general idea about the most common forms, the style, and the technique of verse making. It seems clear that the great majority of the poems are divided into four-line stanzas, each line consisting of eight to ten syllables, and are two to twenty stanzas in length. The rhymes are mostly aabb or abab, and sometimes there is an incremental repetition or a sonnet-like three-line refrain.

Each stanza is a self-sufficient content unit, an independent *parole* in itself, easily moved from one textual context to another. When the authors/compilers routinely piece these units together, like pieces in a quilt, they do not make an effort to fit them smoothly. The authors often do not keep the number of lines and syllables of the borrowed stanzas intact. They extend lines to add emphasis, thus upsetting rhythmic and aesthetic balance—sometimes dilating the verse into bland prose. It often happens that the authors take the model formula and rephrase it, causing infinite variation of the same idea and image. These verses are built on a sequence of ideas and images, like occasional folk poetry, and are unlike folk songs, which are controlled by the rhythm and syllabic balance of the melody.

These verses, following the traditional domestic verse-making custom of both rural and urban, folk and elite women, can be considered folklore as they enter the world of modern mass communications. Like other viable forms of folklore, they multiply through the convenience of print. While they intensify and strengthen the religious family bond and the ideology of "Heaven is our home," memoriams do not spread upward beyond the lower middle class. The memorial ad column, however, accommodates not only these strictly formulaic pieces but also memoriams from self-styled artists, preachers, and moralists, displaying an unmistakable amateurism in their awkward laments studded with Biblical quotations. Although these latter writers of memoriams receive their inspiration from peddlers of bombastic, syrupy religious clichés, these amateurs also exploit the inventory of traditional formulas. What keeps both types of memoriams from refinement through repetition and wear is fixity. The stringency of the model and the respect for the written (printed) word allow personal dilution of the form so that it will apply to the meaning of individual authors/rewriters/adapters, but they do not permit further polishing.

It seems these memoriams, as presented in the Indiana sample, perform a similar function across Middle America. They are part of the ritualization of basic human endeavor—remembering the dead in the hope of eternal life. What they uniformly express is the denial of death: departure—arrival—regeneration. Furthermore, the memoriams have a religious ideological foundation rooted in medieval Christian mythology. A tradition emerged concerning the oneness of the living and dead members of the family as a nuclear social group. Following the British clerical persuasion, pious Protestant convention in America revised the mythology to exclude the concept of evil and damnation; it created a new one about the divine origin of humans, who, like Jesus, after a brief sojourn on earth, victoriously return to Heaven. This idea is the basic theme of consolation literature, which also includes funerary ritual poetry.

Modern American folk religion developed from the church canon in the twentieth century, and its popular interpretations evolved along the lines of the proliferation and multiplication of sects. In the course of time, this ideology was crystallized further, while creating its own folklore in terms of custom, narrative, and poetry. The memorializing of the dead in the language of a highly metaphoric poetry has become a socially sanctioned festive admonition. This poetry continually depends on ecclesiastic-edifying tradition, particularly as related to funerary oratory and writing. It inspired the lay poetic tradition of women—the arbiters of piety and secular domesticity.

While the classified ad memoriams demonstrate a merger of the two intellectual traditions, they cannot be considered simply the mere continuation of earlier forms of consolation lyrics, oral or written. The established newspaper memoriam section gave rise to a modern style of personal communication with the dead. Positive response to the newspaper publicity on the part of the subcultural audience encouraged renewal and maintenance of the tradition. It appears today as a new form of folklore. In seemingly informal, but in fact extremely formal and celebratory cliché letters, the mortal address the immortal by way of the local newspaper, and at the same time communicate the message to the local community.

APPENDIX

Sample Texts of In-Memoriam Advertisements

2. IN MEMORIAM 1975

IN LOVING MEMORY of Linda Lou Gilliland, who passed away fourteen years ago, Jan. 23, 1961. Today as every day we think of one so dear.
Although she is so far away, she seems so very near.
She always cheered and made us smile when we were feeling blue.
So today and every day, Dear Linda we still think of you.
Sadly missed by parents, Mr. & Mrs. Eathel Kinser; sisters, Kathryn, Audrey, Reba, Roberta and Shirley; brother, Sheldon, and son Eddie Ray.

In loving remembrance of OSBIN A. CLAY who left this life Jan. 23, 1972.
Little things that seem to go unnoticed and unsung,
Are the things we all remember Of the days when we were together.
These little things will be A lasting recollection and a cherished memory.
Sadly missed by wife, children and their families.

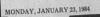

MONDAY, JANUARY 23, 1984

IN MEMORIAM 07

In loving memory of Linda Lou Gilliland, who passed away Jan. 23, 1961. Sadly missed by parents, Mr. & Mrs. Edthel Kinser, sisters; Kathryn, Audrey, Shirley. Brother Sheldon and son Eddie Ray.

IN MEMORIAM 02

In loving memory of Linda Lou Gilliland, who passed away Jan. 23, 1961. Sadly missed by parents, Mr. & Mrs. Edthel Kinser, sisters; Kathryn, Audrey, Reba, Robert and Shirley. Brother, Sheldon and son Eddie Ray.

IN MEMORIAM 04

In Loving Memory of Linda Lou Gilliland who passed away Jan. 23, 1961.

Though she is gone from our presence her sweet voice we don't hear, the memories in our hearts make her seem very near. We loved her so much we could never replace, the joy of her laughter, and her sweet smiling face.
We know she is watin in God's Mansion far away, and our only desire is to be with her, some Glorious day.

Sadly missed by parents: Mr. & Mrs. Eathel Kinser, Sisters: Kathryn, Audrey, Reba, Roberta and Shirley. Brother: Sheldon and son Eddie Ray.

IN MEMORIAM 07

In loving memory of Linda Lou Gilliland, who passed away Jan. 23, 1961. Sadly missed by parents, Mr. & Mrs. Edthel Kinser, sisters: Kathryn, Audrey, Reba, Roberta and Shirley. Brother Sheldon and son Eddie Ray.

H-T
1982 Jan. 23

IN MEMORIAM 02

1979 H-T

In loving memory of Linda Lou Gilliland, who passed away Jan. 23, 1961.

As the snow falls in January we still recall the day, of the one we loved so dearly who God saw fit to call away. He took her from her suffering where pain she would bear no more. There she waits to meet her loved ones on her Master's golden shore.

Sadly missed by parents: Mr. & Mrs. Eathel Kinser, Sisters: Kathryn, Audrey, Reba, and Shirley. Brother; Sheldon, and son Eddie Ray.

IN MEMORIAM 02

In loving memory of Linda Lou Gilliland, who passed away Jan. 23, 1961

The depths of sorrow we cannot tell,
Of the loss of one we loved so well,
And while she sleeps a peaceful sleep,
Her memory we shall always keep.
Sadly missed by parents Mr. & Mrs. Eathel Kinser, sisters Kathryn, Audrey, Reba, Roberta and Shirley. Brother Sheldon and son Eddie Ray

1976 Jan. 23
H-T Fri.

In loving memory of Linda Lou Gilliland, who passed away Jan. 23, 1961. Sadly missed by parents, Mr. & Mrs. Edthel Kinser, sisters; Kathryn, Audrey, Reba, Roberta and Shirley. Brother Sheldon and son Eddie Ray.

In loving Memory of Linda Lou Gilliland, who passed away Jan. 23, 1961.

In all the world we shall not find,
a heart so wonderfully kind,
so soft a voice,
so sweet a smile,
a sympathy so sure,
so deep,
a love so beautiful to keep.

Only a memory of bygone days,
and a sigh for a face unseen,
a constant feeling that God alone knows best what should have been.

Sadly missed by parents, Mr. and Mrs. Eathel Kinser, sisters, Kathryn, Audrey, Reba, Roberta and Shirley, brother, Sheldon and son, Eddie Ray.

H-T 1977

In loving memory of Linda Lou Gilliland who passed away Jan. 23rd, 1961

Though many years have passed since we last saw her lovely face.
We hold memories in our hearts that time cannot erase
Sadly missed by the parents: Mr. & Mrs. Eathel Kinser Sisters: Kathryn, Audrey, Reba, Roberta & Shirley; Son: Eddie Ray
Linda was joined in death by her brother (Sheldon) Aug. 1st, 1988.
We love and miss them both so very, very much.

IN LOVING MEMORY OF
MIKE HOARD
Oct. 3, 1958-June 20, 1980

To My Dad:

Dad,
Looking and reminiscing through the old dusty pictures of you as a child thinking briefly of what could have been .. if you could have stayed for awhile. I see all the trophies, all the champions pictures too. I see the smile on your face, all your happiness shining through. I would give anything to once be able to talk to you ... in person ... instead of photographs but that's just a passing thought; I only have slight memories to last.

I'll see you again one of these days with that smile on your face; all of my pain will go away. I just want you to hold me in your arms and never let go and tell me how you missed me and how you love me so.

Anna

'Mike'
Well another year has passed since you left us. As I sit here writing this it seems like only yesterday when you went out the door ("See you later" you said.) Little did I know it would be 'later.' PARENTS ... love your children ... tell them you love them, hug them, for if you ever lose them life stops for many years. (Well Mike ... later, see you later ... son)

I see his face in a boy playing ball

I hear his laugh in his daughter's voice when she laughs;

I see his image in his brothers' faces when they smile

I see the pain in mine and my wife's heart when we put flowers on his grave ... when we think of what might have been. (He was some boy.)

Love you Mike

Marcia, Jack, Mark, Tom, Susan, Daughter Anna, Jeremy.

Gerald H. Skinner
In Loving Memory Of My Precious Husband, Gerald, Who Passed Away 2 Yrs. Ago., December 15th, 1989

A lonely tomb in Avoca land,
On Hill Tops hill!!
Speak to these curious hearts of ours,
And teach them to be still.
God hath His mysteries of grace,
Ways that we cannot tell,
He hides them deep,
Like the secret sleep,
Of him He loved so well.

Your Family Wishes You A Merry Christmas With Jesus!
We Love You And Miss You!
Wife, Wilma

IN MEMORIAM 07

In memory of Steve "Mike" Detmer who was killed by a bowling ball on January 4, 1985.

We will never forget you.

June Detmer, Ann Detmer & Ernie Detmer

In Loving Memory
of my brother,
Buck Reeves
on his
49th birthday.

I think of you everyday
And the things you
used to say
All the times you took
care of your sister
And all the love you
gave
I'll always have your
memories to save
I know your pain and
hurts have been
taken away,
when you went to be
with God that day.
It's your Birthday and
the family couldn't
miss you more
But I know God and
you are waiting to
open the door.

**Your loving sister
Martha Frame**

In Loving Memory of
Dana R. Crohn
on his birthday October 26

We cannot send a
birthday card
Your hand we
cannot touch
Today there will be
no gifts and cake
For the one we love
so much
The heart is a
house of many rooms
Where things are
stored away
The treasures of
many happy birthdays
The cherished ones
of yesterday
Nothing can ever
take away
The love that a
heart holds dear
Fond memories
linger every day
Remembrance
keeps you near

Happy Birthday
Sadly Missed
We Love You
Thelma, Connie
Gary and Family

In Loving Memory
of Peggy Gilliland
on her Birthday
May 30th

Tho we'll never meet
again
On the earth my Precious
sister
If to God we have been
true
And we've lived above all
sin
Then for us there'll be a
greeting
For there's gonna be a
meeting
I'll see you in the Rapture
Some sweet day
I'll see you in the Rapture
I'll see you in the Rapture
I'll see you at that meeting
in the air
There with our Blessed
Savior
We'll live and reign
forever
I'll see you in the Rapture
some sweet day.
To my loved ones let me
say
That there'll surely come a
day
When the Lord will come
again
And He'll take his Bride
away
So get ready now to meet
Him
With the Hallelujas greet
Him
I'll see you in the Rapture
some sweet day

Sadly missed by
Mother & Dad, Sis-
ters Reva, Kay, Bon-
nie, brother Jerry

OUR UNCLE BUCK

Our Uncle Buck was a
Special Man
He always gave
everyone a helping hand
Whether it was big or
even small
He'd try to answer their
every call

He loved to joke and
carry on and
tell about the fights that
he had won

His favorite thing that he
liked to do was
go to reunions and play
horse shoe

He liked to be around us
and talk to us all
Cheering and yelling as
we played baseball.

Well, as life went on
Uncle Buck got sick
Life for him was a really
hard trick.
He had several strokes
and lost his sight
But he kept on fighting
with all his might

Even though losing a leg
and a wife
He had a strong will to
hang onto his life

Even sick he'd throw
you a joke
as long as you'd give
him a cigarette to smoke

His pain got worse and
his body got weak
Our Uncle Buck just
went fast to sleep

Yes, God took him home
to be with Him
He would not have to
lose another limb

I know now that he is in
pain no more
God has fixed his every
sore
and we will be with him
again some day
so we can tell him all we
forgot to say

He's there waiting for
you and me
and I know he's happier
now than he
could ever be

We miss you
From All Nieces
and Nephews,
Mother and Dad
Written by Donna B.

Sept. 28, Mon.
1987

07 In Memoriam

IN LOVING MEMORY OF STEPHEN R. BARTLETT KILLED BY A DRUNK DRIVER TWO YEARS AGO TODAY, AUGUST 14, 1987

Death took a ray of sunlight from all of our lives.

But I can see his face when I look at blue skies.

He's up there above us, I don't know where,

But if there's a Heaven I know that he's there.

We still hear his voice, we still hear his laughter,

It will remain in our memories for ever after.

It seems that we had him for such a short while —

Oh, what we would give only to see him smile.

The memories he left us, his courage, his will,

He had so many things in his life to fulfill.

The suffering, the anguish, the struggle, the pain,

We ask God over and over, "What can be the gain?"

Why should someone so young and good have to die,

If there is an answer, please, tell us why.

Finally and slowly, I think, we begin to almost understand.

It must be a part of a great and infinite plan.

We're all pieces in a puzzle too big to embrace,

Each one of us can occupy only one certain space.

There's no way to change it, no way to escape,

Someone greater than all of us determines our place and our shape.

He lived a good life, the Minister said,

His spirit still lives, only his body is dead.

The circle has been broken,

There's no way we can ever mend.

Now I think I know why, his life he had to give,

To show the rest of us how to live.

These are the hearts that miss you so,

Dear Son, Brother, Uncle and Friend.

Sadly missed by all of us who were privileged To be your family.

IN LOVING memory of Stephen R. Bartlett who was killed one year ago today August 14, 1987. A splendor shines
On my pathway
Because you're in
My thoughts today.
You're in my plans
And it is true
That when I dream
I dream of you.
You're in my thoughts
And in each prayer
Always my love
Will keep you there.
I Love You
Loving & missing you
Kim

ON AUGUST 14, 1987 the life of a very close friend was taken. Steve 'Budda' Bartlett will always be in our thoughts. No, softball was not, and never will be the same without Budda at 3rd base hitting home run after home run. Even though he was thought of at every practice, every game and every day of our lives.
We never told you how special your friendship and leadership was to us.
You will always be in our thoughts and the wonderful memories of you will never leave us.
We Miss You,
Rich (Kruz), Sherry & Brittany Kuruzovich

**To My Son
STEVE BARTLETT
Killed in an Accident**

The light that was
your life
Has been
extinguished.
The warmth of your
sun no longer
warms me.
The joy of your
presence is not
with me.
How shall I live
without you?
Of course, I must.
At first it is like
a sudden cripple—
Groping, blinded,
I see no beauty
around me,
I feel and taste
nothing—My
laughter is false,
for there is no joy.
And yet it is not
meant that my life
Should only be
bathed in your
reflection.
Gradually but surely,
I must go forward,
Step by Step building
the days to a
fulfillment that you
knew.
Your colorful, busy,
exciting life must
Be my inspiration.
You did not lean on
me for your joys
and neither must I.
God help me to fill
my days with
meaning
And again—in time—
laughter,
So that when we meet
again
You will be proud of
me!!

Love,
Mom

---

07 In Memoriam

IN LOVING MEMORY of our nephew Stephen Bartlett who was killed 1 year ago today. He little thought when leaving home
He would return no more
That he & death so soon would meet
And leave us here to mourn
We do not know the pain he bore
Or why he had to die
We only know he passed away
And could not say goodbye
So put your arms around him Lord
And whisper in his ear
Tell him that we love him
And wish that he were here.
Sadly missed by David & Donna

**For Our Son
Stephen R. Bartlett
who was killed by a drunk driver on August 14, 1987.**

Our thoughts are filled with you, our Dear Boy, you were and are our pride and joy.

It is now one year on this very day that you died because a boy was drunk in such a tragic way.

Where are you now, you Dear One. Whose laughter we miss. In what green fields do you wonder, what do your eyes behold?

Sometimes, in some familiar place we almost feel you near.

Our eyes cannot see you, yet our hearts know your presence, Dear.

Why did you die, we sometimes ask, and to despair we yield.

But then we look at a monument, built from love, and it helps our bruised hearts to heal.

Just now and then we feel doubt which places us in Hell until we see the world God's made and know that all is well.

Love Mom and Dad

In loving memory of
Timothy Jon Bruner
who passed away May
7, 1973.
He was a rose bud in
the garden of life,
That was lent for
just a spell.
He has been trans-
planted in Heaven.
Eternally there to
dwell.

Sadly missed by
parents, grandparents
& brother.

In Loving Memory of
TIMOTHY JON BRUNER
who passed away May 7,
1973.

The memory of his dear
wee ways,
Will linger with us all our
days,
Sweetest Flower too
sweet to stay;
God took him home to
show us the way.

Sadly missed by parents,
grandparents and broth-
er.

TIMOTHY JON BRUNER

In loving memory of Timothy
Jon Bruner who passed away
two years ago today.
When God calls little children
to dwell with Him above,
We mortals sometime
question the wisdom of
His love.
For no heartache compares
with the death of one
small child
Who does so much to make
our world seem wonderful
and mild.
Perhaps God tires of calling
the aged to His fold,
So He picks a rosebud
before it can grow old.
God knows how much we
need them, and so He
takes but few
To make the land of Heaven
more beautiful to view.
Believing this is difficult
still somehow we must try,
The saddest work mankind
knows will always be
"Goodbye."
So when a little child departs,
we who are left behind
Must realize God loves
children. Angels are hard
to find.
Sadly missed by parents,
grandparents & brother.

IN LOVING memory of LILLIE
BORUFF who passed away May
6th, 1967.
The love you gave us many years
will never from us depart.
Though you have gone beyond
our reach,
You're always in our hearts.
Sadly missed by husband,
children, & grandchildren.

In loving memory of
Timothy Jon Bruner on his
birthday, August 27.

We do not know His
reasons;
Someday we'll
understand.
Why God came down so
suddenly
And took our Timmy's
hand,
He bid no one a last
farewell,
He could not say
goodbye,
God took him home to be
with Him
and only He knows why.

Sadly missed by parents,
grandparents and brother.

In loving memory of
Timothy Jon Bruner who
passed away May 7, 1973.

The memory of his
dear wee ways,
Will linger with us
all our days,
Sweetest flower,
too sweet to stay,
God took him home
to show us the way.

Sadly missed by his family.

AIRMAIL TO HEAVEN
Wade V. Baker
Dear Dad:
I've made some new friends
Who didn't know you.
The stories I tell them
They can't believe they are true.
But when I back up my stories
By your friends who knew you so long,
They confirm what I have said
With love ever so strong.
When they hear the love and respect
That your friends have in their voice
They would love to have known you
Had they had the choice.
    I love you,
        Your daughter, Darlene

07 In Memoriam

AIRMAIL TO HEAVEN
Wade V. Baker
3-3-77
Well it's that time again
It's been a long 13 years
You've been gone from me
And I've shed so many tears.

Since I talked to you last
Many things happened in my-life
I'm a new grandma
But I'm no longer a wife.

LynDora has a good husband
Together they gave me a grandson
I wish you could see him
To us he is number one.

You're the only man who never hurt me.
I sure wish you were here
To take me in your arms
And say I love you my dear.
        Sadly missed by
        Your daughter
        Darlene

IN LOVING MEMORY of
William H. Hays Sr., who
entered into eternal rest June 26,
1965.
Dear Bill,
Only God knows why you left us
and could not say goodbye.
He had a way you could not help
loving and a heart that was purer
than gold.
And to those who knew him and
loved him, his memory will
never grow old.
His helping hand was always
first to render any aide he could.
His voice was always raised in
praise, his works were wise and
good.
Dear Dad, since you have gone
away, the ones you loved so true,
Try hard to carry on the way we
know you would have us do.
Sadly missed by all the family.

In Loving Memory of our Papaw
Everett Lake who passed away
April 25, 1986. Written by Grand-
daughter Sherry Lee Meadows.

Hello, Operator
We'd like to place a call
Make it direct to Heaven
So we can talk to Papaw

You see it's been exactly
One year ago today
Since God made His call
And took our Papaw away

We just want to hear his voice
Or see his loving smile
Please Operator
We'll only talk a little while

So won't you help us
Make this call
We just want to say
We love you, to our Papaw.

Sadly missed by other Grandchil-
dren-Kris Sciscoe, David & Laura
Lake, Eugene Meadows, Rose
Harden & 7 Great-Grandchildren

Notes

1. The Variant and the Folklorization Process

1. For example, Cupid and Psyche, Sidi Numan, Festin de Pierre, Amicus and Amelius, Brunhilde, Aladdin, Fortunatus, Crescentia, The Ring of Polycrates, Turandot, Griselda, Alcestis, the Taming of the Shrew, Oedipus, Gregory on the Stone.

2. Such as Cinderella, Bluebeard, Puss in Boots, Jorinde and Joringel, Hansel and Gretel, Rumpelstiltskin, and so on.

3. It is the folklorist's task to observe any spontaneously occurring folklorism of the folk, and these phenomena deserve to be studied (Kirshenblatt-Gimblett 1988); however, it is not the folklorist's task to promote these causes or artificially keep them alive through institutionalization.

2. Magic for Sale

1. In this discussion we will use the term Märchen alternately with folktale and tale, meaning the group of narratives summarily identified as "Ordinary Folk-Tales" (Types 300–1199) in *The Types of the Folktale* (Aarne and Thompson 1961).

2. Stith Thompson noted with mock regret in personal conversations that "fairies did not cross the Ocean," and Reidar Christiansen, surveying the importation of European tales into America, remarked that "whatever folk-tales the first early immigrants knew were more readily forgotten" (1962:57).

3. John Honti elaborated the "world of the Märchen and its central importance for folktale study" as early as 1937 (Honti 1975).

4. To use the term and idea of André Jolles (1965:240).

5. As Roland Barthes does in explaining narrative patterns and implicit legends in margarine and detergent ads (1977:36, 42).

6. Röhrich also notes that the structure of Märchen lends itself to exploitation by commercial advertising: "It is no rarity that the texts and images of industrial promotions follow the structure of the tale. And this is by no means accidental. Advertising imputes to merchandise the same magic powers that the Märchen imputes to magic objects. It invents its own supernatural beings, which, as the personification of the industrial products, are as effective for the people as their counterparts in the magic tale. The wish-fulfillment motif in the Märchen is easily transposed at any time and to any content. The most general scheme that underlies the folktale is: hardship and the overcoming of it, struggle and victory, task and solution, expectation and fulfillment. In this scheme, the happy ending, which is generally cited as characteristic of the tale, is included" (1974: introduction; my translation).

7. "The gap between oral traditional Märchen and its equivalents in the form of trivia were bridged immediately and continually as whole branches of the culture industry developed to promote and satisfy the demand of the growing market in today's society" (Bausinger, *Volkskunde*, 35 ff; my translation).

8. In her survey of Americans' familiarity with tales, Kay Stone ranks as the top six Sleeping Beauty, Snow White, Cinderella, Rumpelstiltskin, Hansel and Gretel, and the

Frog Prince (Stone 1975a:242 ff). For the American adaptation of Grimm tales, see the discussions of Wayland D. Hand (1963) and Linda Dégh (1983b).

9. The explanation of the phenomenon that units of folklore messages temporarily separate from each other and lead independent lives has been offered in Dégh and Vázsonyi (1975).

10. "Incidental folklore is usually a stylistic device and consists of allusions, metaphors, similes, and references which are folkloristic in nature" (Denby 1971:118).

11. "It is reasonable to ask whether all advertising is likely to employ magic. I suppose so," states Howard Gossage in his witty essay (1961).

12. McLuhan quotes an American army officer who wrote for *Printer's Ink* from Italy that "the wall space of Italian cities was given over to political rather than commercial slogans. . . . In fact, he went so far as to say that democratic freedom very largely consists in ignoring politics and worrying about the means of defeating underarm odor, scaly scalp, hairy leg" (1957:435).

13. "The implications [of a soap advertisement] are severe and rather sinister: They are designed to brainwash the viewer into buying the product by using seduction (a positive stroke) and intimidation (a negative stroke) to use the familiar terms associated with transformational psychoanalysis" (Makkai 1974:200).

14. One of the strategies, the "definition of the situation," is discussed in DeFleur (1970:146–49).

3. Magic as a Mail-Order Commodity

1 The term *superstition* is often used by folklorists in the sense of popular or unofficial belief and religion. The consideration of lexical definitions by Gustav Jahoda (1971:1–16) concludes that the term in general expresses a critical, prejudicial, subjective opinion about the belief of others.

2. From the late 1960s onward, magazines like *Newsweek, Der Spiegel, Time,* and others have informed their readership of the return of mysticism and a "new black magic" in western society. *Time* (27 Sept. 1968) offered same interpretations of the amazing spread of supernaturalism in the age of technological advancement and electronic sophistication. While established great religions lose their attraction, people in mass society turn to mystic Oriental religions, Christian fundamentalism, and substitute religions. Social scientists belatedly reported an "occult explosion" (Freedland 1972), the "occult wave" (Assion 1976; Bender 1984), the "high tide of superstition" (Wimmer 1975), "the new nonsense" (Fair 1974); and concentrated effort was launched by leading scientists through the *Skeptical Enquirer,* a bimonthly magazine whose goal since the early 1970s has been to enlighten the gullible public.

3. Some of the best enthnographic documents of present-day witchcraft and magic include Favret-Saada 1979; Schöck 1978; Farrar and Farrar 1987; and Graichen 1986.

4. Psi is a keyword for the whole field of paranormal phenomena—using the twenty-fourth letter of the Greek alphabet.

5. The mass suicide of the settlers of Jonestown, Guyana, at the command of their charismatic pastor, Jim Jones, occurred in 1978. As this book went to press, another charismatic leader, David Koresh—who convinced his flock of an imminent apocalyptic demise—perished with several dozen followers in an apparently self-induced fire at the cult's compound in Waco, Texas, following a shoot-out and months-long standoff with federal law enforcers in 1993.

6. Most American tabloids, such as *Midnight, Globe, Star, Sun, The National Enquirer, The Weekly World News,* and the *National Examiner,* publish these announcements. Similar

classifieds can also be found in British, German, Swiss, Austrian, and French tabloids, evening papers and illustrated magazines. Among the ads promoting sex or marriage partnership, magic solicitations appear under these titles: "Correspondence," "Acquaintances," "Luck-In-Life," or simply "Miscellany."

7. In her paper "Mail Order Magic: The Commercial Exploitation of Folk Belief" (1979), Loudell Snow limits her interest to materials satisfying the needs of black Americans. This limitation seems naive in light of our own observations and data gathering. Something that is so universal cannot be attributed to the manipulation of the descendants of slaves through belief in black magic. The listed magic supplies are equally popular among other American subcultural groups and in the mainstream as well.

8. For a definition of the legend, see Dégh 1965b; Dégh and Vázsonyi 1974. Most advertisement legends are told in first person (even if the speakers do not identify themselves) and can be considered memorates. For the sake of this discussion, it is not necessary to distinguish between memorates and fabulates on the basis of their stylistic differences.

4. Beauty, Wealth, and Power

1. Contributions to the study of women and folklore include, among others, two special issues of the *Journal of American Folklore* (Farrer 1975; Jackson 1987), and the works of Jordan and Kalčik (1985), Jordan and de Caro (1986), and Sawin (1988).

2. For the notion: Kirche, Küche, Kinder, see Friedan 1963:30–32; Weber-Kellermann 1975:102, 127.

3. "The attributes of True Womanhood, by which a woman judged herself and was judged by her husband, her neighbors and society, could be divided into four cardinal virtues—piety, purity, submissiveness and domesticity. Put them all together and they spelled mother, daughter, sister, wife—woman. Without them, no matter whether there was fame, achievement or wealth, all was ashes. With them she was promised happiness and power" (Welter 1981:152).

4. "The chief function of media stereotypes of women is not to sell goods but to reinforce the ideology and therefore the reality of male supremacy—of the economic and sexual subordination of women to men, in the latter's objective interest" (Gornick and Moran 1971:659).

5. See Epstein 1971:52. "From the youngest age in Little League, there is often a denigrating attitude toward girls and women. The worst insult a boy can yell at another boy in Little League is to call him a wuss. If you combine the emphasis on winning at any cost with the negative attitude toward women, it is not at all surprising that approximately one-third of the sexual assaults are by athletes." From an interview with social philosopher Myriam Miedzian, *Time*, 16 Sept. 1991.

6. It is common knowledge that the test of courage that adolescent boys endure at Halloween includes the scaring of his date in order to have her seek shelter from supernatural dangers in his strong arms.

7. Walter Benjamin's term was applied by Schenda to the mass spread of folklore (1992:24–25).

5. Tape-Recording Miracles for Everyday Living

1. The most impressive folkloristic study of Pentecostals has been done by Elaine Lawless. Her two books (1988a, 1988b), several articles, and the award-winning documentary film *Joy Unspeakable*, for which she collected the data in the company of Elizabeth Peterson in 1981, are focused on Pentecostal women and their oral art in the performance

of religious functions, in the same Southern Indiana region where I observed the life of a particular congregation.

2. Encountering Indiana Pentecostals reminded me of my early exposure to another fundamentalist sect, the Jehovah's Witnesses, widespread among large-estate share tenants in east Hungary. During my student years, I conducted fieldwork in this region, where traditional storytellers came from the poorest class of agricultural laborers. Their American import religion was their refuge from the miseries they suffered in the real world. It impressed me at that time how these traditional villagers formed their congregation in private homes, straw-roofed adobe shacks, and talked about their religion, and how articulate and eloquent they were discussing pertinent passages of the Bible. In their literal interpretations of the Bible, everything they argued for followed clear logic and sounded brilliantly intelligent and convincing. I respected them for their openness and courage in resisting the military draft during wartime.

3. According to secular humanist philosopher Paul Kurtz, fundamentalism "refers to any movement or attitude that stresses strict and literal adherence to a set of fundamental principles or values. A fundamentalist is . . . one who professes belief in a creed, doctrine, dogma, code or ideology that he accepts unreservedly and without question. His commitment is firm, inflexible, and unwavering. These principles are taken as absolute, unchanging, eternal. The system of fundamentalist belief, at least in theory if not in practice, is used as a guide for all aspects of life. . . . There is a battle, they believe, between the children of light (their side) and the forces of darkness (the enemy). A kind of self-righteous moral fanaticism can result; for, since the true believer is doing God's work, he believes that he is justified in opposing his enemies in any way he can" (Kurtz 1986–1987:19).

4. "Authentic" pilgrim reports are presented in a pamphlet by Josef Maller (1971); moreover, cases of instant healing from stroke, headache, earache, heart, lung and kidney disease, and the healing of animals at the miracle site were described by Dr. Maria Pinsker (1976), with the authorization of Pope Paul VI.

5. Al Gossan is an optometry student turned Pentecostal minister who has written up the miracles that brought about his conversion in 1986 (Gossan 1986).

6. As an example, Felicitas Goodman (1988:52) notes that the 600,000 inhabitants of Columbus, Ohio, support a Spiritualist, 52 Pentecostal, and 60 Apostolic congregations. According to Nichol's estimation (1974), the number of Pentecostals amounts to eight to twelve million. "Today the Pentecostal Churches are among the most rapidly growing churches" (Horton, Leslie and Larson 1974:137).

7. Originally raised in the Grace Tabernacle Church, this evangelist, with his partner, John Baker, established his own itinerant mission, Frontline Ministries. The recording was made at a service for high school students on the temptations of Satan, in October 1989 at the Agape Community Church in Ellettsville, Indiana. The total service conducted on two consecutive evenings was videotaped by Mitchell and sold to the audience.

8. Lisa is my prime contact with the Grace church. She has been cleaning my house once a week for the last ten years or so, and it was through our conversations that I became interested in the lifestyle and religious ideology of Pentecostals. She is a devout saint of the church who was saved at the age of eleven and used by Jesus to deliver his messages through tongues. She is an extremely articulate, self-conscious, intelligent speaker, generous and patient with my many questions, never minding the tape recorder. She introduced me to her family and friends in the church, who were also very hospitable and accommodating to me, my husband, and the students and colleagues whom we occasionally brought along to the services. I never had a problem asking questions and recording speech or music in and out of church. Lisa and her husband are in their mid-forties; one son is now at home, attending college. I have recorded much of her life history in bits and pieces,

some of which I have presented in this discussion. She is not only a representative of the Pentecostal way of life but also an excellent narrator. She also came to class with me when I spoke of Indiana folk religion; she made comments and answered questions from students in relation to the film *Joy Unspeakable*.

9. Recorded October 12, 1988.

10. From tape, Sept. 12, 1991.

11. The widespread legends about the subliminal satanic seduction of young people by rock music instruments, musicians, and records or cassettes played backwards were little noticed by folklorists before attention was aroused by the overwhelming rumor-panic about a cult of Satan, involving child abuse, drug trafficking and ritual murder (Victor 1989; Hicks 1990).

6. Letters to the Dead

1. I found great similarity among memoriams, framed conspicuously in the fashion of an obituary or simply as common classified ads in British and German daily papers.

2. Lloyd Warner distinguishes between the living and the dead cemetery, a distinction that also pertains to the time span of the relationship between living and dead family members in terms of memoriams. "When cemeteries no longer receive fresh burials which continue to tie emotions of the living to the recently dead and thereby connect the living in a chain of generations to an early ancestry, the graveyards lose their sacred quality and become objects of historical ritual. The lifetime of individuals and the living meanings of cemeteries are curiously interdependent, for both are dependent on an ascription of sacred meaning bestowed upon them by those who live. The symbols of death say what life is and those of life define what death must be" (Warner 1961:215).

3. Douglas (1974:64–66) discusses the idealization and sanctification of the dead in nineteenth-century fiction.

4. "Vacant chair" as Memorial Day tableau (Warner 1953:13).

5. "Papaw" and "Mamaw" are common names for grandfather and grandmother in Indiana.

6. "Almost everywhere religious thought consistently denies the irreversible and terminal nature of death by proclaiming it a new beginning" (Bloch and Parry 1982:9).

7. Among the many descriptions in Phelps's novel about future life in Heaven, this dialogue comes close to the memorial poem's depiction: "I hope to have a home of my own" . . . "Not a house?" "Something not unlike it . . . Christ is truly 'preparing' my home for me. . . . " "In the Father's house are many mansions" (Phelps 1964:94).

8. The mansion metaphor appears also on nineteenth-century Monroe County (Indiana) epitaphs. One stone has a picture of a mansion on the top of it, with the inscription: "In my father's house are many mansions"; another inscription says: "Our father has gone to a mansion of rest to the glorious land the deity blest" (manuscript collection of Mike Diekhoff).

9. The importance of family unity for Americans is well illustrated by family reunions. The festive vacation gathering at the home base of kin scattered all over the country symbolizes the same desire for family cohesion in a mobile society as the desire for return to the celestial home (Swenson 1980).

10. This movement has been describes as the "scribbling women's literary production with lofty patriotism and misty death-oriented and nonsectarian religious fervor" (Douglas 1971:7).

11. Ann McDaniel, Doris's daughter-in-law, allowed me to make a copy of the manuscript.

12. Schneider (1968:71–72) excluded the dead from the category of relatives in the American kinship system because some respondents who filled out his questionnaire asked him if they should also include the dead. The question made him believe that people do not feel they can have relationships with the dead, although it is quite possible that the informants were not sure if the researcher wanted them to list the departed also. The respondents' question may have meant that the dead were very much on their minds, as the conceptualization of family kinship in my study indicates.

13. Cross-American sampling indicates that memoriams are also popular among non-Anglo-Saxon, non-Protestant ethnics. The adoption of the custom is not surprising, but it does not mean acceptance of the "heaven is our home" ideology. Materials from Polish, Ukrainian, Italian, and German Catholic Americans in my sample stress the pain of separation and the continued support of the deceased rather than the domestic heaven.

Bibliography

Aarne, Antti, and Stith Thompson. 1961. *The Types of the Folktale; A Classification and Bibliography.* Folklore Fellows Communications, 184. Helsinki: Suomalainen Tiedeakatemia.

Adorno, T. W. 1972 [1960]. Television and the Patterns of Mass Culture. In *Mass Communications,* ed. Wilbur Schramm, 594–612. Urbana: University of Illinois Press.

Alcock, James E. 1979. Psychology and Near-Death Experiences. *The Skeptical Inquirer* 3(3):25–41.

Alver, Bente Gullveig, 1990. *Creating the Source Through Folkloristic Fieldwork.* Folklore Fellows Communications, 246. Helsinki: Suomalaisen Tiedeakatemia.

André, Rae. 1981. *Homemakers: The Forgotten Workers.* Chicago: The University of Chicago Press.

Angst, B. E. 1972. *Magische Praktiken des Menschen unserer Zeit in ihrer sozialpsychologischen und psychodynamischen Bedeutung.* Frankfurt: Bern.

Apo, Satu. 1986. *Ihmesadun rakenne. Juonien tyypit pääjaksot ja henkilöasetelmat satakuntalaisessa kansansatuaineistossa* (The structure and message of magic tales. A description and interpretation of southwest Finnish folktale material). Helsinki: Suomalaisen Kirjallisunden Seura.

Ariès, Philippe. 1978 [1974]. *Western Attitudes towards Death from the Middle Ages to the Present.* Baltimore: John Hopkins University Press.

Assion, Peter. 1976. Legitimierte Irrationalität. Zur popularisierten Parapsychologie. In *Direkte Kommunikation und Massenkommunikation, Referate und Diskussionsprotokolle des 20. deutschen Volkskunde-Kongresses in Weingarten,* ed. Hermann Bausinger and Elfriede Moser-Rath, 145–55. Tübingen: Tübinger Vereinigung für Volkskunde; E. V. Schloss.

Babcock, Barbara A. 1987. Taking Liberties, Writing from the Margins, and Doing It with a Difference. *Journal of American Folklore* 100:390–411.

Bächtold-Staubli, Hanns and Edward von Hoffman-Krayer. 1927–42. *Handwörterbuch des deutschen Aberglaubens.* 10 vols. Berlin: Walter de Gruyter.

Bainbridge, William Sims. 1988. Is Belief in the Supernatural Inevitable? *Free Inquiry* 8(2):21–26.

Baker, Ronald. 1982. *Hoosier Folk Legends.* Bloomington: Indiana University Press.

Barthes, Roland. 1977. *Mythologies.* New York: Hill and Wang.

Bascom, William. 1953. Folklore and Anthropology. *Journal of American Folklore* 67:283–90.

Bauman, Richard, ed. 1977. *Verbal Art as Performance.* Rowley, Mass.: Newbury House Publishers.

———. 1986. *Story, Performance and Event. Contextual Studies of Oral Narrative.* Cambridge: Cambridge University Press.

————. 1989. Folklore. In *International Encyclopedia of Communication*, ed. Erik Barnouw, vol. 2:177–81. New York: Oxford University Press.

Bausinger, Hermann. 1986. *Volkskunde*. Darmstadt: Carl Habel Verlagsbuchhandlung.

————. 1958. Strukturen des alltäglichen Erzählens. *Fabula* 1:239–54.

————. 1977. Alltägliches Erzählen. In *Enzyklopädie des Märchens*, vol. 1, ed. Kurt Ranke et al., 323–30. Berlin: Walter de Gruyter.

————. 1980. *Formen der "Volkspoesie."* Berlin: Erich Schmidt.

————. 1988. Concluding Remarks. In *Life History as Cultural Construction/Performance*, ed. Tamás Hofer and Peter Niedermüller, 477–88. Budapest: Ethnographic Institute.

Bausinger, Hermann, and Wolfgang Brückner. 1969. *Kontinuität? Geschichtlichkeit und Dauer als volkskundliches Problem*. Berlin: Erich Schmidt.

Becker, E. 1973. *The Denial of Death*. New York: Free Press.

Ben-Amos, Dan. 1971. Toward a Definition of Folklore in Context. *Journal of American Folklore* 84:3–15.

Bender, Hans. 1984. Spuk—Täuschungen und Tatsachen. In *Psi—Was verbirgt sich dahinter? Wissenschaftler untersuchen parapsychologische Erscheinungen*, ed. Eberhard Bauer and Walter von Lucadou, 123–42. Freiburg: Herderbücherei.

Benes, Peter. 1977. *The Masks of Orthodoxy: Folk Gravestone Carving in Plymouth County, Massachusetts 1689–1805*. Amherst: University of Massachusetts Press.

Benjamin, Walter. 1963. Das Kunstwerk im Zeitalter in seiner technischen Reproduzierbarkeit. In *Gesammelte Schriften*, vol. 1, ed. Rolf Tiedemann and Hermann Schweppenhäuser, 431–508. Frankfurt am Main: Suhrkamp.

Berne, Eric. 1972. *What Do You Say After You Say Hello?* New York: Bantam.

Bertaux, Daniel, ed. 1981. *Biography and Society: The Life History Approach in the Social Sciences*. Beverly Hills: Sage Publications.

Bertaux, Daniel, and I. Wiame. 1981. Life Stories in the Baker's Trade. In *Biography and Society: The Life History Approach in the Social Sciences*, ed Daniel Bertaux, 29–46. Beverly Hills: Sage Publications.

Bethke, Robert D. 1970. Narrative Obituary Verse and Native American Balladry. *Journal of American Folklore* 83:61–68.

Bettelheim, Bruno. 1976. *The Uses of Enchantment: The Meaning and Importance of Fairy Tales*. New York: Knopf.

Bloch, Ernst. 1959. *Das Prinzip Hoffnung*. 3 vols. Frankfurt am Main: Suhrkamp.

Bloch, Maurice, and Jonathan Parry. 1982. *Death and Regeneration of Life*. New York: Cambridge University Press.

Bødker, Laurits. 1965. *Folk Literature*. Vol. 2 of *International Dictionary of Regional European Ethnology and Folklore*. Copenhagen: Rosenkilde and Bagger.

Bogatyrev, P., and R. Jakobson. 1929. Die Folklore als eine besondere Form des Schaffens. In *Donum natalicium Schrijnen. Versameling van opstellen door ondleeringen en bevriende vakgenooten opgedragen aan mgr. prof. Dr. Jos. Schrijnen bij gelegenheid van zijn zestigsten verjaardag*. Nijmegen-Utrecht: Dekker & van de Vegt.

Bolte, Johannes. 1921. *Zeugnisse zur Geschichte der Märchen*. Folklore Fellows Communications, 39. Helsinki: Suomalainen Tiedeakatemia.

Bottigheimer, Ruth B. 1987. *Grimms' Bad Girls & Bold Boys: The Moral & Social Vision of the Tales*. New Haven: Yale University Press.

Brednich, Rolf Wilh., Hannjost Lixfeld, Dieter-Rüdiger Moser, and Lutz Röhrich.

1982. *Lebenslauf und Lebenszusammenhang: Autobiographische Materialien in der volkskundlichen Forschung.* Freiburg im Breisgau: Abteilung Volkskunde des deutschen Seminars der Universität Freiburg i Br.

Bringéus, Nils-Arvid. 1982. *Volkstümliche Bilderkunde.* München: Callwey.

Brunvand, Jan Harold. 1981. *The Vanishing Hitchhiker: American Urban Legends and their Meanings.* New York: Norton.

———. 1986. *The Mexican Pet: More "New" Urban Legends and Some Old Favorites.* New York: Norton.

Buchan, David. 1981. The Modern Legend. In *Language, Culture and Tradition.* Papers on Language and Folklore Presented at the Annual Conference of the British Sociological Association, April 1978, ed. A. E. Green and J. D. A. Widdowson, 1–15. Leeds: Instiute of Dialect and Folklife Studies, University of Leeds.

Bünker, Reinhold. 1906. *Schwänke, Sagen und Märchen in heanzischer Mundart.* Leipzig.

Burns, Tom. 1969. Folklore in the Mass Media. *Folklore Forum* 2:90–106.

Le Cabinet des fées; ou Collection choisie des contes des fées, et autres contes merveilleux. 1785. Amsterdam & Paris: Rue de Hotel Serpente.

Carr, David. 1986. *Time, Narrative and History.* Bloomington: Indiana University Press.

Caughey, John L. 1984. *Imaginary Social Worlds: A Cultural Approach.* Lincoln: University of Nebraska Press.

Chodorow, Nancy. 1974. Family Structure and Feminine Personality. In *Woman, Culture and Society,* ed. Michelle Zimbalist Rosaldo and Louise Lamphere, 43–66. Stanford: Stanford University Press.

Choi, In-Hak. 1979. *A Type Index of Korean Folktales.* Seoul: Myong Ji.

Christiansen, Reidar. 1962. *European Folklore in America.* Oslo: Universitetsforlaget.

Clements, William M. 1974. The American Folk Church. Ph.D. diss., Indiana University, Bloomington.

———. 1978. The American Folk Church in Northeast Arkansas. *Journal of the Folklore Institute* 15:161–80.

———. 1981. Ritual Expectation in Pentecostal Healing Experience. *Western Folklore* 40:139–48.

Clifford, James, and George E. Marcus. 1986. *Writing Culture. The Poetics and Politics of Ethnography.* Berkeley: University of California Press.

Cocciardi, Carol, et al., eds. 1977. *The Psychic Yellow Pages.* Saratoga, CA: Out of the Sky.

Cohen, Daniel. 1988 *Phone Call from a Ghost: Strange Tales from Modern America.* New York: Pocket Books.

Cone, F. M. 1968. What's Bad for TV is Worse for Advertising. In *Sight, Sound and Society,* ed. D. M. White and R. Averson, 263–70. Boston: Beacon Press.

Danforth, Loring M. 1982. *The Death Rituals of Rural Greece.* Princeton: Princeton University Press.

de Beauvoir, Simone. 1952 [1949]. *The Second Sex.* Translated and edited by H. M. Parshley. New York: Bantam Books.

Deemer, Polly Stewart. 1975. A Response to the Symposium. *Journal of American Folklore* 88:101–109.

DeFleur, Melvin L. 1970 [1966]. *Theories of Mass Communication.* New York: David McKay.

Dégh, Linda. 1946–1947. Népmese és ponyva. *Magyar Nyelvör* 1946:68–72 and 143–47; 1947:3–7, 43–45, and 88–92.

———. 1965a. *Folktales of Hungary*. Chicago: University of Chicago Press.

———. 1965b. Processes of Legend Formation. *Laographica* 22:77–87.

———. 1972. Folk Narrative. In *Folklore and Folklife: An Introduction*, ed. Richard M. Dorson, 53–83. Chicago: University of Chicago Press.

———. 1975. Stadt-Land Unterschiede in den USA, dargelegt am Beispiel moderner Sagenbildung. In *Stadt-Land-Beziehungen*, ed. Gerhard Kaufman, 93–108. Göttingen: Otto Schwartz.

———. 1977. UFO's and How Folklorists Should Look at Them. *Fabula* 18:242–48.

———. 1979a. Biologic des Erzählguts. In *Enzyklopädie des Märchens*, vol. 2, ed. Kurt Ranke et al., 386–406. Berlin: Walter de Gruyter.

———. 1979b. Conduit-Theorie. In *Enzyklopädie des Märchens*, ed. Kurt Ranke, vol. 3:124–25. Berlin: Walter de Gruyter.

———. 1980. *People in the Tobacco Belt: Four Lives*. New York: Arno Press.

———. 1981. The Magic Tale and its Magic. *International Folklore Review* 1:71–76.

———. 1983a. What Is Folklore? In *Folklore, Myth and Oral History. The Harvard Advocate* 117(3A):38–39.

———. 1983b. Zur Rezeption der Grimmschen Märchen in den USA. In *Über Märchen für Kinder von heute*, ed. Klaus Doderer, 116–28. Weinheim und Basel: Beltz.

———. 1984. Erzählen, Erzähler. In *Enzyklopädie des Märchens*, vol. 4, ed. Kurt Ranke et al., 315–42. Berlin: Walter de Gruyter.

———. 1985a. Frauenmärchen. *Enzyklopädie des Märchens*, vol. 5, part 1, ed. Kurt Ranke, 211–20. Berlin: Walter de Gruyter.

———. 1985b. When I Was Six We Moved West: The Theory of Personal Experience Narrative. *New York Folklore* 11:99–109.

———. 1986. Introduction. *Journal of Folklore Research* 25:77–86.

———. 1988. What Did the Grimm Brothers Give to and Take from the Folk? In *The Brothers Grimm and Folktales*, ed. J. M. McGlathery, 66–90. Chicago: University of Illinois Press.

———. 1989. [1969]. *Folktales and Society: Story-Telling in a Hungarian Peasant Community*. Bloomington: Indiana University Press.

———. 1990. How Storytellers Interpret the Snakeprince Tale. In *The Telling of Stories. Approaches to a Traditional Craft: A Symposium*, ed. Morten Nojgaard et al., 47–62. Odense: Odense University Press.

Dégh, Linda, and Andrew Vázsonyi. 1973. The Dialectics of the Legend. *Folklore Preprint Series* I.6. Bloomington: Folklore Publications Group.

———. 1974. The Memorate and the Proto-Memorate. *Journal of American Folklore* 87:225–39.

———. 1975. The Hypothesis of Multi-Conduit Transmission in Folklore. In *Folklore Performance and Communication*, ed. Dan Ben-Amos and Kenneth S. Goldstein, 207–252. The Hague: Mouton.

———. 1976. Legend and Belief. In *Folklore Genres*, ed. Dan Ben-Amos, 93–123. Austin: University of Texas Press.

———. 1979. Magic for Sale: Märchen and Legend in TV Advertising. *Fabula* 20:47–68.

———. 1983. Does the Word 'Dog' Bite? Ostensive Action: A Means of Legend-Telling. *Journal of Folklore Research* 20:5–34.

De Martino, Ernesto. 1958. *Morte e pianto rituale nel mondo antico.*

Denby, Priscilla. 1971. Folklore in the Mass Media. *Folklore Forum* 4:113–25.

Dobos, Ilona. 1978. True Stories. In *Studies in East European Folk Narrative*, ed. Linda Dégh, 167–205. Publications of the American Folklore Society, Bibliographical and Special Series, 30. American Folklore Society.

————. 1984. *Egy folkórgyüjtö feljegyzései.* Budapest: Kozmosz.

————. 1986. *Paraszti szájhagyomány, városi szóbeliség.* Budapest: Gondolat.

Doderer, Klaus (ed). 1983. *Über Märchen für Kinder von heute.* Weinheim und Basel: Beltz.

Dolby-Stahl. 1989. *Literary Folkloristics and the Personal Narrative.* Bloomington: Indiana University Press.

Dorson, Richard M. 1945. Print and American Folklore. *California Folklore Quarterly* 4:207.

————. 1971. *American Folklore and the Historian.* Chicago: University of Chicago Press.

Douglas, Ann. 1971. The 'Scribbling Women' and Fanny Fern: Why Women Wrote. *American Quarterly* 23:3–24.

————. 1975. Heaven Our Home: Consolation Literature in the Northern United States, 1830–1880. In *Death in America*, ed. D. Stannard, 30–48. Philadelphia: University of Pennsylvania Press.

Douglass, William A. 1969. *Death in Murélaga: Funerary Ritual in a Spanish Basque Village.* Seattle: University of Washington Press.

Dow, James, and Hannjost Lixfeld. 1986. *German Volkskunde. A Decade of Theoretical Confrontation, Debate, and Reorientation (1967–1977)* Bloomington: Indiana University Press.

Dowling, Colette. 1981. *The Cinderella Complex.* New York: Pocket Books.

Dundes, Alan. 1963 Advertising and Folklore. *New York Folklore Quarterly* 19:143–51.

————. 1966. Metafolklore and Oral Literary Criticism. *The Monist* 50:505–16.

————. 1971. Folk Ideas as Units of Worldview. *Journal of American Folklore* 84:93–103.

————. 1986. The Anthropologist and the Comparative Method in Folklore. *Journal of Folklore Research* 23:125–46.

———— (ed). 1989. *Little Red Riding Hood: A Casebook.* Madison: University of Wisconsin Press.

Dundes, Alan, and Carl R. Pagter. 1978 [1975]. *Work Hard and You Shall Be Rewarded: Urban Folklore from the Paperwork Empire.* Bloomington: Indiana University Press.

Ellis, Bill. 1983. Adolescent Legend-Tripping. *Psychology Today* (Aug.): 68–69.

Ellwood, Robert S. 1979. *Alternative Altars. Unconventional and Eastern Spirituality in America.* Chicago: University of Chicago Press.

Epstein, Cynthia Fuchs. 1971. *Woman's Place: Options and Limits in Professional Careers.* Berkeley: University of California Press.

Erikson, Erik. 1964. *Insight and Responsibility.* New York: Norton.

Fair, Charles. 1974. *The New Nonsense.* New York: Simon and Schuster.

Faragó, József. 1969. *Kurcsi Minya havasi mesemondó* (Alpine storyteller M. Kurcsi). Bucharest: Irodalmi Könyvkiadó.

Farrar, Janet, and Stewart Farrar. 1987. *The Life & Times of a Modern Witch.* London: Piatkus.

Farrer, Claire, ed. 1975. Women and Folklore. (Special Issue.) *Journal of American Folklore* 88.

Favret-Saada, Jeanne. 1979. *Die Wörter, der Zauber, der Tod: Der Hexenglaube im Hainland von Westfrankreich.* Translated by Eva Moldenhauer. Frankfurt: Suhrkamp.

Finnegan, Ruth. 1977. *Oral Poetry: Its Nature, Significance and Social Context.* Cambridge: Cambridge University Press.

Freedland, Nat. 1972. *The Occult Explosion.* New York: Berkeley Medallion Books.

Friedan, Betty. 1963. *The Feminine Mystique.* New York: Dell.

Gardner, Martin. 1989. Glossolalia. *Free Inquiry* 9(2):46–48.

Geiger, Klaus, Utz Jeggle, and Gottfried Korff. 1970. *Abschied vom Volksleben.* Tübingen: Vereinigung für Volkskunde.

Georges, Robert A. 1969. Toward an Understanding of Storytelling Events. *Journal of American Folklore* 82:313–28.

———. 1986. The Pervasiveness in Contemporary Folklore Studies of Assumptions, Concepts and Constructs Usually Associated with the Historic-Geographic Method. *Journal of Folklore Research* 23:87–104.

Gillon, Edmund V. 1972. *Victorian Cemetery Art.* New York: Dover.

Goffman, Erving. 1959. *The Presentation of Self in Everyday Life.* New York: Doubleday Anchor.

———. 1967. *Interaction Ritual.* New York: Doubleday Anchor.

———. 1971. *Relations in Public Places.* New York: Harper & Row.

Goldberg, Christine. 1984. The Historic-Geographic Method: Past and Future. *Journal of Folklore Research* 21:1–18.

Golowin, Sergius. 1964. *Magische Gegenwart. Forschungsfahrten durch modernen Aberglauben.* Bern: Francke.

Goodman, Felicitas D. 1972. *Speaking in Tongues: A Cross-Cultural Study of Glossolalia.* Chicago: University of Chicago Press.

———. 1988. *How About Demons? Possession and Exorcism in the Modern World.* Bloomington: Indiana University Press.

Gordon, George. 1971. *Persuasion: The Theory and Practice of Manipulative Communication.* New York: Hastings House.

Gornick, Vivian, and Barbara K. Moran, eds. 1971. *Woman in Sexist Society: Studies in Power and Powerlessness.* New York: Basic Books.

Gosnell, Lynn, and Suzanne Gott. 1989. San Fernando Cemetery: Decorations of Lore and Loss in a Mexican-American Community. In *Cemeteries and Gravemarkers: Voices of American Culture,* ed. Richard E. Meyer, 217–36. Ann Arbor: UMI Research Press.

Gossage, Howard. 1961. The Magic Twig: Black, White and Pango Peach Magic in Advertising. *Harper's* (March): 10–20.

Gossan, Al, Jr. 1986. *My Search: The True Story of a Young Man Who Was Directed to the Truth through Visions and Voices from Heaven.* Nederland, Tex.: The National Pentecostal Church Growth Institute.

Gottschalk, Louis, Clyde Kluckhohn and Robert Angell. 1945. *The Use of Personal Documents in History, Anthropology and Sociology.* New York: Social Science Research Council.

Graichen, Gisela. 1986. *Die neuen Hexen: Gesprächen mit Hexen.* Hamburg: Hoffmann und Campe.

Greene, Gayle, and C. Kahn, eds. 1985. *Making a Difference: Feminist Literary Criticism.* London: Methuen.

Greverus, Ina-Maria. 1990. *Neues Zeitalter oder verkehrte Welt. Anthropologie als Kritik.* Darmstadt: Wissenschaftliche Buchgesellschaft.

Grider, Sylvia. 1980. The Hatchet Man. In *Indiana Folklore: A Reader,* ed. Linda Dégh, 147–78. Bloomington: Indiana University Press.

———. 1984. The Razor Blades in the Apples Syndrome. In *Perspectives on Contemporary Legend,* vol. 1, ed. Paul Smith, 128–40. Sheffield: The Center for English Cultural Tradition and Language, University of Sheffield.

Haag, Ernest van der. 1957. Of Happiness and of Despair We Have No Measure. In *Mass Culture: The Popular Arts in America,* ed. Bernard Rosenberg and David Manning White, 504–36. New York: The Free Press.

Halpert, Herbert. 1971. Definition and Variation in Folk Legend. In *American Folk Legend: A Symposium,* ed. Wayland D. Hand, 47–54. Berkeley: University of California Press.

Hand, Wayland D. 1963. Die Märchen der Brüder Grimm in den Vereinigten Staaten. *Hessische Blätter für Volkskunde* 54:525–44.

———. 1965. Status of European and American Legend Study. *Current Anthropology* 6:439–46.

Haring, Lee. 1982. *Malgasy Tale Index.* Folklore Fellows Communications, 231. Helsinki: Suomalainen Tiedeakatemia.

Harkort, Fritz. 1966. Volkserzählungstypen und-motive und Vorstellungsberichte. *Fabula* 8:208–23.

Harris, Marvin. 1981. *America Now: The Anthropology of a Changing Culture.* New York: Simon and Schuster.

Herranen, Gun. 1984. Aspects of a Blind Storyteller's Repertoire. Auditive Learning—Oral Tradition. In *Le Conte. Pourquoi? Comment?* (Folktales: how and why), ed. Genevieve Calame-Griaule et al., 511–25. Paris: Editions du Centre National de la Recherche Scientifique.

Hesseltine, Patricia. 1982. The 1980 Lady as Depicted in TV Commercials. In *Researching American Culture: A Guide for Student Anthropologists,* ed. Conrad Phillip Kottak, 236–45. Ann Arbor: University of Michigan Press.

Hicks, Robert D. 1990. Police Pursuit of Satanic Crime. *Skeptical Inquirer* 14(3):276–86.

Hofer, Tamás, and Peter Niedermüller, eds. 1988. *Life History as Cultural Construction/Performance.* Budapest: Ethnographic Institute.

Hohmann, Delf Maria. 1985. Jennifer and Her Barbies: A Contextual Analysis of a Child Playing Barbie Dolls. *Canadian Folklore Canadien* 7:111–20.

Holbek, Bengt. 1987. *Interpretation of Fairy Tales: Danish Folklore in European Perspective.* Folklore Fellows Communications, 239. Helsinki: Suomalainen Tiedeakatemia.

Honti, John. 1975. *Studies in Oral Epic Tradition.* Budapest: Akadémiai Kiadó.

Horkheimer, M. 1936. *Autorität und Familie.* Paris.

Horkheimer, M. and Th. Adorno. 1947. *Dialektik der Aufklärung.* Amsterdam.

Horton, Paul B., Gerald R. Leslie and Richard F. Larson. 1974. *The Sociology of Social Problems.* Englewood Cliffs, N.J.: Prentice-Hall.

Horton, Robin. 1960. A Definition of Religion and its Uses. *Man* 90:201–26.

Hultkrantz, Ake. 1960. *International Dictionary of Regional European Ethnology and Folklore.* Copenhagen: Rosenkilde and Bagger.

Huntington, R., and P. Metcalf. 1979. *Celebration of Death: The Anthropology of Mortuary Ritual*. Cambridge: Cambridge University Press.

Jackson, Bruce, ed. 1987. Folklore and Feminism. (Special Issue). *Journal of American Folklore* 100.

Jacobs, Joseph. 1967. *English Fairy Tales*. 3rd rev. ed. New York: Schocken.

Jahner, Elaine. 1985. Woman Remembering: Life History as Exemplary Pattern. In *Women's Folklore, Women's Culture*, ed. Rosan A. Jordan and Susan J. Kalcik, 214–33. Philadelphia: University of Pennsylvania Press.

Jahoda, Gustav. 1971 [1969]. *The Psychology of Superstition*. Baltimore: Penguin Books.

Jakobson, Roman. 1964 [1960]. Closing Statement: Linguistics and Poetics. In *Style in Language*, ed. Thomas A. Sebeok, 350–77. Cambridge, Mass.: M. I. T. Press.

Jarvie, I. C. 1977 [1970]. Explaining Cargo Cults. In *Rationality*, ed. Bryan R. Wilson, 50–61. Oxford: Basil Blackwell.

Jeggle, Utz. 1984. *Feldforschung. Qualitative Methoden in der Kulturanalyse*. Tübingen, Vereinigung für Volkskunde.

Jolles, André. 1965 [1930]. *Einfache Formen*. Tübingen: Max Niemeyer.

Jones, Stephen Swann. 1986. Structural and Thematic Application of the Comparative Method. *Journal of the Folklore Institute* 23:147–62.

Jordan, Rosan, and Frank de Caro. 1986. Women and the Study of Folklore. *Signs* 11:500–16.

Jordan, Rosan A. and Susan J. Kalčik, eds. 1985. *Women's Folklore, Women's Culture*. Philadelphia: University of Pennsylvania Press.

Kálmány, Lajos. 1914–1915. *Hagyományok*. 2 vols. Szeged.

Kastenbaum, R. J. 1977. *Death, Society and Human Experience*. St. Louis: Springer.

Keil, Charles. 1979. The Concept of "The Folk." *Journal of the Folklore Institute* 16:209–10.

Key, Wilson Bryan. 1973. *Subliminal Seduction: Ad Media's Manipulation of a Not So Innocent America*. Englewood Cliffs, N.J.: Prentice-Hall.

Kirshenblatt-Gimblett, Barbara. 1988. Mistaken Dichotomies. *Journal of American Folklore* 101:140–55.

———. 1989. Authoring Lives. *Journal of the Folklore Research* 26:123–50.

Klass, Philip J. 1988. *UFO-Abductions: A Dangerous Game*. Buffalo, N.Y.: Prometheus Books.

Klintberg, Bengt af. 1976. Folksänger i dag. *Fataburen*: 269–96.

Klymasz, Robert B. 1975. Ukrainian Folklore in Canada. *Canadian Ethnic Folklore* 7(2):50–56.

König, René. 1976 [1969]. Soziologie der Familie. In *Handbuch zur empirischen Sozialforschung*, vol. 7, ed. René König, 1–217. Stuttgart: Ferdinand Enke.

Kosko, Maria. 1966. *Le fils assassiné (AT 939A): Etude d'un theme legendaire*. Folklore Fellows Communications, 198. Helsinki: Suomalainen Tiedeakatemia.

Kübler, H. D. 1975. *Unterhaltung und Information im Fernsehen. Dargestellt am Beispiel der Abendschau Baden-Württemberg*. Untersuchungen des Ludwig-Uhland-Instituts der Universität Tübingen 37 (especially 148-62). Tübingen: Tübinger Vereinigung für Volkskunde.

Kübler-Ross, Elizabeth. 1975. *Death, the Final Stage of Growth*. Englewood Cliffs, N.J.: Prentice-Hall.

Kurth, Wolfram. 1976. *Menschen und Massen*. Saarbrücken: Universitäts-und Schulbuchverlag; Aloys Henri Verlag.

Kurtz, Paul. 1986–1987. The Growth of Fundamentalism Worldwide: A Humanist Response. *Free Inquiry* 7(1):18–24.

Lang, Andrew. 1892. Comment. In *International Folk-Lore Congress, 1891,* 66. London: Nutt.

Langness, L. L. 1965. *The Life History in Anthropological Sciences.* New York: Holt, Rinehart and Winston.

Langness, L. L., and G. Frank. 1988. *Lives: An Anthropological Approach to Biography.* Novato, Calif.: Chandler and Sharp.

Lawless, Elaine K. 1985. Oral "Character" and "Literary" Art: A Call for a New Reciprocity Between Oral Literature and Folklore. *Western Folklore* 44:77–96.

———. 1988a. *God's Peculiar People: Women's Voices and Folk Tradition in a Pentecostal Church.* Lexington: University Press of Kentucky.

———. 1988b. *Handmaidens of the Lord: Pentecostal Women Preachers and Traditional Religion.* Philadelphia: University of Pennsylvania Press.

Lazarsfeld, P. F., B. Berelson, and H. Gaudet. 1948. *The People's Choice.* New York: Columbia University Press.

Lehmann, Albrecht. 1983. *Erzählstruktur and Lebenslauf: Autobiographische Untersuchungen.* Frankfurt/Main and New York: Campus Verlag.

Lord, Albert. 1960. *The Singer of Tales.* New York: Atheneum.

Lucaites, J. L., and C. M. Condit. 1985. Re-Constructing Narrative Theory: A Functional Perspective. *Journal of Communication* 35:90–108.

Lüthi, Max. 1966. *Volksmärchen und Volkssage: Zwei Grundformen erzählender Dichtung.* Bern: Francke.

———. 1976 *Märchen.* 6th ed. Stuttgart: Metzlersche Verlagsbuchhandlung.

———. 1981 [1947]. *Das europäische Volksmärchen. Form und Wesen.* München: Francke.

Lynd, R. S. and H. M. Lynd. 1937. *Middletown in Transition: A Study in Cultural Conflicts.* New York: Harcourt, Brace and World.

———. 1956 [1929]. *Middletown, a Study in American Culture.* New York: Harcourt, Brace and World.

Makkai, Adam. 1974. Madison Avenue Advertising: A Scenario. In *The First Lacus Forum 1974,* ed. Adam Makkai and Valerie Becker Makkai, 197–208. Columbia, S. C.: Hornbeam Press.

Maller, Josef. 1971. *Wunder um Eisenberg: Authentische Pilgerberichte.* Vienna: Josef Maller.

Marcus, George E., and Michael M. J. Fischer. 1986. *Anthropology as Cultural Critique: An Experimental Moment in the Human Sciences.* Chicago: University of Chicago Press.

Marzolph, Ulrich. 1984. *Typologic des persischen Volksmärchens.* Beirut (Wiesbaden): Steiner.

Mayer, Martin. 1958. *Madison Avenue: USA.* New York: Harper.

McLuhan, Marshall. 1951. *The Mechanical Bride: Folklore of Industrial Man.* New York: Vanguard Press.

———. 1957. American Advertising. In *Mass Culture: The Popular Arts in America,* ed. Bernard Rosenberg and David Manning White, 435–42. New York: Free Press.

McLuhan, Marshall, and Quentin Fiore. 1967. *The Medium Is the Massage: An Inventory of Effects.* New York: Bantam Books.

Mead, Margaret. 1935. *Sex and Temperament in Three Primitive Societies*. New York: New American Library.

Meletinsky, E. M. 1958. *Geroi volshebnoy skazki*. Moscow: Izd-vo vostochnoi litery.

Mieder, Wolfgang. 1979. *Grimm Märchen—modern, Prosa, Gedichte, Karikaturen*. Stuttgart: Reclam.

Mitford, Jessica. 1963. *The American Way of Death*. New York: Simon and Schuster.

Montenyohl, Eric L. 1986. Andrew Lang and the Fairy Tale. Ph.D. diss., Indiana University, Bloomington.

Moody, Raymond A. 1976. *Life after Life: The Investigation of a Phenomenon-Survival of Bodily Death*. Harrisburg, Pa.: Stackpole Books.

Moore, R. Laurence. 1977. *In Search of White Crows: Spiritualism, Parapsychology and American Culture*. New York: Oxford University Press.

Moser-Rath, Elfriede. 1964. *Predigtmärlein der Barockzeit*. Berlin: Walter de Gruyter.

Motz, Marilyn Ferris. 1983. The Cultural Significance of the Barbie Doll. In *The Popular Culture* Reader, 3d ed., ed. Christian D. Geist and Jack Nachbar. Bowling Green, Ohio: Bowling Green University Press.

Mullen, Patrick B. 1978. The Folk Idea of Unlimited Good in American Buried Treasure Legends. *Journal of the Folklore Institute* 15:209–20.

Nichol, John Thomas. 1966. *Pentecostalism*. New York: Harper and Row.

———. 1974. Pentecostal Churches. *Encyclopaedia Britannica*, vol. 14, 30–35.

Nicolaisen, William F. H. 1984a. Perspectives on Contemporary Legend, A Panel Discussion. Introduction. In *Papers II, The 8th Congress of the International Society for Folk Narrative Research*, ed. Reimund Kvideland and Torunn Selberg, 113–17. Bergen. N.p.

———. 1984b. Legend as Narrative Response. In *Perspectives on Contemporary Legend*, vol. 1, ed. Paul Smith, 167–79. Sheffield: The Center for English Cultural Tradition and Language, University of Sheffield.

Oinas, Felix. 1973. The Problem of Aristocratic Origin of Russian Byliny. *Slavic Review* 30:513–22.

Ong, Walter J. 1980. Literacy and Orality in Our Times. *Journal of Communication* 30:197–205.

Oring, Elliott. 1982. Forest Lawn and the Iconography of American Death. *Southwest Folklore* 6:62–72.

———. 1986. *Folk Groups and Folklore Genres: An Introduction*. Logan: Utah State University Press.

Ortner, Sherry B. 1974. Is Female to Male as Nature Is to Culture? In *Woman, Culture and Society*, ed. Michelle Zimbalist Rosaldo and Louise Lamphere, 67–87. Stanford: Stanford University Press.

Ortutay, Gyula. 1959. Principles of Oral Transmission in Folk Culture. *Acta Ethnographics* 8:175–221.

———. 1972. *Hungarian Folklore: Essays*. Budapest: Akadémiai Kiadó.

Packard, Vance. 1957. *The Hidden Persuaders*. New York: Pocket Books.

———. 1959. *The Status Seekers*. New York: Simon and Schuster.

Panttaja, Elisabeth. 1988. Making Reality Evident: Feminine Disempowerment and Reempowerment in Two Grimm's Fairy Tales. *Folklore Forum* 21:166–80.

Parker, Adrian. 1975. *States of Mind: ESP and Altered States of Consciousness*. New York: Taplinger Publishing.

Pentikäinen, Juha. 1970. Quellenanalytische Probleme der religiösen Überlieferung. *Temenos* 6:89–118.

———. 1980. Life History—A Neglected Folklore Genre. In *Folklore on Two Continents: Essays in Honor of Linda Dégh*, ed. Nikolai Burlakoff and Carl Lindahl, 150–59. Bloomington, Ind.: Trickster Press.

Personal Narrative Group, The. 1989. *Interpreting Women's Lives: Feminist Theory and Personal Narratives*. Bloomington: Indiana University Press.

Phelps, Elizabeth Stewart. 1964. *The Gates Ajar*. Ed. H. Sootin Smith. Cambridge: Belknap Press.

Piaget, Jean. 1976 [1929]. *The Child's Conception of the World*. Totowa, N.J.: Littlefield, Adams & Co.

Pinsker, Maria. 1976. *Segen über Eisenberg*. Vienna: Kreuz-Verlag.

Porterfield, Amanda. 1980. *Feminine Spirituality in America from Sarah Edwards to Martha Graham*. Philadelphia: Temple University Press.

Pratt, Mary Louise. 1986. Fieldwork in Common Places. In *Writing Culture: The Poetics and Politics of Ethnography*, ed. James Clifford and George E. Marcus, 27–50. Berkeley: University of California Press.

Propp, Vladimir. 1946. *Istoricheskie korni volsebnoj skazki*. Leningrad: [Izd-vo Leningradskogo gos. ordena Lenina Universiteta]

———. 1968. *Morphology of the Folktale*. Rev. and ed. with a preface by Louis A. Wagner. New introduction by Alan Dundes. Austin: University of Texas Press.

———. 1984. *Theory and History of Folklore*. Transl. Ariadne Y. Martin and Richard P. Martin. Ed. Anatoly Liberman. Minneapolis: University of Minnesota Press.

Ranke, Kurt. 1955–1962. *Schleswig-holsteinische Volksmärchen*. 3 vols. Kiel: F. Hirt.

———. 1967. Kategorienprobleme der Volksprosa. *Fabula* 9:4–12.

Regush, Nicholas and June Regush. 1974. *PSI: The Other World Catalogue*. n.p.

Rentz, Patricia M. 1982. A Picture is Worth a Thousand Words. In *Researching American Culture: A Guide for Student Anthropologists*, ed. Conrad Phillip Kottak, 227–35. Ann Arbor: University of Michigan Press.

Rihtman-Augustin, Dunja. 1978. Novinske osmrtnice. *Narodna Umjetnost* 15:117–75.

———. 1987. Ethnographic Items in Yugoslav and Italian Death Notices. Paper presented at conference, Life History as Cultural Performance, Aug. 12–17, Budapest.

Röhrich, Lutz. 1962–67. *Erzählungen des späten Mittelalters und ihr Weiterleben in Literatur und Volksdichtung bis zur Gegenwart*. 2 vols. Bern: Francke.

———. 1974. *Märchen und Wirklichkeit*. 3d ed. Wiesbaden: Franz Steiner.

———. 1985. Zur Deutung und Be-Deutung von Folklore-Texten. *Fabula* 26:3–28.

———. 1988. The Quest of Meaning in Folk Narrative Research. In *The Brothers Grimm and Folktale*, ed. James M. McGlathery, 1–15. Urbana: University of Illinois Press.

Rojcewicz, Peter M. 1991. Between One Eye Blink and the Next: Fairies, UFOs, and Problems of Knowledge. In *The Good People: New Fairylore Essay*, ed. Peter Narváez, 479–514. New York: Garland.

Rölleke, Heinz. 1975. *Die älteste Märchensammlung der Brüder Grimm*. Cologny-Genève: Fondation Martin Bodmer.

Rosaldo, Michelle Zimbalist, and Louise Lamphere, eds. 1974. *Woman, Culture and Society*. Stanford: Stanford University Press.

Rosenfeld, Hans-Friedrich. 1958. Zur Arbeitweise der Brüder Grimm in ihren Deutschen Sagen. *Deutsches Jahrbuch für Volkskunde* 4:82–90.

Ruitenbeek, Hendrik M. 1967. *The Male Myth*. New York: Dell.

Samuelson, Sue C. 1982. Festive Malaise and Festive Participation: A Case Study of Christmas Celebrations in America. Ph.D. diss., University of Pennsylvania, Philadelphia.

Sanday, Peggy Reeves. 1981. *Female Power and Male Dominance: On the Origins of Sexual Inequality*. Cambridge: Cambridge University Press.

Sanderson, Stewart F. 1981. *The Modern Urban Legend*. Katharine Briggs Lecture No. 1, delivered Nov. 3 to the Folklore Society at University College London. London: Folklore Society.

Sawin, Patricia E. 1988. Ethnicity and Women's Status: An Exploratory Bibliography. *Folklore Forum* 21:114–65.

Schenda, Rudolf. 1970a. *Volk ohne Buch. Studien zur Sozialgeschichte der populären Lesestoffe 1770–1910*. Frankfurt: Klostermann.

———. 1970b. Einheitlich-Urtümlich-Noch Heute. Probleme der volkskundlichen Befragung. In *Abschied vom Volksleben*, ed. Klaus Geiger et al., 124–54.

———. 1976. *Die Lesestoffe der kleinen Leute*. Munich: Beck.

———. 1985. *Die Märchen der Brüder Grimm*. Zürich: Artemis.

———. 1992. Folklore und Massenkultur. In *Tradition and Modernisation*. Plenary Papers Read at the 4th International Congress of the Société Internationale d'Ethnologie et de Folklore, ed. Reimund Kvideland, 23–38. Turku: Nordic Institute of Folklore.

Schneider, David M. 1968. *American Kinship: A Cultural Account*. Englewood Cliffs, N.J.: Prentice-Hall.

Schöck, Inge. 1978. *Hexenglaube in der Gegenwart*. Tübingen: Tübinger Vereinigung für Volkskunde; E. V. Schloss.

Sebestyén, Ádám. 1979–1984. *Bukovinai székely népmesék* (Bucovina Székely folktales). 4 vols. Szekszárd: Tolna megyei tanács.

Sirovátka, Oldrich. 1964. Zur Morphologie der Sage und Sagenkatalogisierung. *Acta Ethnographica* 13:99–108.

Smith, Paul. 1984. On the Receiving End: When Legend Becomes Rumour. In *Perspectives on Contemporary Legend*, vol. 1, ed. Paul Smith, 197–215. Sheffield: The Center for English Cultural Tradition and Language, University of Sheffield.

Snow, Loudell. 1979. Mail Order Magic: The Commercial Exploitation of Folk Belief. *Journal of the Folklore Institute* 16:44–73.

Stahl, Sandra Dolby. 1977. The Oral Personal Narrative in Its Generic Context. *Fabula* 18:18–39.

Stannard, David, ed. 1975. *Death in America*. Philadelphia: University of Pennsylvania Press.

Stark, Rodney, and William Sims Bainbridge. 1985. *The Future of Religion, Secularization, Revival, and Cult Formation*. Berkeley: University of California Press.

Stolz, Benjamin A., and Richard S. Shannon III. 1976. *Oral Literature and the Formula*. Ann Arbor, Mich.: Center for the Coordination of Ancient and Modern Studies.

Stone, Kay. 1975a. Romantic Heroines in Anglo-American Folk and Popular Literature. Ph.D. diss., Indiana University, Bloomington.

———. 1975b. Things Walt Disney Never Told Us. In *Women and Folklore* (Special issue), ed. Claire R. Farrer. *Journal of American Folklore* 88:42–50.

———. 1983. Missbrauchte Verzauberung—Aschenputtel als Weiblichkeitsideal in

Nordamerika. In *Über Märchen für Kinder von heute*, ed. Klaus Doderer, 78–96. Weinheim and Basel: Beltz.

———. 1985. The Misuses of Enchantment: Controversies on the Significance of Fairy Tales. In *Women's Folklore, Women's Culture*, ed. Rosan A. Jordan and Susan J. Kalčik, 125–48. Philadelphia: University of Pennsylvania Press.

Sullenberger, Tom E. 1974. Ajax Meets the Jolly Green Giant: Some Observations on the Use of Folklore and Myths in American Mass Marketing. *Journal of American Folklore* 87:53–65.

Swenson, Greta E. 1980. Family Identity and Transmission in a Mobile Society. Ph.D. diss., Indiana University, Bloomington.

Szenti, Tibor. 1985. *Parasztvallomások. Gazdák emlékezése Vásárhelyről*. Budapest: Gondolat.

Tagung. 1962. International Society for Folk-Narrative Research. Antwerp. 6–8 September. Berichte und Referate. Antwerp: Centrum voor Studie en Documentatie, 1965.

Tagung. 1963. Sagenkommission der International Society for Folk-Narrative Research. Budapest, 14–16 October. *Acta Ethnographica* 13 (1964).

Tatar, Maria. 1987. *The Hard Facts of the Grimm's Fairytales*. Princeton: Princeton University Press.

Thompson, Stith. 1949. Variant. In *Funk & Wagnalls Standard Dictionary of Folklore Mythology and Legend*, Vol. 2, ed. Maria Leach, 1154–55. New York: Funk and Wagnalls.

———. 1955–58. *Motif-Index of Folk Literature. A Classification of Narrative Elements in Folktales, Ballads, Myths, Fables, Medieval Romances, Exempla, Fabliaux, Jest-Books, and Local Legends*. 6 vols. Bloomington: Indiana University Press.

Titon, Jeff Todd. 1991. Review of *God's Peculiar People: Women's Voices and Folk Tradition in a Pentecostal Church*, by Elaine J. Lawless; and *Diversities of Gifts: Field Studies in Southern Religion*, ed. Ruel W. Tyson Jr., James L. Peacock, and Daniel W. Patterson. *Journal of American Folklore* 104:121–22.

Toelken, Barre. 1979. *Dynamics of Folklore*. Boston: Houghton Mifflin.

Turner, Victor. 1969. *The Ritual Process: Structure and Anti-Structure*. Chicago: Aldine.

Uther, Hans-Jörg, ed. 1990. *Märchen in unserer Zeit. Zur Erscheinungsformen eines populären Erzählgenres*. Munich: Diederichs.

Verrier, Jean. 1984. Contes à lire à conter. *Le français aujourd'hui* 68.

Victor, Jeffrey S. 1989. A Rumor-Panic About a Dangerous Satanic Cult in Western New York. *New York Folklore* 15:23–48.

Virtanen, Leea. 1976. Paranormale Spontanerlebnisse in der modernen Erzähltradition. *Studia Fennica* 20:338–47.

———. 1990. *"That Must Have Been ESP!"* Bloomington: Indiana University Press.

Voigt, Vilmos. 1972. *A folklór alkotások elemzése* (Analysis of folklore products). Budapest: Akadémiai Kiadó.

———. (ed). 1974. *A szájhagyományozás törvényszerüségei* (Rules of oral tradition). Nemzetközi szimpozion Budapesten, 1969, május 28–30. Budapest: Akadémiai Kiadó.

———. 1980. Orality, a Form of Communication, and the Three Main Forms of It. In *Oralità: Cultura, letterature, discorso*, Atti del convegno internazionale, 509–34. Urbino.

Wagner, Roy. 1981. *The Invention of Culture.* Rev. ed. Chicago: University of Chicago Press.

Warner, Marina. 1990. Mother Goose Tales: Female Fiction, Female Fact? *Folklore* 101:3–25.

Warner, W. Lloyd. 1953. *American Life, Dream and Reality.* Chicago: University of Chicago Press.

————. 1961 [1959]. *The Family of God: A Symbolic Study of Christian Life in America.* New Haven: Yale University Press.

Watson, Lawrence C., and Maria-Barbara Watson-Franke. 1985. *Interpreting Life Histories: An Anthropological Inquiry.* New Brunswick, N.J.: Rutgers University Press.

Weber-Kellermann, Ingeborg. 1975 [1974]. *Die deutsche Familie. Versuch einer Sozialgeschichte.* Frankfurt am Main: Suhrkamp.

————. 1983. *Frauenleben im 19. Jahrhundert.* Munich: Beck.

Wehse, Rainer, ed. 1983. *Märchenerzähler, Erzählgemeinschaft.* Kassel: Erich Röth.

Welter, Barbara. 1966. The Cult of True Womanhood: 1820–1860. *American Quarterly* 18:151–74.

Wesselski, Albert. 1925. *Märchen des Mittelalters.* Berlin.

————. 1931. *Versuch einer Theorie des Märchens.* Reichenberg i.B.: Sudetendeutsche Verlag Franz Kraus.

————. 1936. *Klaret und sein Glossator. Böhmische Volks-und Mönchs-märlein im Mittelalter.* Brünn: R. M. Rohrer.

Williams, Melvin D. 1974. *Community in a Black Pentecostal Church: An Anthropological Study.* Prospect Heights, Ill.: Waveland Heights.

Wimmer, Wolf. 1975. Parapsychologie, Aberglaube und Verbrechen. In *Zeitschrift für Volkskunde* 71:181–202.

Winkelman, Michael. 1982. Magic: A Theoretical Reassessment. *Current Anthropology* 23:37–66.

Wuthnow, Robert. 1978. *Experimentation in American Religion: The New Mysticisms and Their Implications for the Churches.* Berkeley: University of California Press.

Zipes, Jack. 1979–1980. Who's Afraid of the Brothers Grimm? Socialization and Politization Through Fairy Tales. *The Lion and the Unicorn* 3(2):4–36.

————. 1980. The Instrumentalization of Fantasy: Fairy Tales and the Mass Media. In *The Myths of Information: Technology and Postindustrial Culture,* ed. Kathleen Woodward, 88–110. Madison, Wis.: Coda Press.

————. 1982. *Rotkäppchens Lust und Leid: Biographie eines europäischen Märchens.* Köln: Diederichs.

————. 1989 [1986]. *Don't Bet on the Prince: Contemporary Feminist Fairy Tales in North America and England.* New York: Routledge, Chapman and Hall.

Index

LINDA DÉGH, Distinguished Professor of Folklore at Indiana University, is an internationally known folk narrative scholar, specializing in folktale and legend studies in traditional and modern industrial societies in Europe and North America.